Y0-DBO-682

New Japanese Architecture

Egon Tempel

Praeger Publishers
New York · Washington

NA1555
T4

Published in the United States of America in 1969

by Praeger Publishers, Inc.

111 Fourth Avenue, New York, N. Y. 10003

All rights reserved

Copyright in Stuttgart, Germany, 1969, by Verlag Gerd Hatje, Stuttgart

Library of Congress Catalog Card Number: 69-19187

Printed in Germany

Translation into English by E. Rockwell

Contents

Inhalt

Japanese architectural development up to 1945

No building deserving the label of architecture existed in Japan before the introduction of Buddhism around the middle of the 6th century AD. An impression of the architecture of the pre-Buddhist era can be gained from the Inner Ise Shrine (Fig. 1) at Ujiyamada on the island of Honshu. This is the most important centre of Shintoism, a religion which developed from the worship of Nature and Heaven to a cult of tribal and ancestral deities, closely linked with an Emperor Myth. The buildings of the shrine, dating back to the year 5 BC or, according to other sources, the late 3rd century. AD have, since the 7th century, been demolished at intervals of twenty years and re-built from new materials on an immediately adjacent site. This custom cannot be explained by the rapid decay of wood — Japanese timber buildings dating back to the 7th century are still standing; it would seem rather to stem from Shinto religious beliefs, being regarded as a symbol for the growth and decay of nature. In this way, the buildings have been renewed 59 times in 1200 years, and the 60th reconstruction is due in 1974. Although, each time, structure and details of the preceding building are slavishly copied, some minor deviations and alien ingredients have crept in over the centuries. The present copy, however, can still be regarded as a comparatively authentic example of early Japanese architecture.

The Shoden — the main building in the group — reflects the type of dwelling then in use: a gabled house, on a rectangular plan, built entirely from pale-yellow, round and smooth but otherwise untreated cypress logs which were driven into the ground without foundations. The floor is about 2 metres above the ground, the space below being left open. Around the house is a verandah, protected by an oversailing thatched saddle roof. Ridge and gable reveal the characteristic symbols of a Shinto Shrine: intersecting gable rafters projecting above the roof (Chigi), and the timber logs placed across the ridge beam (Katsuogi), designed to prevent the roof from being torn off in a storm.

A list of such details would comprise a number of characteristics which, with certain modifications, continued to feature in the architecture of all Japanese houses, palaces and temples far into the 19th century: framework construction with posts and beams; deliberate emphasis on the structural members; conversion of certain structural elements into sculptural shapes with an aesthetic identity of their own, and accentuation of the oversailing roof. Because of the heavy rains in Japan, the protective function of the roof is of special importance. Even in formal buildings the roof has always played an important part and has been correspondingly decorated. In spite of its simplicity and austerity, however, the Ise Shrine shows a very subtle design both in its overall concept and detail. An exceptional feeling for building materials and an intuitive understanding of laws of harmony are characteristic of Japanese architecture. These features are evident particularly in what is perhaps the most important example of Japanese domestic architecture, the 17th century Villa Katsura (Fig. 2), near Kyoto, which embodies the arts of proportions and simplicity in perfect harmony.

Wood was almost the only building material used in Japan until the second half of the 19th century. With extensive forests, building in timber continued to be an economic proposition. Wood was, in addition, extremely well suited to the particular climatic conditions. A structural frame raised above the ground was especially suitable for hot and humid summers; it ensured the best possible ventilation of both the lower part of the structure and of the house itself, for the paper-lined sliding doors in the bays between the frames could be opened completely. The wooden houses were, moreover, less vulnerable than stone or brick houses to the frequent earthquakes — though at the greatly increased risk of life. Building in timber was a vital part of the Japanese aesthetic sense; not only was the material appreciated for itself, but the system enabled the house to be opened to the garden on all sides. Removable partitions, simple furniture (consisting mainly of low tables and wall cupboards) and a free use of rooms provided considerable flexibility, even inside, where the size of rooms was governed by the module of the Tatami mat (approx. 6 x 3 feet).

With the advent of Buddhism, which reached Japan first from India via China and Korea in 552 AD, Japanese art and culture came under the influence of China for more than a thousand years. Apart from the acceptance of Chinese styles of architecture, this resulted in ever increasing building activity, apparent in numerous Buddhist temples of increasing size. Towards

1. The Shoden (main building) of the Inner Ise Shrine. Reconstruction of the early Shintoist sanctuary.

1. Der Shoden (Hauptgebäude) des inneren Ise-Schreins. Rekonstruktion des frühshintoistischen Heiligtums.

Die Entwicklung der japanischen Architektur bis 1945

2. The Katsura Palace, one of the imperial villas in Kyoto, 17th Century.

2. Der Katsura-Palast, eine der kaiserlichen Villen in Kyoto, 17. Jahrhundert.

Aus der Zeit vor der Einführung des Buddhismus (um die Mitte des 6. Jahrhunderts n. Chr.) haben sich in Japan keine Bauwerke erhalten, denen ein architektonischer Wert zugesprochen werden könnte. Eine Vorstellung darüber, wie die Architektur der vorbuddhistischen Frühzeit ausgesehen hat, kann am ehesten der innere Ise-Schrein (Abb. 1) in Ujiyamada auf der Insel Honshu vermitteln. Er ist das bedeutendste Zentrum der altjapanischen Shinto-Religion, die sich aus der Verehrung von Natur- und Himmelsgottheiten zu einem Kult der Sippen- und Ahnengötter entwickelte und eine enge Verbindung mit dem Kaisermythos einging. Die Bauten dieses Heiligtums, dessen Gründung auf das Jahr 5 v. Chr. oder, nach anderen Quellen, auf das späte 3. Jahrhundert n. Chr. zurückgeht, werden seit dem 7. Jahrhundert im Turnus von zwanzig Jahren abgerissen und auf einem Bauplatz unmittelbar daneben aus neuem Baumaterial wieder aufgebaut. Dieser Brauch läßt sich keineswegs mit dem raschen Verfall des Baustoffes Holz erklären — in Japan haben sich Holzbauten aus dem 7. Jahrhundert erhalten —, er entspringt vielmehr den religiösen Vorstellungen des Shintoismus, die darin ein Sinnbild für das Werden und Vergehen der Natur sehen. So wurde die Anlage in 1200 Jahren neunundfünfzigmal erneuert, die 60. Rekonstruktion ist 1974 fällig. Wenn auch jedesmal die Konstruktion und die Details des Vorgängerbaus genau übernommen wurden, so haben sich im Lauf der Jahrhunderte natürlich doch kleinere Abweichungen und fremde Zutaten eingeschlichen. Im ganzen darf die heutige Kopie aber dennoch als relativ authentisches Zeugnis der frühen japanischen Baukunst gelten.

Der Shoden, das Hauptgebäude der ganzen Anlage, spiegelt den damaligen Wohnhaustyp wider: einen Giebelbau mit rechteckigem Grundriß, ganz aus blaßgelbem, geglättetem, aber sonst unbehandeltem Zypressenholz errichtet, mit Rundpfosten, die ohne Fundament einfach ins Erdreich getrieben wurden. Der Fußboden ist etwa zwei Meter über den Baugrund hochgelegt, der Raum darunter offen. Ringsum läuft eine Veranda, die von dem weit ausladenden, mit Schilf gedeckten Satteldach geschützt wird. Dachfirst und Giebel tragen die charakteristischen Merkmale eines Shinto-Schreins: die über das Dach hinausgezogenen, sich überkreuzenden Giebelsparren (Chigi) und die quer über den Firstbalken gelegten Holzwalzen (Katsuogi), die bei Sturm ein Abdecken des Daches verhüten sollen.

In diesen Details lassen sich eine ganze Reihe von Charakteristika fassen, die mit gewissen Abwandlungen bis weit in das vorige Jahrhundert hinein für die ganze japanische Wohn-, Palast- und Tempelarchitektur ihre Gültigkeit behalten haben: die Skelettbauweise mit Ständer- und Rahmenkonstruktionen, das Sichtbarmachen und Hervorheben der Strukturglieder, das Umwandeln einzelner Konstruktionselemente in skulpturale Formen von ästhetischem Eigenleben und die Akzentuierung des weit überstehenden Daches. Da seine Schutzfunktion bei den großen Niederschlagsmengen, die in Japan fallen, besonderes Gewicht hat, wurde die Dachzone auch bei der formalen Gestaltung sehr wichtig genommen und entsprechend ausgeschmückt.

Im übrigen zeigt der Ise-Schrein bei aller Einfachheit und Schlichtheit doch eine sehr subtile Durchbildung des Ganzen und der Einzelform. Die außergewöhnliche Sensibilität für Materialreize und das intuitive Erfassen harmonikaler Gesetzmäßigkeiten waren für die japanische Architektur zu allen Zeiten bezeichnend. Sie gelten in ganz besonderem Maß für das wohl bedeutendste Beispiel des japanischen Wohnhausbaus, die Villa Katsura (Abb. 2) bei Kyoto aus dem 17. Jahrhundert, die die Kunst des Maßes und der Einfachheit in vollendeter Harmonie verkörpert.

Bis in die zweite Hälfte des 19. Jahrhunderts verwendete man in Japan fast ausschließlich Holz als Baumaterial. Reiche Waldbestände machten den Holzbau wirtschaftlich, und zugleich eignete er sich hervorragend für die besonderen klimatischen Bedingungen des Landes. In den extrem feuchten und heißen Sommern erwies sich die vom Boden abgehobene Rahmenbauweise als die günstigste: Sie sicherte die bestmögliche Durchlüftung der Unterkonstruktion und des Hauses selbst, da die Felder zwischen den Rahmen großenteils mit Hilfe papierbespannter Schiebetüren geöffnet werden konnten. Auch waren die Holzkonstruktionen weniger gegen die häufigen Erdbeben anfällig als Stein- oder Ziegelbauten, allerdings um den Preis der stark erhöhten Brandgefahr. Und nicht zuletzt entsprach der Holzbau in besonderem Maß dem ästhetischen Empfinden des Japaners, sowohl von der Materialwirkung her als auch

the end of the 7th century, more than five hundred Buddhist temples and monasteries had been built in Japan.

As centres of education and science, as well as social welfare, these temples are comparable to the monasteries of the West — large, rectangular temple areas surrounded by earth mounds, with gates on all four sides and an inner precinct with a cloistered quadrangle containing the 'Golden Hall' with the principal statue of Buddha and a Pagoda enshrining a Buddha relic or marking a holy place. The reconstruction of such an early Buddhist temple (Fig. 3) — the Shitennoji temple at Osaka dating back to 593 A.D — shows the cloisters surrounding the inner precinct which is entered by the two-storeyed inner gate. Along the north-south axis are the Pagoda, the Golden Hall (Main Hall), the extension of that Hall built into the north wing of the cloisters and the auditorium for readings of the Buddhist canon. However extensive a Buddhist temple area may be — with festival halls, dining halls, treasuries, stores and bathhouse or, as at the Shitennoji temple, an old people's home, an orphanage, an alms house and a pharmacy — the gatehouse, Pagoda, Golden Hall, Auditorium and Cloisters always form an inter-related, harmoniously dimensioned ensemble of sculpturally treated volumes and related open spaces. A view of the world's oldest timber structure, the Horyuji temple (Fig. 4) of 608 AD, shows the Gatehouse on the left, the Auditorium on the right and, between them, the Main Hall and Pagoda.

The differences between Buddhist structures and Shinto architecture are described by Tetsuro Yoshida in his book on Japanese Architecture: 'The individual buildings are placed on a stone platform. They are regular post-and-beam structures, rectangular in plan, with plastered walls and a widely overhung tiled roof. The roof is slightly concave and the caves turn up gently at the corners. The overhanging roof is characterised by the extension of the rafters and the provision of special brackets known as Masugumi or Kumimono which, though basically functional in character, have assumed great decorative importance. Externally as well as internally, the buildings are painted in vivid colours: posts and other wood-work are, on the outside, vermilion, except for their intersections which are yellow; latticework and balustrades are blue-green. These colours are in strong contrast to the white-plastered walls'.

For a period of 1400 years — from the introduction of Buddhism until the middle of the 19th century — new styles in Japanese architecture were always developed by a slow transformation of existing ones. Western architecture exhibits distinct breaks between successive periods of design (e. g. between Gothic and Renaissance) or even between certain variants of the same style (e. g. between High-Renaissance and Mannerism), often embodying a radical rejection of the characteristics of the preceding style. The Japanese, however, regarded each new style as a minor variation of an older form. Never was there a complete rejection of an existing style; old and new co-existed harmoniously. At the height of the feudal system, towards the end of the 12th century, for example, two new styles — Karayo and Tenjikuyo — were evolved, yet the traditional Wayo style persisted. Although there was an interval of nine centuries between the construction of the Main Hall of the Toshodaiji Temple in the middle of the 8th century (Fig. 5), and that of the Kiyomizu-dera Temple (Fig. 6), both were built in the same Wayo style, the use of different roof materials apart.

Such a scheme of development, it must be admitted, resulted in a degree of mannerism and, regarding construction, to complete stasis of technique. Around the middle of the 19th century, the policy of strict isolation that the members of the Tokugawa family, as trustees and military leaders (Shoguns) of the Emperor (Tenno) had adopted for over two centuries towards the West began to loosen. In 1853-54, commercial treaties with the United States, Britain, Netherlands and Russia brought the first amicable contacts with the West. The isolation policy of the Tokugawa period came to an end with the so-called Meiji Restoration in 1867, when the political power was restored to the Emperor Meiji. The feudal system was replaced by an absolute monarchy which became a constitutional monarchy in 1889.

Japan, eager now to catch up with the industrial revolution, was open to Western influence. The Japanese began to use stone and brick. The first brick buildings, of very simple design, were ironworks and textile mills, usually erected under the supervision of European experts. The cotton mill at Kagoshima (1866; Fig. 7) was built under the direction of an Englishman; but there were also American, French and Dutch advisers. During the 1860's and 1870's, the Japanese Government commissioned a number of foreign architects to plan public buildings, schools and factories. In two years the English architect, T. Waters, erected 1400 two-storey brick houses, colonnades on the ground floor, terraces above, in the Ginza district of Tokyo which had been razed by fire in 1872 (Fig. 8). From France came C. de Boinville, from Italy G. V. Capelletti, from Germany H. Emde and W. Böckmann. All of them introduced the historic-ising styles prevailing in their own countries.

An Englishman, Josiah Condor, who went to Japan in 1877, exerted the greatest influence, as the lecturer at the Faculty of Architecture of Tokyo Technical University, and there trained

3. Reconstruction of the Buddhist Shitennoji Temple at Osaka, 593 AD.

3. Rekonstruktion des buddhistischen Shitennoji-Tempels in Osaka, 593 n. Chr.

4. The Buddhist Horyuji Temple, the oldest still existing timber structure in the world, 608 AD.

4. Der buddhistische Horyuji-Tempel, ältester erhaltener Holzbau der Welt, 608 n. Chr.

5. Main Hall of the Toshodaiji Temple, founded 759 AD.

5. Haupthalle des Toshodaiji-Tempels, gegründet 759 n. Chr.

6. The Kiyomizu-dera Temple at Kyoto, 1633.

6. Der Kiyomizu-dera-Tempel in Kyoto, 1633.

wegen der Möglichkeit, das Haus nach Belieben zum Garten hin zu öffnen. Das System der beweglichen Trennwände, die einfache Innenausstattung (die außer niedrigen Tischen und Wandschränken keine Möbel kannte) und die variable Nutzung der Räume boten auch im Hausinneren eine sehr weitgehende Flexibilität, wobei die Raumgrößen nach der Maßeinheit der aus Reisstroh hergestellten Tatamimatte (etwa 190×95 cm) und deren Vielfachem bestimmt wurden.

Mit der 552 n. Chr. beginnenden Übernahme des Buddhismus, der Japan von seinem Mutterland Indien aus auf dem Weg über China und Korea erreichte, kam die japanische Kunst und Kultur für mehr als tausend Jahre unter den Einfluß Chinas. Das bedeutete neben der Aufnahme chinesischer Architekturformen eine schnell anwachsende Bautätigkeit, die sich in zahlreichen buddhistischen Tempelanlagen von immer größeren Abmessungen manifestierte. Gegen Ende des 7. Jahrhunderts gab es in Japan schon über fünfhundert buddhistische Tempel und Klöster. Als Stätten der Bildung und der Wissenschaft, aber auch der sozialen Fürsorge sind sie den abendländischen Klosteranlagen vergleichbar: große rechteckige, von Erdmauern umgebene Bezirke, mit Toren nach allen Himmelsrichtungen und einem inneren Tempelbereich, in dessen Hof, von Wandelgängen umschlossen, die »goldene Halle« mit der wichtigsten Buddhastatue und die Pagode zur Aufbewahrung einer Buddha-Reliquie oder als Markierung eines heiligen Ortes steht. Die Rekonstruktion einer solchen frühbuddhistischen Tempelanlage (Abb. 3), des Shitennoji-Tempels in Osaka von 593 n. Chr., zeigt den Wandelgang um den inneren Bezirk, den man durch das zweigeschossige innere Tor betritt. In der Nord-Süd-Achse stehen hintereinander die Pagode und die goldene Halle (Haupthalle) und in ihrer Verlängerung, eingebaut in den Nordflügel des Wandelgangs, die Aula für die Vorlesungen des buddhistischen Kanons. Wie umfangreich das Raumprogramm einer buddhistischen Tempelanlage auch sein mag — mit Festräumen, Speisesälen, Schatzhäusern, Speichern und Badehaus oder, wie beim Shitennoji-Tempel, mit Altersheim und Waisenhaus, Armenhospital und Armenapotheke —, immer bilden Torgebäude, Pagode, Haupthalle, Aula und Wandelhalle ein beziehungsreiches, in den Proportionen harmonisch ausgewogenes Ensemble aus plastischen Volumen und den entsprechenden Freiräumen. Ein Blick auf den ältesten erhaltenen Holzbau der Welt, den Horyuji-Tempel (Abb. 4) von 608, zeigt links die Torhalle und rechts die Aula, dazwischen Haupthalle und Pagode.

Was die buddhistischen Bauwerke von der Shinto-Architektur unterscheidet, beschreibt Tetsuro Yoshida in seinem Buch über »Japanische Architektur«: »Die einzelnen Bauten stehen auf einer steinernen Plattform. Sie sind im Grundriß rechteckige, regelmäßige Ständerbauten mit verputzten Wänden und einem weit ausladenden Ziegeldach. Die Dachfläche hat eine leicht konkave Krümmung und die Traufkanten eine sanfte, nach oben gerichtete Schweifung an den Ecken. Der große Dachüberstand wird durch die Verlängerung der Sparren und durch eine besondere Konsolenbildung, Masugumi oder auch Kumimono genannt, gestaltet, beides eigentlich rein konstruktive Elemente, die aber sehr bedeutsame dekorative Bedeutung erlangt haben. Das Äußere wie das Innere der Bauten haben einen lebhaften Farbanstrich: außen sind Pfosten und andere Holzteile zinnoberrot gestrichen, deren Schnittfläche aber gelb; Gitterwerk und Geländer sind blau-grün. Gegen die weiß verputzte Wand heben sich diese Farben stark ab.«

Über eine Zeitspanne von 1400 Jahren — seit der Einführung des Buddhismus bis zur Mitte des 19. Jahrhunderts — hat die japanische Architektur neue Stile stets dadurch geschaffen, daß sie die bestehenden Stilrichtungen ganz allmählich abwandelte. Während wir aus der abendländischen Architekturgeschichte deutliche Einschnitte zwischen Epochenstilen (etwa zwischen Gotik und Renaissance) oder auch zwischen Stilstufen (etwa zwischen Hochrenaissance und Manierismus) gewohnt sind, die manchmal eine radikale Abwendung von den vorangehenden Stilmerkmalen bedeuten, sah der Japaner jeden neuen Stil nur als nuancierende Abwandlung von älteren Stilformen. Niemals wurde das Bestehende völlig verworfen, vielmehr konnte Altes und Neues einträchtig nebeneinander existieren. Als zum Beispiel gegen Ende des 12. Jahrhunderts, in der Blütezeit des Feudalsystems, zwei neue Stile — Karayo und Tenjikuyo — geschaffen wurden, hielt sich der traditionelle Wayo-Stil weiter. Obwohl zwischen dem Bau der Haupthalle des Toshodaiji-Tempels aus der Mitte des 8. Jahrhunderts (Abb. 5) und der Errichtung des Kiyomizu-dera-Tempels (Abb. 6) eine Zeitspanne von neun Jahrhunderten liegt, sind doch beide — abgesehen von den unterschiedlichen Materialien der Dächer — im gleichen Wayo-Stil gehalten.

Man wird allerdings nicht übersehen dürfen, daß diese Art kultureller Entwicklung einem gewissen Manierismus Vorschub leistete und im Bereich der Konstruktion nahezu jeden Fortschritt lahmlegte.

Um die Mitte des neunzehnten Jahrhunderts begann sich die strenge Abschließung zu lockern, mit der die Mitglieder der Familie Tokugawa als Treuhänder und Feldherren (Shogune) des Kaisers (Tenno) mehr als zwei Jahrhunderte lang fast jede Berührung mit der westlichen Zivilisation vermieden hatten. Handelsabkommen mit den USA, England, Holland und Rußland

Japanese students in the same way as in the European architectural schools. At the same time, as a member of the Building Department in the Ministry for Engineering Construction, he designed numerous public buildings, mostly in brick. In accord with Western academic tradition, he reproduced a range of historical styles ranging from the Gothic to Baroque. The Government, however, was anxious to promote the spread of Western architecture, which was regarded as a symbol of the efficiency of the new administration. It wished also to demonstrate that the country was no longer backward.

In the 1880's, the first Japanese graduates went into practice. They had been trained in the spirit of European historism. Condor's disciple, Otokuma Katayama (1853–1917) combined elements of French 17th century architecture and English Palladianism in his Hiyokeikan Museum (Fig. 9). Other architects attempted a mixed Japanese-Western style (Fig. 10), in which a European plan (with solid walls and rooms strung along corridors) was combined with historicising facades (including random rubble and pilasters) and traditional Japanese roofs. With the spread of brick construction, the Japanese were faced with the problem of developing earthquake-proof building techniques. The Nobi earthquake of 1891 showed that brick buildings offered little resistance to earthquakes, whilst wooden buildings stood up surprisingly well — as might have been expected from the experience of Japanese building history. The first architect who dealt effectively with the problem of earthquake-proof construction was J. Condor, who strengthened brick walls with reinforcing iron bars and hoops. After many experiments, the Japanese began to use steel frame construction or composite brick and steel frame structures. The first examples of these two methods date back to the mid-1890's. Around the turn of the century, Rikichi Sano developed a systematic theory of earthquake proofing based on the use of reinforced concrete. His Maruzen building, completed in 1909, was one of the first reinforced concrete frame structures. Such new building techniques gave Japan's new building industry a great impetus.

The spread of Western architecture was not unopposed. With the growth of national consciousness, many critics rejected even the mixed Japanese-European compromise and, emphasising their own architectural tradition, tried to promote the construction of houses and public buildings of timber alone. Nationalism was further reinforced by a victory over Russia in the war of 1904–05. Even those architects who were little concerned to preserve the historic heritage began, in the early years of the 20th century, to discuss the direction in which Japanese architecture should develop. They were in a dilemma: Western-influenced buildings were alien to their mentality; traditional wooden buildings constituted a fire risk and were outdated.

In 1909, the architect Chuta Itoh, who had studied the old buildings of Japan and East-Asia, argued that Japan should rid itself of European influences and should revive its own traditional style so as to arrive at a new formal language through a gradual adaptation of Western-style building methods. A year later, the critic Yashuharu Ohtsuka voiced the opposite thesis; that Japan should begin by accepting Western architecture, and then modify it. Both had the same objective; to create a new, specifically Japanese style. Rikichi Sano, who upheld a rational theory of architecture, was critical of both proposals. The purpose of a building, he argued, was for practical use. Japanese architects should therefore become engineers with a rational outlook. Their chief aim should be to create useful buildings at a minimum cost. His point of view was developed in Toshihiko Noda's book 'Kenchiku Hi-Geijutsu Ron' ('Architecture is not an Art'). Noda rejected any form of decoration, laying even more emphasis on a rational approach, on structure and functionalism in architecture. Although these ideas had no immediate effect, they eased the transition in modern architecture in the 1920's. The controversy about future Japanese architecture dragged on well into the 1950's. Some architects looked forward to a synthesis of the different standpoints, others aimed at a preservation of the national heritage. The early 1920's are marked by a milestone in architecture: Frank Lloyd Wright's Imperial Hotel in Tokyo (Fig. 11, 12). The effect of this building, erected between 1919 and 1922, was at first indirect. It provided the younger Japanese architects with a forceful example of modern architecture and made them aware of the high originality of a great artistic personality. But the organic concept of architecture put forward by Wright found no immediate echo. Not for another thirty years was Japanese architecture able to boast of buildings with a similarly rich and plastic complexity.

In 1920, the interest of progressive architects focussed on Jugendstil. Twenty years after the Vienna Secession, the movement of the Japanese Secession was started by a group of architects who had just completed their studies at Tokyo University; these included Sutemi Horiguchi (born in 1895) and Mamoru Yamada (1894–1966). The formation of this group marks the beginning of the modern movement in Japan. Horiguchi and Yamada were, in fact, two important representatives of the pioneer generation, born in the early 1890's. The activities of the group were confined, for a while, to the exhibition of plans and models. But their ideas eventually took form in a series of buildings, all in the Tokyo area: Horiguchi's Memorial

7. Cotton Mill at Kagoshima, 1866.

7. Baumwollspinnerei in Kagoshima, 1866.

8. T. Waters: Two-storey row houses in the Ginza district of Tokyo, 1872-74.

8. T. Waters: Hauszeile im Ginza-Bezirk in Tokio, 1872-74.

9. Otokuma Katayama: Hiyokeikan Museum at Tokyo, 1908.

9. Otokuma Katayama: Hiyokeikan-Museum in Tokio, 1908.

10. Contest design for a building of the Nisshin Life-Insurance Company, 1916.

10. Wettbewerbsentwurf für das Gebäude der Nisshin-Lebensversicherungsgesellschaft, 1916.

brachten in den Jahren 1853-54 die ersten freundschaftlichen Kontakte mit dem Westen. Ihr definitives Ende fand die Isolationspolitik der Tokugawa-Periode mit der sogenannten Meiji-Restauration von 1867, die dem Kaiser Meiji die politische Gewalt zurückgab. An die Stelle des Feudalstaates trat damit die absolute Monarchie, die 1889 in eine konstitutionelle Monarchie umgewandelt wurde.

Jetzt war der Weg frei für das Einströmen westlicher Einflüsse, denen sich Japan nun bereitwillig öffnete, um möglichst rasch die industrielle Revolution nachzuholen. Auf dem Gebiet der Architektur lernten die Japaner, die bis dahin nur die Technik des Holzbaus kannten, mit Steinen und Ziegeln umzugehen. Die ersten, noch sehr einfachen Mauerwerksbauten waren Eisenwerke und Textilfabriken, vorwiegend aus Backsteinen. Sie entstanden meist unter der Aufsicht von europäischen Fachleuten. So war bei der Baumwollspinnerei in Kagoshima (Abb. 7) von 1866 ein englischer Baumeister beteiligt; aber auch Amerikaner, Franzosen und Holländer wirkten als Berater. Für die Planung von öffentlichen Bauten, Schulen und Fabriken berief die Regierung in den sechziger und siebziger Jahren eine ganze Reihe ausländischer Architekten, unter ihnen den Engländer T. Waters, der innerhalb von zwei Jahren im 1872 abgebrannten Ginza-Bezirk von Tokio 1400 zweigeschossige Backsteinhäuser baute (Abb. 8), mit Kolonnaden im Erdgeschoß und Terrassen darüber. Aus Frankreich kam C. de Boinville, aus Italien G. V. Capelletti, aus Deutschland H. Emde und W. Böckmann. Sie alle brachten die Vorliebe für historisierende Stilimitationen mit, wie sie damals die Architektur ihrer Heimatländer beherrschte. Den größten Einfluß übte der Engländer Josiah Condor aus, der 1877 nach Japan ging. Als Dozent an der Architekturfakultät der Technischen Hochschule in Tokio bildete er japanische Studenten nach dem Muster europäischer Architekturschulen aus. Zugleich entwarf er als Mitglied der Bauabteilung im Ministerium für Ingenieurwesen zahlreiche Regierungsgebäude, meist Backsteinbauten. Ganz im Sinne des akademischen Historismus rekapitulierte er dabei die verschiedensten abendländischen Stile, von der Gotik über die Renaissance bis zum Barock.

Die Regierung förderte nachdrücklich die Ausbreitung der westlichen Baukunst, und damit natürlich auch den herrschenden Eklektizismus. Architektur »im westlichen Stil« galt als höchster Inbegriff für die Tüchtigkeit der neuen Verwaltung. Außerdem wollte man der Welt zeigen, daß Japan nicht länger als zurückgebliebenes Land betrachtet werden durfte.

Als im Lauf der achtziger Jahre die ersten japanischen Hochschulabsolventen in die Praxis gingen, waren sie völlig im Geist des europäischen Historismus ausgebildet. So vereinigte zum Beispiel der Condor-Schüler Otokuma Katayama (1853–1917) in seinem Hiyokeikanmuseum (Abb. 9) Elemente der französischen Architektur des 17. Jahrhunderts mit Merkmalen des englischen Palladianismus. Oder aber sie praktizierten einen japanisch-europäischen Mischstil (Abb. 10), bei dem westliche Grundrißschemata (mit massiven Wänden und an Korridoren aufgereihten Räumen) mit historisierenden Fassaden (mit Rustika und Pilasterordnungen) und traditionellen japanischen Dachformen verbunden wurden.

Die Ausbreitung des Mauerwerksbaus konfrontierte die Japaner mit dem Problem, erdbebensichere Bauweisen zu entwickeln. Das Erdbeben von Nobi im Jahr 1891 hatte nämlich gezeigt, daß Backsteinbauten wenig widerstandsfähig waren, während sich Holzbauten — wie nach den Erfahrungen der japanischen Baugeschichte zu erwarten — überraschend gut hielten. Als erster befaßte sich J. Condor mit der Erdbebensicherung: Er versteifte die Backsteinwände mit eisernen Zugstäben und Eisenbändern. Nach manchen Experimenten gingen die Japaner schließlich dazu über, reine Stahlskelettbauten zu errichten oder eine Verbundbauweise aus Stahlskelett und Backsteinmauerwerk anzuwenden. Mitte der neunziger Jahre entstanden die ersten Beispiele für die eine wie für die andere Methode. Um die Jahrhundertwende entwickelte Rikichi Sano eine systematische Theorie der Erdbebensicherung mit Hilfe von Stahlbeton. Sein 1909 fertiggestelltes Maruzengebäude war eines der ersten Bauwerke mit einem Stahlbetonskelett. Die neuen Konstruktionsverfahren gaben der jungen Bauindustrie Japans einen kräftigen Auftrieb.

Die Verbreitung westlicher Bauformen vollzog sich nicht ohne Widerspruch. Im Zeichen des erstarkenden Nationalbewußtseins gab es genug kritische Stimmen, die auch den Kompromiß eines japanisch-europäischen Mischstils ablehnten und unter Berufung auf die eigene Architekturtradition Wohnhäuser und öffentliche Bauten in möglichst reiner Holzbauweise propagierten. Der Sieg über Rußland im Krieg von 1904—05 verstärkte die nationalistischen Tendenzen noch mehr. Aber auch diejenigen Architekten, die keineswegs das historische Erbe konservieren wollten, begannen zu Anfang des zwanzigsten Jahrhunderts immer lebhafter die Frage zu diskutieren, in welcher Richtung sich die japanische Architektur künftig entwickeln solle. Man stand vor einem Zwiespalt: Bauten im westlichen Stil waren dem japanischen Gefühl mehr oder weniger fremd, auf der anderen Seite waren die herkömmlichen Holzbauten feuergefährlich und veraltet.

Der Architekt Chuta Itoh, der sich bei seinen historischen Studien sehr eingehend mit der Baukunst Japans und Ostasiens befaßt hatte, vertrat 1909 leidenschaftlich den Standpunkt,

Tower at the Peace Exhibition (1922), Yamada's Central Telegraph Office (1926; Fig. 13), and Kikuji Ishimoto's Asahi Newspaper Building (1927). The designs were influenced not only by the Jugendstil, but even more by German Expressionism to which the young architects were particularly attracted as they felt that it allowed them greater freedom to develop their structural ideas and detail design.

While an understanding of Jugendstil and Expressionism came late, the Japanese avant-garde of 1925 made contact promptly with international architectural movements. Through visits abroad and detailed reports, critics became acquainted with the Esprit Nouveau, de Stijl and the Bauhaus. Japanese architects born ten years later than the pioneers studied at the Bauhaus or went to Paris to work with Le Corbusier. Two important representatives of modern Japanese architecture worked in Le Corbusier's studio: Kunio Mayekawa (b. 1905) from 1928 to 1930, and Junzo Sakakura (b. 1904) from 1929 to 1936. In Japan itself, Walter Gropius' book on International Architecture, published in 1925, had considerable influence. The new movement was also joined by members of the Japanese Secession such as Horiguchi and Yamada who made their own contribution towards the final break-through to modern architecture. However, the period during which the Japanese produced architecture in the so-called International Style was confined to a decade, before it was overthrown by a new wave of nationalism.

Between 1928 and 1936 several well-designed, functional buildings were put up in Japan — Sutemi Horiguchi's Meteorological Station on the island of Oshima (1928; Fig. 14), Tetsuro Yoshida's Central Post Office, Tokyo (1931; Fig. 15), Togo Murano's Sogoh Department Store, Osaka (completed in 1935; Fig. 16), and Mamoru Yamada's Theishin Hospital, Tokyo (1937; Fig. 17). Of special interest was Junzo Sakakura's Japanese Pavilion (Fig. 18) at the Paris World Exhibition of 1937 which showed the Western World how high a standard could be achieved by the Japanese.

Japan was greatly affected by the economic crisis of 1929. The pressure of population increase and the need to export at any price created problems which, in view of the political position at that time, could be solved only by force of arms. In 1932, the Japanese went to war with China. This imperialistic policy dictated a relapse in art into national romanticism. The conservative classes, consisting mainly of officers, civil servants and landowners, acquired such an ascendancy that progressive developments in architecture became more and more difficult. All building activities were coloured by ideals of Japanese nationalism; pseudo-Japanese symbols were used everywhere. There was a great predilection for the so-called Imperial Crown style (Fig. 19), which derived its name from the fact that reinforced concrete structures were crowned with traditional tiled roofs.

11, 12. Frank Lloyd Wright: Imperial Hotel in Tokyo, finished in 1922.

11, 12. Frank Lloyd Wright: Imperial Hotel in Tokio, fertiggestellt 1922.

13. Mamoru Yamada: Central Telegraph Office in Tokyo, 1926.

13. Mamoru Yamada: Telegrafenamt in Tokio, 1926.

m...
gesetz...
dieses an...
die Entwicklu...
strukturellen Arch...
eines Gebäudes sei s...
ten vor allem als wissen...
die Erstellung funktional ri...
wurde in Toshihiko Nodas Buch...
Künsten) weiterentwickelt. Noda leh...
tung von Rationalität, Struktur und Fun...
auch keinen unmittelbaren Widerhall fanden...
gang zur Moderne in den zwanziger Jahren. ...
den japanischen Baustil der Zukunft noch bis üb...
der politischen Konstellation und der persönlichen Übe...
Blick mehr nach vorn auf eine Synthese der Standpunkte ...
nationalen Erbes.

Am Beginn der zwanziger Jahre steht ein Markstein des neuen ...
in Tokio (Abb. 11, 12) von Frank Lloyd Wright. Die Wirkung des zwischen...
fenen Bauwerks war zunächst eher indirekt. Es machte die jüngeren Arc...
einem kraftvollen Beispiel der modernen Baukunst bekannt und ließ sie begre...
originellen schöpferischen Leistungen eine große Künstlerpersönlichkeit fähig s...
Dagegen fand die organische Architekturauffassung Wrights keine direkte Nachfolge. E...
dreißig Jahre später gibt es in der japanischen Architektur Bauten, die eine ähnlich ...
fältige räumliche Durchdringung aufweisen, eine vergleichbare plastische Gliederung mit reichen...
Licht- und Schattenspiel und ebenso expressive kubische Formen aus liegenden und stehenden
Blöcken.

Um 1920 wandte sich das Interesse der fortschrittlich orientierten Architekten erst einmal dem
Jugendstil zu. Mit zwei Jahrzehnten Abstand zur Wiener Sezession schlossen sich 1920 Sutemi
Horiguchi (geb. 1895) und Mamoru Yamada (1894–1966) sowie einige andere Kollegen, die
gerade das Studium an der Tokio-Universität beendet hatten, zur japanischen Gruppe »Sezes-
sion« zusammen. Diese Vereinigung markiert den Beginn der modernen Bewegung in Japan.
Mit Horiguchi und Yamada hat sie zwei wichtige Repräsentanten der um 1890–95 geborenen
Pioniergeneration hervorgebracht. Der Einfluß der Gruppe war beträchtlich; er hat das Ende
des Eklektizismus und der historisierenden Stilimporte wesentlich beschleunigt. Die Mitglieder
der Sezession trugen ihre Ideen zunächst mit Plänen und Modellen auf Ausstellungen vor.
Schließlich konnten sie ihre Vorstellungen aber auch in Bauten verwirklichen, die alle in Tokio
entstanden: Horiguchi 1922 mit dem Gedenkturm der Friedensausstellung, Yamada 1926 mit
dem Telegrafenamt (Abb. 13) und Kikuji Ishimoto 1927 mit dem Asahi-Zeitungsgebäude. Diese
Entwürfe waren übrigens nicht nur vom Jugendstil, sondern mehr noch vom deutschen Expressionismus beeinflußt. Von ihm fühlten sich die jungen Architekten der Sezessionsgruppe deshalb so besonders angezogen, weil er ihnen in der Konstruktion und im Detail den größten
Spielraum für die Entfaltung ihrer schöpferischen Kräfte ließ.

Während die Auseinandersetzung mit dem Jugendstil und dem Expressionismus erst mit größerem zeitlichen Abstand begann, fanden die japanischen Avantgardisten um 1925 den unmittelbaren Anschluß an die internationale Architekturentwicklung.

Auf Studienreisen und durch ausführliche Berichte wurden japanische Architekten und Kritiker
rasch und genau mit den Ideen des »Esprit Nouveau«, des Stijl und des Bauhauses vertraut.
Junge Japaner, die etwa zehn Jahre später als die Pioniergeneration geboren waren, studier-
ten am Bauhaus oder gingen nach Paris, um bei Le Corbusier zu arbeiten. Zwei große
Repräsentanten der neuen japanischen Architektur waren längere Zeit Mitarbeiter in Corbusiers
Atelier: Kunio Mayekawa (geb. 1905) von 1928–30 und Junzo Sakakura (geb. 1904) von 1929–36.
In Japan selbst hatte das 1925 erschienene Buch von Walter Gropius über »Internationale
Architektur« nachhaltige Wirkung. So wandten sich auch Mitglieder der japanischen Sezessions-
gruppe wie Horiguchi und Yamada der neuen Richtung zu und trugen gleichfalls dazu bei,
der modernen Architektur endgültig zum Durchbruch zu verhelfen.

Allerdings war die Zeitspanne, in der die Japaner im Sinne des sogenannten »Internationalen
Stils« entwerfen konnten, auf ein knappes Jahrzehnt beschränkt. Dann verdrängte eine neue
nationale Welle den »Funktionalismus«, wie diese internationale Richtung wegen ihres Ver-
suches, die Baukunst durch ein logisches System mit einfachen Regeln zu funktionalisieren,
auch in Japan bezeichnet wurde.

14. Sutemi Horiguchi: Meteorological Station in
the island of Oshima, 1928.
15. Tetsuro Yoshida: Central Post Office in Tokyo,
1931.

14. Sutemi Horiguchi: Metereologische Station
auf der Insel Oshima, 1928.
15. Tetsuro Yoshida: Hauptpostamt in Tokio, 1931.

...lion
...efore
...signed
...ds and
...ials and
...ructures.

...' (Fig. 22)
...ased on the
...floor area of
...was available

module...
55 sq. metres. .
for \$ 1,000 (US), inclu...
Another minimum sized pre... member of the
younger generation of architects wi... ...sign of low-price
houses. His minimal timber house for a ra... . 23) is evidence
of the efforts made to overcome the housing sho... ...on methods.
All the houses designed during the early post-war perio... ...t construction and
minimal floor area. A particular feature was the combination of li... ...om and kitchen — a
move, it was thought, to make Japanese family life more democratic. This detail was a
reflection of an overall move towards democracy beginning in 1945 with the abolition of the
Tenno system. In the process, traditional ideas of house building were abandoned and the
nationalistic tendencies in architecture rejected. The architectural movement took up the
development that had been interrupted during the 1930's. Reflecting the general economic
position before the boom of 1950, progress in housing construction was slow. Steel and concrete were rationed and unavailable for private building work. Architects had little work.
Many sought work in government or municipal offices or with the occupation authorities. An
exception to the general rule were the reinforced concrete council flats, built in 1948, not
subject to government control. One of the first architects to resume free-lance activities was
Mayekawa. In 1947, he built the Kinokuniya Book Store and in 1948 the Keio Hospital, which,
in spite of their size, were entirely of timber. Both as a designer and thinker Mayekawa
had a great and uplifting influence on the younger architects, who admired, in particular,
his consistency of approach and evident faith in the new architecture.
With no commissions, architects concerned themselves largely with theory and sought a new
basis for their work. In 1947, a 'New Architects' Union' (NAU) with 500 members was founded.
The NAU became the leading group of the late 1940's and made a great contribution towards
democratization in the sphere of architecture. It became a forum for discussion, especially
between the protagonists of the revived Functionalism and those of the new Social Realism.
Their struggle led eventually to the dissolution of the organization in 1951. The confrontation
between the Eastern and Western blocs before and during the Korean War led the Social
Realists, including many young architects, to take up an extreme standpoint, rejecting func-
tionalist architecture as cosmopolitan, reactionary and undemocratic. Most of the Social
Realists, however, admitted that the new architecture of the Communist countries offered
no convincing alternative. During the post-1950 building boom, they gave no convincing

16. Togo Murano: Department Store Sogoh in Osaka, 1935.
17. Mamoru Yamada: Teishin Hospital in Tokyo, 1937.
18. Junzo Sakakura: Japanese Pavilion at the Paris World Exhibition of 1937.

16. Togo Murano: Warenhaus Sogoh in Osaka, 1935.
17. Mamoru Yamada: Teishin-Hospital in Tokio, 1937.
18. Junzo Sakakura: Japanischer Pavillon auf der Weltausstellung in Paris, 1937.

19. Hitoshi Watanabe: National Museum in Tokyo, 1937.

19. Hitoshi Watanabe: Nationalmuseum in Tokio, 1937.

20. Kunio Mayekawa: Contest design for the National Museum in Tokyo, 1931.
21. Kenzo Tange: Contest design for a Sino-Japanese Cultural Centre, 1943.

20. Kunio Mayekawa: Wettbewerbsprojekt für das Nationalmuseum in Tokio, 1931.
21. Kenzo Tange: Wettbewerbsprojekt für ein japanisch-chinesisches Kulturzentrum, 1943.

Immerhin entstanden zwischen 1928 und 1936 eine ganze Reihe gelungener funktionalistischer Bauten, mit denen sich Japan erfolgreich der internationalen Architekturbewegung anschloß. Als Beispiele seien genannt: Sutemi Horiguchis Meteorologische Station auf der Insel Oshima (Abb. 14) von 1928, Tetsuro Yoshidas Hauptpostamt in Tokio (Abb. 15) von 1931, das 1935 fertiggestellte Warenhaus Sogoh in Osaka (Abb. 16) von Togo Murano und Mamoru Yamadas Theishin-Hospital in Tokio (Abb. 17) von 1937. Besondere Bedeutung erlangte Junzo Sakakuras japanischer Pavillon (Abb. 18) auf der Weltausstellung von 1937 in Paris. Er zeigte dem Westen, welchen hohen Stand die moderne japanische Architektur in ihren Spitzenleistungen zu erreichen vermochte.

Die 1929 einsetzende Weltwirtschaftskrise hatte Japan besonders stark getroffen. Der Druck des Bevölkerungsüberschusses und der Zwang, um jeden Preis zu exportieren, schufen Probleme, die den maßgeblichen politischen Kräften nur mit Waffengewalt lösbar schienen. So begannen die Japaner 1932 den Krieg gegen China, das man sich als Versorgungs- und Absatzmarkt sichern wollte. Die imperialistische Politik war auf kulturellem Gebiet von einem Rückfall in nationalromantische Vorstellungen begleitet. Die konservativen Elemente des Tenno-Systems, das sich vorwiegend auf die Militärs, die Beamten und die Großgrundbesitzer stützte, gewannen allmählich so sehr die Oberhand, daß auf dem Gebiet der Architektur eine progressive Entwicklung immer mehr erschwert wurde. Statt dessen geriet das Baugeschehen zunehmend in den Sog eines nationalistisch gefärbten Eklektizismus, der mit pseudo-japanischen Symbolformen nationales Selbstbewußtsein demonstrieren wollte. So wurde beispielsweise die Verwendung des »Imperial-Crown«-Stils stark gefördert (Abb. 19). Er hat seinen Namen davon, daß ein Stahlbetonbau ein historisierendes Ziegeldach wie eine Krone aufgesetzt bekam.

Als Reaktion auf diese Entwicklung gründeten 1937 führende Architekten und Kritiker, unter ihnen Hideo Kishida, Shinji Koike, Sutemi Horiguchi, Yoshiro Taniguchi, Takeo Satow und Kunio Mayekawa, den japanischen Werkbund »Kosaku Bunka Renmei« und gaben die Publikation »Kosaka Bunka« (Werkkultur) heraus. Über die Verteidigung der modernen Architektur hinaus suchte der japanische Werkbund auch auf den Gebieten der industriellen und kunsthandwerklichen Formgebung nach fortschrittlichen Lösungen, die den zeitgenössischen Wohn- und Lebensverhältnissen besser gerecht wurden. Seine Tätigkeit fand jedoch bald ein Ende, als der militaristische Nationalismus die politische und kulturelle Szene vollends beherrschte. Mayekawa, der nicht nur die architektonischen Ideen Le Corbusiers nach Japan gebracht hatte, sondern auch dessen Vorstellungen vom sozialen Aspekt des Bauens, versuchte immer wieder gegen die chauvinistischen Tendenzen zu opponieren. Seine radikale Ablehnung des offiziell geförderten Pseudo-Monumentalstils trat bei seinem Wettbewerbsentwurf für das Nationalmuseum in Tokio (Abb. 20) deutlich zutage. Sein Entwurf hatte jedoch keine Chance. Gebaut wurde 1937 das mit dem 1. Preis ausgezeichnete Projekt von Hitoshi Watanabe (Abb. 19): ein Musterbeispiel für den Imperial-Crown-Stil.

Nach dem Ausbruch des zweiten Weltkriegs blieb auch den avantgardistischen Architekten nur noch die Möglichkeit, sich dem herrschenden Geschmack anzupassen. Kenzo Tanges Wettbewerbsprojekt für ein japanisch-chinesisches Kulturzentrum von 1943 (Abb. 21) ist ein historisches Beispiel für die situationsbedingte Anpassung.

Die Neuorientierung der japanischen Architektur nach 1945

Bei Kriegsende am 15. August 1945 waren in Japan 2,7 Millionen Häuser zerstört. Rund 4,2 Millionen Wohnungen fehlten, und etwa 14 Millionen Menschen hatten nur eine behelfsmäßige Unterkunft. Es war also die nächstliegende Aufgabe, die Wohnungsnot so schnell wie möglich zu beheben, und zwar mit geringen Kosten, ökonomischen Herstellungsmethoden und kurzen Bauzeiten. In ihren Projekten gingen die Architekten den einzig richtigen Weg: Sie entwickelten Kleinwohnungen als Übergangslösung und wollten mit Hilfe der Vorfabrikation und der industriellen Massenproduktion eine rationelle Fertigung in Gang bringen. In der Praxis kamen diese Bemühungen allerdings wegen der Materialknappheit und dem Fehlen geeigneter Produktionsstätten nicht über die Anfänge hinaus. Statt dessen wurden die ersten Häuser der Nachkriegszeit nach wie vor in rein handwerklicher Methode nach traditionellen Vorbildern in Holzbauweise ausgeführt. Was an vorgefertigten Bauten erstellt werden konnte, erreichte bei weitem keine Stückzahlen, die den Nachholbedarf spürbar verringert hätten. Als dann um 1950 der Wohnungsbau, zum Teil mit staatlicher Finanzhilfe, in größerem Umfang einsetzte, gingen die Wohnwünsche der Bevölkerung bereits über die Minimallösungen hinaus. Kleinhäuser waren als Provisorium kaum mehr gefragt.

Unter den ersten Nachkriegsversuchen mit präfabrizierten Häusern galten die von Kunio Mayekawa und seiner Gruppe zwischen 1945 und 1950 entworfenen und auch hergestellten präfabrizierten »Premos«-Typen (Abb. 22) als eine Meisterleistung. Die Holzhäuser, die in einer

expression to their ideas. Discussion turned once again from the controversy between Functionalists and Social Realists, to the question of creating, in the face of international influences, a specifically Japanese style.

The beginning of the Japanese building boom and the inception of a new building style, 1950-1955

The inflationary period came to an end with the beginning of the Korean War in 1950. A boom followed. There was a rapid increase in the production of basic materials — cement, steel and glass — and rationing came to an end. Throughout the country building activity was resumed. Architectural theorising gave way to practical construction. Apart from housing, a spate of large projects was initiated by regional and municipal administrations; town halls, administrative centres, libraries, museums, concert halls and hospitals. Private enterprise required factories, offices and banks. Most of these new buildings were of reinforced concrete, making extensive use of industrial methods of prefabrication.

Within a few years a number of buildings had been put up that reflected international architectural developments. The first was Antonin Raymond's Reader's Digest building in Tokyo (Fig. 24), of 1951. The Reader's Digest building incorporated exposed concrete work of a hitherto unknown perfection. The principle of the cantilevered floor and glazed curtain-walling was likewise new to the Japanese. Born in 1890 in Vladno, Bohemia, Raymond went in 1910 to America and, in 1919, with Frank Lloyd Wright to Tokyo, where he became the site-architect to the Imperial Hotel. He remained in Japan after its completion, started a practice, and exerted a considerable influence. Many Japanese architects who have since acquired a considerable reputation, such as Mayekawa, Yoshimura and Masuzawa, worked in his office. Kunio Mayekawa's Nippon Sogo Bank in Tokyo, finished in 1952 (Fig. 25), was a pioneering example of post-war architecture, notable not so much for its formal design qualities (it is a sober, straightforward building) but rather for the technological advances which were incorporated, forcing the building industry to adopt new methods of construction. Mayekawa used a steel frame clad with prefabricated concrete panels. The sliding windows had aluminium frames; perforated plywood was used for sound-insulating partitions and acoustic ceilings were designed using aluminium sheets. Such details are now commonplace. But at the time their introduction was difficult, for the building industry was not geared to their production.

Another of the early classics of Japanese post-war architecture was Mayekawa's concert hall and library building at Yokohama (1954; Fig. 26). The strongly expressed and contrasted volumes and the vigorous appearance of the exposed concrete columns were harbingers of the forceful handling of concrete characteristic of his later works. An important example of the modern architecture of the early 1950's is Junzo Sakakura's Museum of Modern Art in Kamakura (Fig. 27), the first part of which was finished in 1951. The square building appears to float above the water on slender steel columns, not unlike the pilotis used by Le Corbusier, with whom Sakakura had worked between 1929 and 1937.

With the completion of Sakakura's museum, another pioneer of the modern movement emerged in Togo Murano. Since the construction of the Sogoh Department store in 1935 (Fig. 16), he had been continuously concerned with their design. The first post-war result of this preoccupation was the Takashima-Ya Branch in Tokyo (1952; Fig. 28). The interiors are regarded as functional entities. Because the sales areas have artificial lighting, the interiors are screened completely from the outside world — a measure adopted in all Murano's later designs. In the Takashima-Ya building, narrow vertical windows in the glass brick walls do allow occasional glimpses of the outside, but the Sogoh Department Store in Tokyo, completed in 1957, is entirely enclosed, so that even the number of floors is no longer discernible from the outside. In many designs prepared by Murano in the 1950's — such as the Nihon' Seimei administration building (1958; p. 150) or the Kobuki Theatre in Osaka (1959), his special artistic architectural abilities are evident: he attempts to combine functionalism and the traditional Japanese heritage by including a range of traditional motifs.

Murano was not alone. After 1950, increasing attention was paid to Japanese traditions. There is however, a clear distinction to be drawn between the progressives who aimed at a synthesis of modern Western architecture and indigenous building motifs and these conservative traditionalists. The new men did not intend a revival of traditional motifs or an acceptance of historic clichés, but rather a re-interpretation of the Japanese cultural tradition. They wished to create a specifically Japanese architectural style, based on contemporary methods of building.

The revival of interest in indigenous architecture is no doubt a reflection of the country's efforts to stay neutral in the East-West confrontation. Certainly, the Peace Treaty of San Francisco in 1951, which gave Japan her independence of the United States, strengthened

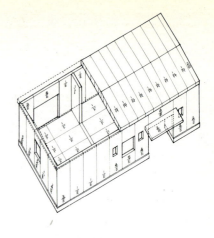

22. Kunio Mayekawa: Prefabricated timber house types 'Premos, type 7', 1945-50.

22. Kunio Mayekawa: Vorfabrizierte Holzhaustypen »Premos, Typ 7«, 1945-1950.

Woche montiert werden konnten und nach der Maßeinheit der Tatamimatte geplant waren, hatten eine Wohnfläche von 55 m². Mayekawa entwickelte eine ganze Reihe von Typenvarianten. So war beispielsweise der Typ Nr. 7 im Jahr 1949 mit komplettem Innenausbau für rund 1000 US-Dollar zu kaufen.

Ein weiteres Beispiel für vorgefertigte Minimalwohnungen bieten die Arbeiten von Kiyoshi Ikebe. Er gehört zu der Generation jüngerer Architekten und hatte mit seinen Entwürfen für das Existenzminimum beträchtlichen Einfluß. Holzhaustypen wie seine Kleinwohnung für eine Familie mit Kind von 1950 (Abb. 23) sind historische Belege für die damaligen Versuche, mit rationellen Methoden dem Wohnungsmangel entgegenzuwirken.

Die in der ersten Nachkriegszeit geplanten Häuser hatten durchweg minimale Grundrisse und waren sehr leicht gebaut. Eines ihrer Merkmale war die Wohnküche, mit der die Japaner versuchten, das Familienleben demokratischer zu gestalten. Ein solches Detail spiegelt den umfassenden Demokratisierungsprozeß wider, der nach 1945 mit der Abschaffung des absolutistischen Tenno-Systems einsetzte. So wie er im Wohnungsbau mit den feudalistischen Vorstellungen brach, so verdrängte er auf dem Gebiet der Architektur ganz allgemein die nationalistischen Tendenzen. Statt dessen knüpfte man dort wieder an, wo die Entwicklung in den dreißiger Jahren unterbrochen worden war: beim Funktionalismus.

Da es auf dem Wohnbausektor, wie überall in der japanischen Volkswirtschaft in den Inflationsjahren vor 1950, nur schleppend voranging, suchten viele Architekten bei staatlichen oder städtischen Ämtern Unterschlupf oder sie arbeiteten für die Besatzungsbehörden. Denn solange Stahl und Beton rationiert waren und von der Privatwirtschaft nicht als Baustoffe verwendet werden durften, fehlte es für freischaffende Architekten an der Existenzgrundlage. Lediglich die Wohnbauten der Gemeindebehörden, die von 1948 an wieder in Stahlbeton ausgeführt wurden, bildeten eine Ausnahme, da die Stadtverwaltungen nicht der Regierungskontrolle unterstanden. Als einer der ersten nahm Mayekawa seine Tätigkeit als freier Architekt wieder auf. 1947 baute er die Kinokuniya-Buchhandlung, 1948 das Keio-Hospital, beides reine Holzbauten, trotz ihrer relativen Größe. Mit seinen Planungen und theoretischen Arbeiten stärkte Mayekawa vor allem die Moral der jüngeren Architekten, die seine konsequente Haltung und sein klares Bekenntnis zu einer neuen Architekturauffassung bewunderten.

Der Auftragsmangel führte dazu, daß sich die Architekten vorwiegend theoretisch mit ihren Berufsproblemen beschäftigten und neue Grundlagen für ihre Arbeit suchten. So kam es 1947 zur Gründung der »New Architect's Union« (NAU) mit 500 Mitgliedern. Die NAU avancierte zur führenden Gruppenbewegung der späten vierziger Jahre und hat viel für die Demokratisierung im Bereich der Architektur getan. Sie entwickelte sich zum wichtigsten Diskussionsforum für aktuelle architektonische und soziale Probleme. So wurde auch die ideologisch gefärbte Auseinandersetzung zwischen den Verfechtern des wiederbelebten Funktionalismus und den Anhängern des sogenannten Sozialrealismus in der NAU ausgetragen — ein Kampf, der 1951 schließlich zur Auflösung dieser Organisation führte. Die Konfrontation der politischen Machtblöcke von Ost und West vor und während des Koreakrieges ließ die Sozialrealisten, unter ihnen viele junge Architekten, einen extremen Standpunkt einnehmen, von dem aus sie die funktionalistische Architektur als kosmopolitisch, reaktionär und undemokratisch ablehnten. Die meisten Anhänger des Sozialrealismus räumten jedoch ein, daß die neue Architektur der kommunistischen Länder keine überzeugenden Alternativen bot. Im Bauboom, der nach 1950 einsetzte, gelang es den Sozialrealisten allerdings nicht, ihre Ideen überzeugend zu verwirklichen. In der ersten Hälfte der fünfziger Jahre verschob sich dann die Diskussion vom Gegensatz »Funktionalismus — Sozialrealismus« wieder zu der Fragestellung, wie sich gegenüber den internationalen Einflüssen ein eigenständiger nationaler Architekturstil schaffen lasse.

Der Beginn der Hochkonjunktur im japanischen Bauen und die Anfänge eines neuen Baustils 1950-1955

Das Ende der inflationistischen Phase, das zeitlich etwa mit dem Beginn des Koreakrieges 1950 zusammenfiel, brachte einen allgemeinen Aufschwung des Wirtschaftslebens. Auch die Produktion der Grundbaustoffe Zement, Stahl und Glas nahm rasch zu, so daß die Rationierungsmaßnahmen der Regierung aufgehoben werden konnten. Das gab der Bautätigkeit überall im Lande starken Auftrieb, und für die Architekten trat nun die reale Bauaufgabe an die Stelle der theoretischen Beschäftigung.

Neben dem Wohnungsbau kamen jetzt auch Großprojekte der Bezirks- und Stadtverwaltungen in Gang, wie Rathäuser, Verwaltungszentren, Bibliotheken, Museen, Konzerthallen und Krankenhäuser, ferner als Aufträge privater Unternehmen Industriebauten, Bürogebäude und Banken. Dabei handelte es sich überwiegend um Stahlbetonbauten, unter ausgiebiger Verwendung industrieller Vorfertigungsverfahren.

23. Kiyoshi Ikebe: Prefabricated minimum-house for a family with one child, 1950.

23. Kiyoshi Ikebe: Vorfabriziertes Minimalhaus für eine Familie mit Kind, 1950.

24. Antonin Raymond: Reader's Digest Publishing House in Tokyo, 1951.

24. Antonin Raymond: Reader's Digest Verlagsgebäude in Tokio, 1951.

national awareness. This has stimulated younger architects with a desire for new forms of expression entirely their own; the older generation has revived its opposition to influence from America and Europe. Critics claimed that Japan's post-war architecture showed no national characteristics and was in danger of merely imitating what was built in other countries. Compared with the international architectural development, Japanese post-war buildings were not particularly advanced.

Conservative traditionalists tried to restore the native building tradition and its forms — which they sometimes copied direct. Examples are the memorial for the writer Tohson Shimazaki (1949; Fig. 29), designed by Yoshiro Taniguchi (b. 1904); and the Hasshokan Hotel at Nagoya (Fig. 30) by Sutemi Horiguchi (b. 1895) of the late 1950's.

Such designs, however, stimulated considerable opposition, especially among younger architects. They regarded them as products of a bourgeois mentality, an escape from the tasks of the present. While willing to recognize the spiritual force of historic architecture, they believed that its formal language had to be translated into a new idiom. The first efforts were made in the design of houses, such as that designed by Kiyoshi Seike for Professor Saito in Tokyo (1951; Fig. 31). Adopting traditional Japanese spatial concepts, efforts were made to evolve new designs, and these efforts were extended from house design to larger projects.

These progressive architects, responsible for the reputation of Japanese architecture today, regarded the basic structure and the spatial concepts as the important characteristics of their historic heritage — not the detail. Noboru Kawazoe, editor of the journal Shinken-Shiku, one of the spokesmen of the Metabolists, writes on this subject in 'Japanese Culture and Architecture': 'Stone and brick walls are structural components which have the function of enclosing a room. Steel and reinforced concrete, in the form of columns and beams, provide framed structures and are, in this respect, akin to traditional timber constructions. A frame structure allows a room to be more open and flexible and obviates the need for solid walls as a structural element. In the continuity of interior and exterior, in the flexibility of a room design using movable partitions, traditional Japanese architecture has pioneered many solutions, such as the integration of the garden and the interior, the protection of the interior by large, oversailing roofs, the use of the verandah as a link between interior and garden, the connection of different parts of a building by corridors, the introduction of the sliding wall (Fusuma) by means of which a room can be enlarged or reduced in size, the use of screens (Byobu) for visual protection, and the Tatami mat serving as a module of floor area. Not only for the sake of industrialization but also for the sake of flexibility, it is necessary to resort to standardization — something that the builders of the past have already done. In traditional architecture, 'Kiwari' signifies a modular order and a 'grammatical' determination of components for the layout and design of rooms.'

It is in the work of Kenzo Tange (b. 1913) that the synthesis of the Japanese architectural tradition and modern design finds its first and most successful expression. To this one-time pupil of Mayekawa, the acceptance of Western architecture was a matter of course. His feeling for the work of Le Corbusier is especially apparent, in particular in his use of 'Beton brut'. Tange's outstanding talent as both engineer and architect is evident in his first post-war buildings.

25. Kunio Mayekawa: Central Administration of the Nippon Sogo Bank in Tokyo, 1952.

25. Kunio Mayekawa: Hauptverwaltung der Nippon Sogo Bank in Tokio, 1952.

Innerhalb weniger Jahre entstand so nach 1950 eine ganze Reihe bedeutender Bauwerke, mit denen Japan den Anschluß an die internationale Architekturentwicklung der Nachkriegszeit zu gewinnen suchte.

Den Anfang machte 1951 Antonin Raymond mit seinem Bürogebäude für den Verlag Reader's Digest in Tokio (Abb. 24). In Vladno in Böhmen (1890) geboren, ging Raymond 1910 nach Amerika und 1919 mit Frank Lloyd Wright nach Tokio, wo er die Bauleitung des Imperial Hotel übernahm. Er blieb in Japan und beeinflußte seit den zwanziger Jahren durch eine Reihe vorbildlicher Bauten die japanische Architektur. Viele Japaner, unter ihnen Architekten, die inzwischen einen bedeutenden Namen haben — wie Mayekawa, Yoshimura und Masuzawa —, sind durch sein Büro gegangen. Die Verwaltung von Reader's Digest war das erste Gebäude in Japan, bei dem Sichtbeton in einer bis dahin unbekannten Perfektion ausgeführt wurde. Auch das Konstruktionsprinzip der auskragenden Boden- und Deckenplatten mit völliger Verglasung der Außenwände war für Japan neu.

Eine weitere Pionierleistung der japanischen Nachkriegsarchitektur war das 1952 fertiggestellte Gebäude der Nippon Sogo Bank in Tokio (Abb. 25) von Kunio Mayekawa — nicht so sehr wegen der formalen Gestaltung (es ist ein eher nüchtern wirkender, funktionsbetonter Bau), sondern wegen der bautechnischen Fortschritte, die hier erstmals verwirklicht wurden und die der japanischen Bauindustrie neue Wege erschlossen. Mayekawa entwarf ein Stahlskelett, das mit Betonelementen ummantelt wurde. Für die Außenwände verwandte er Betonfertigteile. Auch beim Innenausbau setzte er neue Materialien ein: Schiebefenster mit Aluminiumrahmen, perforiertes Sperrholz für Schallschluckwände und Akustikdecken aus Aluminiumplatten. Inzwischen sind das längst Selbstverständlichkeiten, aber damals war es schwierig, bei dem noch nicht sehr hoch entwickelten Stand der japanischen Bauindustrie solche Details zu verwirklichen.

Von Mayekawa stammt noch ein weiterer Bau, der zu den klassischen Frühwerken der Nachkriegsarchitektur gehört: die Konzerthalle und Bibliothek in Yokohama von 1954 (Abb. 26). In der kontrastreichen räumlichen Differenzierung und in den kraftvollen, schalungsrauh belassenen Betonsäulen kündigt sich schon die expressive Anwendung des Stahlbetons an, die seine späteren Werke charakterisiert.

Zu den wichtigen Beispielen moderner Architektur in den frühen fünfziger Jahren gehört auch Junzo Sakakuras Museum für moderne Kunst in Kamakura (Abb. 27), dessen erste Bauetappe 1951 fertiggestellt wurde. Das quadratische Gebäude mit einem Atriumhof für Skulpturen scheint auf dünnen Stahlstützen über dem Wasser zu schweben — eine Reminiszenz an die Pilotis Le Corbusiers, in dessen Atelier Sakakura von 1929 bis 1937 gearbeitet hatte.

Zur gleichen Zeit, in der Sakakuras Museum entstand, trat auch Togo Murano, einer der Pioniere der modernen japanischen Architektur, mit neuen Arbeiten hervor. Seit er 1935 mit dem Kaufhaus Sogoh (Abb. 16) eine der Inkunabeln des neuen Bauens in Japan geschaffen hatte, nahm diese Bauaufgabe einen zentralen Platz in seinem Werk ein. Das erste Nachkriegsergebnis war die Takashima-Ya-Filiale in Tokio (Abb. 28) von 1952. Bei seinen Warenhäusern sieht Murano das Gebäudeinnere als Funktionseinheit. Da die Verkaufsflächen künstlich beleuchtet sind, können die Innenräume völlig gegen die Außenwelt abgeschirmt werden — ein Schritt, den er bei seinen späteren Entwürfen denn auch konsequent geht. Während beim Takashima-Ya schmale vertikale Fensterstreifen in den Außenwänden aus Glasbausteinen noch gelegentliche Ausblicke gestatten, ist der Bau des 1957 entstandenen Kaufhauses Sogoh in Tokio vollkommen ummantelt, so daß die Anzahl der Geschosse von außen nicht mehr abgelesen werden kann. In vielen Projekten, die Murano in den fünfziger Jahren ausarbeitete — etwa beim Nihon'Seimei-Verwaltungsgebäude von 1958 (Seite 150) oder beim Kobuki-Theater in Osaka von 1959 —, wird die Eigenart dieses sensiblen Künstler-Architekten sichtbar: Er versucht, seinen Avantgardismus funktionalistischer Prägung mit der Pflege des traditionellen Erbes zu verbinden, indem er eine breite Skala altjapanischer Motive in sein Schaffen einbezieht.

Murano steht damit nicht allein. Nach 1950 läßt sich ganz allgemein eine erneute Hinwendung zur japanischen Architekturtradition beobachten. Dabei müssen jedoch deutlich zwei Richtungen unterschieden werden, die aus recht gegensätzlichen Motiven auf die Vergangenheit zurückgreifen: einerseits die mehr konservativ eingestellten Traditionalisten, und auf der anderen Seite die progressiven Kräfte, die nach einer Synthese zwischen der modernen Architektur des Westens und der alten einheimischen Baukunst streben. Sie wollen keine Wiederbelebung traditioneller Architekturmotive im wörtlichen Sinn, keine Übernahme historischer Klischees, sondern eine moderne Interpretation der Kulturtradition. Ihr Ziel ist es, mit den Gestaltungsmitteln unserer Zeit einen eigenständigen japanischen Architekturstil zu schaffen. Sicherlich stand die Besinnung auf die Baukunst des eigenen Landes auch mit dem Neutralitätsstreben im Zusammenhang, durch das sich die Japaner aus der Konfrontation der Machtblöcke von Ost und West herauszuhalten versuchten. Und zweifellos stärkte der Friedensvertrag von San Francisco, der Japan 1951 die Unabhängigkeit von den USA zurückgab, das nationale Bewußtsein. Bei den jüngeren Menschen wuchs dadurch das Verlangen nach neuen, eigenen

26. Kunio Mayekawa: Entrance of the library and concert hall in Yokohama, 1954.
27. Junzo Sakakura: Museum of Modern Art in Kamakura, 1951.
28. Togo Murano: Department Store Takashima-Ya in Tokyo, 1952.

26. Kunio Mayekawa: Eingangshalle der Bibliothek und Konzerthalle in Yokohama, 1954.
27. Junzo Sakakura: Museum für moderne Kunst in Kamakura, 1951.
28. Togo Murano: Kaufhaus Takashima-Ya in Tokio, 1952.

In his Peace Memorial, Hiroshima (Fig. 32), designed in competition in 1949, the traditional frame is interpreted in reinforced concrete. At the printing works in Haramachi (1955; Fig. 33), an elegant steel structure was devised, with cantilevered beams supported on a pair of central columns. At the meeting hall in Shizuoka (1957; Fig. 34), he spanned the square room with a shell roof in the form of a hyperbolic paraboloid. These early works, revealing his mastery and wide structural repertoire, lead in a consistent line to the famous halls for the Tokyo Olympics (1964; page 78), the Metabolist structure of his urban development projects (Tokyo plan, page 219) and individual buildings such as the Communication Centre at Kofu (page 194). Tange's significance as an engineer-architect lies in the fact that structure and design are completely integrated.

Tange's public buildings represent a second line of development. First, his numerous town halls, beginning with that of Shimizu (1954), that of Kurayoshi (1956), and the City Hall in Tokyo, completed in 1957 (Fig. 35). In combining a multi-storey office block (for the internal administrative departments) with a low-rise building (for meeting halls and common services), Tange provided a new interpretation of the Town Hall theme which was soon adopted by other Japanese architects.

The administration building of the Kagawa Prefecture at Takamatsu (page 182), built in 1959, where this type was fully developed for the first time, is also an example of the integration of Japan's historic heritage with modern architectural ideals. In making the core of the building alone the bracing member, Tange is able to reduce the facade to a slender framework of lines, familiar to the aesthetic sense of the Japanese, but far from mere reproduction of a traditional feature.

Tange has given his countrymen great stimulus — even before becoming Professor of Architecture and Town Planning at Tokyo University. He has reversed the relationship of give-and-take between the West and Japan. The Western World has overwhelmed him with prizes, distinctions and honorary memberships of architectural associations and colleges. He has entered and won many international contests (such as that for the reconstruction of Skopje in 1965).

The consolidation of the new style after 1955

Since the mid-1950's, efforts have intensified to produce a specifically Japanese interpretation of modern architecture. The revival of functionalism, which initiated the post-war building boom around 1950, was accepted as a necessary resumption of an interrupted development from the 1930's. But efforts were made to progress further. Following a revival of interest in native building traditions, attention was directed to that of neighbouring countries in East-Asia and extra-European cultures such as Africa or Mexico. The intention was not to make any direct borrowing, but rather to find corroborative analogies for Japan's own need for more imaginative spatial relationships. At the same time, attention was directed increasingly towards sociological aspects. Efforts to deal with formal problems were accompanied by attempts to reflect the social revolution; large multi-functional community and administration centres were designed.

As expressions of a democratic resurgence and as symbols of a new community consciousness, they are the highlights of contemporary Japanese architecture. These town halls and district

29. Yoshiro Taniguchi: Tohson Shimazaki Memorial Pavilion, 1949.

29. Yoshiro Taniguchi: Gedächtnispavillon für Tohson Shimazaki, 1949

30. Sutemi Horiguchi: Hasshokan Hotel in Nagoya, around 1955.

30. Sutemi Horiguchi: Hotel Hasshokan in Nagoya, um 1955.

31. Kiyoshi Seike: House Saito in Tokyo, 1951.

31. Kiyoshi Seike: Wohnhaus Saito in Tokio, 1951.

32. Kenzo Tange: Peace Memorial in Hiroshima. Memorial for atomic bomb victims and museum, 1955-56.

32. Kenzo Tange: Friedenszentrum in Hiroshima. Gedächtnismal für die Opfer der Atombombe und Museum, 1955-56.

33. Kenzo Tange: Printing works in Haramachi, 1955.

33. Kenzo Tange: Druckerei in Haramachi, 1955.

34. Kenzo Tange: Meeting hall in Shizuoka, 1957.

34. Kenzo Tange: Versammlungshalle in Shizuoka, 1957.

Ausdrucksformen; bei der älteren Generation verdichtete sich der Widerstand gegen Einflüsse aus Amerika und Europa. Es wurden Stimmen laut, die unzufrieden feststellten, die japanische Nachkriegsarchitektur zeige keine nationalen Merkmale und gerate in Gefahr, lediglich das nachzuempfinden, was in anderen Ländern gebaut wurde. Und zudem seien die japanischen Nachkriegsbauten im Vergleich mit der internationalen Architekturentwicklung des Westens noch nicht einmal besonders modern.

Vor diesem Hintergrund bemühten sich die konservativen Traditionalisten um eine Restauration der heimischen Baukunst, deren Formenapparat sie in teilweise direkten Zitaten wieder aufgriffen. Der 1949 gebaute Gedächtnispavillon für den Schriftsteller Tohson Shimazaki (Abb. 29) von Yoshiro Taniguchi (geb. 1904) bietet dafür ebenso ein Beispiel wie das Hotel Hasshokan in Nagoya (Abb. 30) von Sutemi Horiguchi (geb. 1895), das — nach der Mitte der fünfziger Jahre entstanden — eine subtile Nachempfindung altjapanischer Wohnarchitektur ist.

Dieses Gestalten auf der Grundlage überlieferter Stilelemente weckte aber auch kräftigen Widerspruch, vor allem unter den jüngeren Architekten. Sie sahen darin eine bürgerlich-reaktionäre Gesinnung, eine Flucht vor den Aufgaben der eigenen Zeit. Man wollte zwar die geistige Substanz der historischen Architektur übernehmen, ihre Formensprache sollte jedoch in ein neues Idiom übersetzt werden. Die ersten Ansätze in dieser Richtung zeigten sich im Wohnungsbau, etwa in Kiyoshi Seikes Wohnhaus für Professor Saito in Tokio von 1951 (Abb. 31). Ausgehend von den traditionellen japanischen Raumvorstellungen versuchte man, neue Bauformen zu schaffen, wobei diese Bemühungen dann bald vom reinen Wohnbau auf größere Projekte übertragen wurden.

Was den fortschrittlich eingestellten Architekten, denen die moderne japanische Architektur ihre heutige Weltgeltung verdankt, an dem historischen Erbe wichtig erschien, war nicht das Detail, sondern die Grundstruktur und die Raumkonzeption. Der Architekturkritiker Noboru Kawazoe, Chefredakteur der Zeitschrift Shinken-Shiku und später einer der Wortführer der Metabolisten, schreibt darüber in seinem Buch »Japanische Kultur und Architektur«:

»Stein- und Ziegelmauerwerk sind raumabschließende konstruktive Wandteile. Stahl und Stahlbeton in Form von Stütze und Träger sind Rahmenkonstruktionen. Auch der traditionelle Holzbau gehört zu den Rahmenkonstruktionen. Die Rahmenkonstruktion gibt dem Raumgefüge mehr Offenheit und Flexibilität und macht die massive geschlossene Wand als konstruktives Element überflüssig. Für die Kontinuität zwischen Innen- und Außenraum, für die Wandelbarkeit des Raumes mit Hilfe beweglicher Trennwände hat schon die traditionelle japanische Architektur viele richtungweisende Lösungen gefunden: zum Beispiel die Verbindung des Gartens mit dem Innenraum, den Schutz des Hausinnern durch große Dachvorsprünge, die Veranda als Bindeglied zwischen Innenraum und Garten, die Verbindung einzelner Gebäudeteile durch Korridore, die Schiebewand (Fusuma) zur Raumvergrößerung oder Raumverkleinerung, die Verwendung von Wandschirmen (Byobu) als optischen Schutz, die Tatamimatte zur Bestimmung der Raumgröße. Nicht nur wegen der Industrialisierung, sondern auch wegen der Flexibilität des Raumes ist es notwendig, zu standardisieren, was die Baumeister der Vergangenheit ebenfalls bereits getan haben. ›Kiwari‹ bedeutet in der traditionellen Architektur eine modulare Ordnung und die ›grammatikalische‹ Bestimmung der verschiedenen Ausbauteile zur Gestaltung der Räume.«

Die Synthese aus der japanischen Architekturtradition und einer konsequent modernen Gestaltungsweise hat im Werk von Kenzo Tange (geb. 1913) eine ihrer frühesten und gelungensten Ausprägungen gefunden. Als ehemaligem Mitarbeiter von Mayekawa war die schöpferische Auseinandersetzung mit der Architektur des Westens für ihn eine Selbstverständlichkeit. Besonders deutlich sind seine Beziehungen zu Le Corbusier, vor allem in der Anwendung des Béton brut. Tanges geniale Doppelbegabung als Ingenieur und Architekt ist schon in den ersten Nachkriegsbauten zu erkennen. Bei der Friedensgedenkstätte in Hiroshima (Abb. 32), für die er 1949 auf Grund eines Wettbewerbs den Auftrag erhielt, übertrug er die traditionelle Rahmenkonstruktion auf das Betonskelett. Bei der Druckerei in Haramachi (Abb. 33) von 1955 schuf er eine elegante Stahlkonstruktion, deren Kragträger auf einem mittleren Stützenpaar aufliegen, und bei der 1957 fertiggestellten Versammlungshalle in Shizuoka (Abb. 34) überspannte er den quadratischen Raum mit einer Dachschale in Form eines hyperbolischen Paraboloids. Von diesen frühen Arbeiten, die bereits ein breites und sicher beherrschtes Repertoire konstruktiver Möglichkeiten erkennen lassen, führt eine konsequent verfolgte Entwicklungslinie weiter zu den berühmten Hallenbauten für die Olympiade (Seite 78) in Tokio von 1964 und zu den metabolistischen Strukturen der städtebaulichen Projekte (Tokio-Plan, Seite 219) und Bauten (Pressezentrum in Kofu, Seite 194). Was Tanges Bedeutung als Ingenieur-Architekt ausmacht, ist die Tatsache, daß bei ihm der Anteil der Konstruktion restlos in der Form aufgeht.

Einen zweiten Entwicklungsstrang, der in seiner Vorbildlichkeit von großem Einfluß auf die japanische Architektur war, bilden Tanges Bauten für die Gemeinschaft. Hierher gehört vor allem die lange Reihe seiner Rathäuser, beginnend mit der Stadtverwaltung von Shimizu von

administrative buildings are evidently not strongholds of bureaucracy but genuine citizens' forums where the barriers between civil servants and population have largely disappeared. They are not only the administrative, but the cultural centres of communities. In addition to Offices and council chambers, they almost always contain one or more auditoria equipped for plays, concerts, films and lectures, as well as libraries, exhibition rooms, space for adult education, associations and groups, and frequently also a cafeteria or restaurant. Even wider is the range of facilities offered in the cultural centres proper which, in the larger cities, were built as independent buildings.

In view of the importance these centres have acquired in public life, it may be taken for granted that their design is suitably representative. That it has been possible to maintain so high a standard is owing to the involvement of the best Japanese architects and their attempt to use these community buildings as a kind of symbol for the modern spirit. Instead of involving themselves in the unnecessary decorative details, they have worked almost exclusively with exposed concrete and glass, and have created a surprisingly rich variety of spatial relationships, excellent planning and a range of strong forms. Such features, together with the detailed handling of the concrete in the stairs and balconies and upsweeping roofs (Fig. 36), the deliberate and traditional expression of the structural framework (Fig. 37) and the modulated perforation of walls to provide a counterpoint of light and shade, constitute a list of the most important characteristics of modern architecture.

The crystallization of this movement occurred in the late 1950's. Once again a European architect, Le Corbusier, acted as catalyst. His late works, the church at Ronchamp and buildings at Chandigarh (India), strongly affected the Japanese. The impact, however, was different from that made first by Le Corbusier in the 1930's.

Then the Japanese had still to learn the vocabulary of the international style; now they turned to Le Corbusier with a sense of spiritual affinity. He was no longer a guide, but a mentor releasing forces already instilled. One aspect of these forces concerned the search for a dynamic architecture. Beginning around 1960, a number of buildings were designed with walls and ceilings of flowing shapes. The traditional frame was replaced by curved concrete planes, overriding the discipline of the rectangle.

One of the first of these plastically designed buildings was Kunio Mayekawa's Cultural Centre at Fukushima (1956; Fig. 38) where the undulating roof is upheld by crinkle-crankle walls, pierced through by extensions of the horizontal beams of the foursquare building alongside. The right-angle was abandoned also in Togo Murano's town hall at Yonago, finished in 1960 (Fig. 39). Al flat segmental arch motif recurs throughout the building. The rise of the seating tiers is clearly expressed externally. The effect of such dynamic expression internally is demonstrated in the large auditorium of the municipal Festival Hall in Tokyo (Fig. 40) built by Mayekawa between 1958 and 1961. The sharp angles of the walls flanking the auditorium are contrasted with the drawn out curves of the acoustic ceiling, which consists of a series of concave and convex elements. By the time Kenzo Tange built the golf club at Totsuka (1962; Fig. 41), with its concrete roof upturned like a gigantic gutter, the style was already established. Numerous examples are illustrated here.

From 1960, the repertoire of sculptured, dynamic forms was further enlivened by the advent of a new theory of aesthetics, Metabolism.

35. Kenzo Tange: House in Tokyo, 1955-57.

35. Kenzo Tange: Stadthaus in Tokio, 1955-57. 22

36. Kunio Mayekawa: Town hall in Kyoto, 1958-60.
37. Kiyonori Kikutake: Museum and Art Gallery of the Shimane prefecture in Matsue, 1958-60.

36. Kunio Mayekawa: Stadthalle in Kyoto, 1958-60.
37. Kiyonori Kikutake: Museum und Kunstgalerie des Bezirks Shimane in Matsue, 1958-60.

1954, dem Rathaus von Kurayoshi von 1956 und dem 1957 fertiggestellten Stadthaus von Tokio (Abb. 35). Mit der Kombination von Bürohochhaus (für die internen Verwaltungsabteilungen) und Flachbau (für Säle und Gemeinschaftseinrichtungen) hat Tange eine neue Interpretation des Themas Rathaus gegeben, die unter den japanischen Architekten rasch Schule machte. Das Verwaltungsgebäude der Präfektur Kagawa in Takamatsu (Seite 182) von 1959, das diesen Typus erstmals voll entwickelt zeigt, bietet auch ein Beispiel für die Integration des historischen Erbes in die moderne Architekturkonzeption: Indem Tange die Aussteifung des Bauwerks auf den massiven Gebäudekern konzentriert, kommt er in der Fassade mit schlanken Rahmenkonstruktionen aus, die dem ästhetischen Empfinden der Japaner vertraut, in dieser Art der Umsetzung aber doch kein banales Formenzitat sind.
Als Anreger und Vorbild hat Tange seinen Landsleuten viele Impulse gegeben, und das nicht erst, seit er als Professor für Architektur und Städtebau an der Universität von Tokio wirkt. In seiner Person vollzog sich so etwas wie eine Umkehrung des bisherigen Verhältnisses von Geben und Nehmen zwischen dem Westen und Japan. Die westliche Welt hat ihn mit Preisen, Auszeichnungen und Ehrenmitgliedschaften von Architektenverbänden und Architekturschulen überhäuft, 1959–60 lehrte er als Gastprofessor am Massachusetts Institute of Technology in Cambridge/USA, und internationale Wettbewerbe erfahren stets eine Bereicherung, wenn er teilnimmt (und gewinnt, wie beim Wettbewerb für den Wiederaufbau von Skopje, 1965).

Die Ausbildung und Festigung einer neuen Stiltradition nach 1955

Seit der Mitte der fünfziger Jahre verdichteten sich die Bemühungen, die zu einer spezifisch japanischen Interpretation der modernen Architektur drängten. Die Rekapitulation des Funktionalismus, die um 1950 das Bauen der Nachkriegszeit eingeleitet hatte, wurde zwar als notwendiges Wiederanknüpfen an die unterbrochene Entwicklung der dreißiger Jahre akzeptiert, aber nun strebte man energisch darüber hinaus. Neben der Besinnung auf die heimische Bautradition richtete sich der Blick jetzt auch auf die asiatischen Nachbarländer und auf außereuropäische Kulturkreise wie Afrika oder Mexiko. Dabei ging es nicht um irgendwelche direkten Anleihen aus dem fremden Formenrepertoire, sondern um bestätigende Analogien für den eigenen Wunsch nach imaginativeren Raumvorstellungen.
Zugleich wandte sich die Aufmerksamkeit der Auftraggeber und Architekten in verstärktem Maß dem soziologischen Aspekt des Bauens zu. Neben die formalen Probleme traten die erfolgreichen Bemühungen, in großen, multifunktionalen Gemeinschafts- und Verwaltungszentren der gesellschaftlichen Umschichtung Ausdruck zu geben. Als Kristallisationspunkte der demokratischen Erneuerung und als Symbole für das ausgeprägte Gemeinschaftsbewußtsein der Japaner stellen diese Bauten die bedeutendste Leistung ihrer Architektur dar.
Die Rathäuser und Bezirksverwaltungen sind in ihrer architektonischen Erscheinung keine Hochburgen der Bürokratie mehr, sondern echte Bürgerforen, in denen die Schranken zwischen Beamten und Bevölkerung weitgehend gefallen sind. Sie bilden nicht nur das administrative, sondern auch das kulturelle Zentrum der Gemeinde. Außer Publikumsräumen, Büros und Ratssaal enthalten sie deshalb fast immer auch ein oder mehrere Auditorien mit den notwendigen Einrichtungen für Theatervorstellungen, Konzerte, Filmvorführungen und Vorträge, ferner Bibliothek, Ausstellungsräume, Räume für die Erwachsenenbildung, für Vereine und Gruppen und häufig sogar eine Cafeteria oder ein Restaurant. Noch vielgestaltiger ist das Angebot in den reinen Kulturzentren, die in den großen Städten als selbständige Komplexe errichtet wurden. Mit anderem Raumprogramm, bei dem Club-, Spiel- und Hobbyräume bis hin zum Musikstudio den Schwerpunkt bilden, gehören auch die Jugendzentren in die Reihe der Gemeinschaftsbauten. Angesichts der Bedeutung, die alle diese Zentren im öffentlichen Leben haben, versteht sich eine entsprechend repräsentative Gestaltung von selbst. Daß ein so außergewöhnlich hoher Qualitätsstandard gehalten werden kann, erklärt sich einerseits aus der Berufung der besten japanischen Architekten und zum anderen aus dem Bemühen, mit derartigen Gemeinschaftsbauten gerade in mehr provinziellen Gemeinden eine Art Zeichen für den Geist der Moderne zu setzen. Anstatt sich in dekorativen Exzessen zu verlieren, wie man das bei Rathausbauten im Westen häufig findet, arbeiten die Japaner fast nur mit Sichtbeton und Glas. Dabei bieten sie erstaunlich reiche räumliche Beziehungen, überraschende Raumfolgen und eine kraftvolle plastische Modellierung der Baukörper, innen wie außen. Nimmt man zu diesen Charakteristika noch die expressive Behandlung des Betons auch im Detail hinzu, etwa bei den Dachaufbiegungen, Treppen und Balkonen (Abb. 36), ferner die vom traditionellen Holzbau inspirierte Sichtbarmachung der konstruktiven Glieder, das betonte Offenlegen von Stützen und Balken (Abb. 37) und schließlich die kontrapunktische Helldunkelwirkung, wie sie sich bei der rhythmischen Durchlöcherung der Wand- und Fassadenflächen ergibt, so hat man damit die wichtigsten Wesenszüge der neuen japanischen Architekturtradition beisammen.

Metabolism

Much attention was paid at the International Design Congress in Tokyo, 1960, to an exhibition of the work of a group of young architects who called themselves 'Metabolists'. At the time of the exhibition they published a manifesto 'Metabolism 1960 — The Proposals for New Urbanism'. Among the group were Masato Otaka (b. 1923). Kiyonori Kikutake (b. 1928), Fumihiko Maki (b. 1928), Noriaki Kurokawa (b. 1934) and the critic Noboru Kawazoe (b. 1926). Four years later, the Metabolists were joined by Kenzo Tange and his pupil, Arata Isozaki (b. 1931).

The notion of Metabolism, derived from the Greek (meaning change or conversion), is interpreted as a process of continuous or cyclic transformation. The Metabolists insist that building for the community at large must be regarded as a metabolic process because, from a biological point of view, human society itself is in a continuous process of renewal so that it defies any fixed or schematized design principles. As Kikutake stated in 1964, one should cease to think in terms of form and (fixed) function and should, instead, be guided by concepts of dynamic and variable space and functional change.

The 'fixed', individual building — however good it may be — is of less interest to the Metabolists than the 'Group Form', serving as a structural framework, unharmed even if some of the members were removed or changed. Focus is directed not on the individual design, but on the whole urban fabric, an environment of changing components. In an essay 'Towards Group Form' which was published first in 'Metabolism 1960', Maki and Otaka interpret 'Group Form' as an entity which must be in equilibrium with all its individual parts, capable nonetheless of easy adaptation to social and economic change. Interior and exterior should be conceived as one to avoid both the sprawl and the standardized monotony of existing cities. A visual mode of expression was called for to reflect the concentration of urban energy. Before the Metabolists exhibition and Manifesto, some members of the group had already published designs conceived in the spirit of Metabolism. Kenzo Tange, even, had made an important contribution to urban structuring with a project, prepared during the late 50's, for the development of the Bay of Tokyo (cf. page 219).

Early in 1959, Kiyonori Kikutake, among the most successful and progressive of the Metabolists, published his project for a Tower City (Fig. 42), followed a month later by Floating City (Fig. 43) in which he proposed urban development at sea on floating islands of concrete. This project is, as it were, the counterpart to Tower City. In fact, Kikutake combined both under the name of Unabara. The combined services of Floating City were to be concentrated on a platform, above water level which would also serve as helicopter landing ground. Housing units, for 3,000, were to be grouped in cylindrical towers suspended in water from the artificial islands, receiving sunlight from circular shafts in their centres. Local transport was to be provided by submarine.

In 1962, Arata Isozaki — one of Kenzo Tange's collaborators on the Tokyo Bay Plan — suggested that housing units could be supended from masts (Fig. 44). The units were to be hung freely in mid-air from beams of different length, projecting on four sides of towers of different height. The fusion of Japanese architectural tradition with a modern formal language is expressed here with exemplary clarity. The structure of the mast buildings is reminiscent — and this is not a coincidence — of the timber structures of early Buddhist temples and pagodas (Fig. 45).

Noriaki Kurokawa, the youngest of the founder members of the Metabolism and, like Isozaki, a disciple of Tange, published his Wall City project in 1959 (Fig. 46). This consists of a gigantic megastructure reduced in height at the periphery, with an integrated traffic system. In 1960, Kurokawa made a more remarkable proposal with Agrarian City (Fig. 47), showing how the concentration of cities could be maintained even in agricultural areas. Agrarian City consists of lattice structures, each covering an area 500 x 500 metres, divided into a 'production level', a 'community level' and a 'private level'. Kurokawa's boldest project, which made his international reputation, is Helix City, published in 1961 (Fig. 48): — a gigantic three-dimensional city for living and working, consisting of helicoidal towers in the form of fan-shaped bearing structures of light metal which contain individual units of dwellings, offices and commercial buildings. The shafts of the helical towers contain all the necessary installations and vertical traffic elements. Monorail lines on different levels intersect the superstructure like arteries, branching out in a network of secondary traffic routes. The towers themselves are also connected, on every tenth floor, by bridge-like connectors. In this way, according to its inventor, Helix City could become a dynamic 'city creating three-dimensional, organic, vertical land' — an artificial landscape where the dynamic process of nature is simulated by modern technology.

In practice, the activities of the Metabolists have been confined to individual buildings, which are

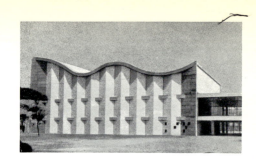

38. Kunio Mayekawa: Cultural Centre at Fukushima, 1956.
39. Togo Murano and Tyuichi Mori: Town hall at Yonago, 1959-60.

38. Kunio Mayekawa: Kulturzentrum in Fukushima, 1956.
39. Togo Murano und Tyuichi Mori: Stadthalle in Yonago, 1959-60.

42. Kiyonori Kikutake: Project for a Tower City, 1959.

42. Kiyonori Kikutake: Projekt Turmstadt, 1959.

40. Kunio Mayekawa: Municipal Festival Hall in Tokyo, 1958-61. Interior view of the main concert and theatre hall.
41. Kenzo Tange: Golf club house at Totsuka, 1962.

40. Kunio Mayekawa: Städtische Festhalle in Tokio, 1958-61. Innenansicht des großen Konzert- und Theatersaals.
41. Kenzo Tange: Golfklubhaus in Totsuka, 1962.

43. Kiyonori Kikutake: Project for a Floating City, 1959.

43. Kiyonori Kikutake: Projekt Schwimmende Stadt, 1959.

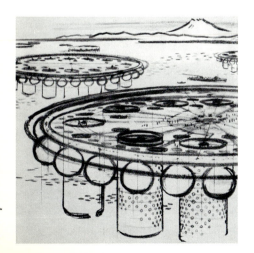

Ihre endgültige Ausbildung setzte nach der Mitte der fünfziger Jahre ein. Dabei stand übrigens noch einmal ein europäischer Architekt Pate: Le Corbusier. Sein Spätwerk, insbesondere die Wallfahrtskirche von Ronchamp und die Bauten in Chandigarh (Indien), hatte in Japan eine nachhaltige Wirkung. Gegenüber der ersten Konfrontation mit Le Corbusier in den dreißiger Jahren bestand nun allerdings ein wesentlicher Unterschied: Während die Japaner sich damals das Vokabular des »Internationalen Stils« fast wie eine Fremdsprache aneignen mußten, entsprang die neuerliche Hinwendung zu Le Corbusier einer geistesverwandten Grundhaltung. Bei dieser zweiten Begegnung war der große Franzose nicht so sehr das richtungweisende Vorbild als vielmehr der Katalysator, der bereits angelegte eigene Kräfte freisetzte.

Eine der Stoßrichtungen, in denen sich diese Kräfte entfalteten, ist durch die Suche nach dynamisch bewegten Formen gekennzeichnet. Um und nach 1960 entstanden eine ganze Reihe von Bauten, bei denen Decke und Wand plastisch durchgebildet wurden; gekurvte Betonflächen traten an die Stelle der Rahmenkonstruktion und hoben den Zwang des rechten Winkels auf. Eines der ersten Beispiele für die freie plastische Ausbildung eines Baukörpers bietet Kunio Mayekawas Kulturzentrum in Fukushima (Abb. 38) von 1956, dessen Wellendach von zickzackförmig gefalteten Außenwänden getragen wird, während die Geschoßplatten des anschließenden Rechteckbaus, als horizontale Balken weitergeführt, die Faltwand durchstoßen. Auch Togo Murano verläßt bei seiner 1960 fertiggestellten Stadthalle von Yonago (Abb. 39) den rechten Winkel. Das Motiv des flachen Segmentbogens kehrt am ganzen Bau wieder, der in seiner plastischen Durchformung das Ansteigen der Zuschauerränge von außen ablesbar macht. Wie sich die dynamische Ausbildung von Decke und Wand auf die Gestaltung des Innenraums auswirkt, kann der große Saal der städtischen Festhalle in Tokio (Abb. 40) verdeutlichen, die von Mayekawa zwischen 1958 und 1961 gebaut wurde. Die Schrägstellung der Wände von Bühnenportal und Bühne wird kontrapunktiert durch das langgestreckte Kurvenband der Akustikdecke aus konvex und konkav gewölbten Teilen. Mit dem letzten Beispiel, Kenzo Tanges 1962 eröffneten Golfklubhaus in Totsuka (Abb. 41), dessen Betondach wie eine riesige Regenrinne aufgebogen ist, sind wir bereits mitten in dem Zeitraum, aus dem dieses Buch weitere vergleichbare Bauten vorstellt.

Neben die Bereicherung, die das Repertoire der neuen japanischen Architektur durch skulpturell durchgebildete und dynamisch bewegte Formen erfuhr, treten von 1960 an auch noch die ästhetischen Konsequenzen, die sich aus der Gestaltungslehre des Metabolismus ergeben.

Der Metabolismus

Auf dem International Design Congress in Tokio 1960 fand eine Ausstellung große Beachtung, mit der eine Gruppe junger Architekten unter dem Sammelbegriff »Metabolismus« ihre Entwürfe der Öffentlichkeit vorstellte. Zu dieser Gruppe gehörten Masato Otaka (geb. 1923), Kiyonori Kikutake (geb. 1928), Fumihiko Maki (geb. 1928), Noriaki Kurokawa (geb. 1934) und der Architekturkritiker Noboru Kawazoe (geb. 1926). Vier Jahre später schlossen sich auch Kenzo Tange und sein Schüler Arata Isozaki (geb. 1931) den Metabolisten an. Etwa gleichzeitig mit der Ausstellung erschien ihr Manifest »Metabolism 1960 — The Proposals for New Urbanism«.

Der aus dem Griechischen übernommene Begriff Metabolismus (Veränderung, Umwandlung) bedeutet im Sinne der Gruppe ständige oder zyklische Transformation. Die Metabolisten gehen von der Überlegung aus, daß das Bauen für die Gemeinschaft als metabolischer Prozeß aufzufassen sei, weil die menschliche Gemeinschaft selbst, biologisch gesehen, in ständiger Erneuerung begriffen ist und sich deshalb allen fixierten und schematisierten Gestaltungsprinzipien entzieht. Wie Kikutake 1964 postulierte, müsse man aufhören, in den Begriffen von Form und (fixierter) Funktion zu denken und sich statt dessen von den Gesetzen des (dynamischen und variablen) Raumes und des Funktionswandels leiten lassen.

Über das statische Einzelbauwerk hinaus — und sei es noch so qualitätvoll — richtet sich das Interesse der Metabolisten auf die Gruppenform als strukturellem Überbau, der es sogar verträgt, wenn einzelne Glieder weggenommen oder ausgetauscht werden. Das Ziel ist die städtebauliche Großstruktur, die Umwelt aus nicht endgültig fixierten Teilen, nicht die Einzelform. In einem Aufsatz »Toward Group Form«, der erstmals in der Publikation »Metabolism 1960« erschien, interpretierten Maki und Otaka den Begriff »Gruppenform« als Ganzheit, die im Gleichgewicht mit den Einzelelementen sein müsse und sich trotzdem flexibel an soziale und wirtschaftliche Veränderungen anpassen lasse. Der innere und der äußere Raum seien gleichzeitig zu gestalten, damit die wuchernde Unordnung, aber auch die schablonisierte Monotonie bestehender Städte vermieden würden. Ferner komme es darauf an, für die Gruppenarchitektur eine Ausdrucksform zu finden, die den Eindruck konzentrierter städtischer Energie vermittle.

Bevor die Metabolisten 1960 mit ihrer Ausstellung und ihrem Manifest gemeinsam auftraten, hatten einzelne Mitglieder schon Projekte publiziert, die im Sinne des Metabolismus konzipiert

scarcely expressive of their tenets as compromise has been called for. Nevertheless, they have demonstrated that Metabolistic theories are applicable to individual buildings, e. g. by separating the fixed from the variable components or by creating space for multi-functional purposes. Convincing examples are Kikutake's houses (pages 32 and 38) or the administrative building for the Izumo Shrine (page 133), or Kurokawa's Leisure Time Centre at Yamagate (page 72, and Kenzo Tange's Communication Centre at Kofu (page 194). With its volumes suspended from a structure of sixteen reinforced concrete cylinders, Tange comes nearest to the vision of Metabolist urbanism.

In view of the urgency with which the rapid population increase throughout the world calls for new urbanistic concepts, the Metabolists must indisputably be given credit for having pointed the way, and for having indicated the scale by which future urbanism must be governed.

Norio Nishimura and Egon Tempel

44. Arata Isozaki: Project for housing units suspended from masts, 1962.
45. Corner in an early Buddhist Temple. Brackets and short cantilevered beams accentuate the corner.

44. Arata Isozaki: Projekt für Wohnquartiere in Mastenbauweise, 1962.
45. Eckausbildung in einem frühbuddhistischen Tempel. Konsolen und kurze Kragarme betonen den Eckpunkt.

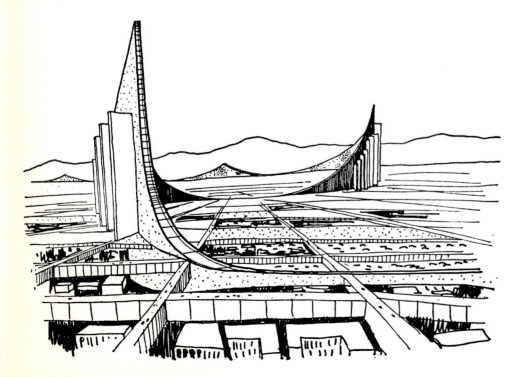

46. Noriaki Kurokawa: Project for a Wall City, 1959.

46. Noriaki Kurokawa: Projekt Wandstadt, 1959.

47. Noriaki Kurokawa: Project for an Agrarian City, 1960.

47. Noriaki Kurokawa: Projekt Agrarstadt, 1960.

48. Noriaki Kurokawa: Project for a Helix City, 1961.

48. Noriaki Kurokawa: Projekt Helix-City, 1961.

waren. Auch Kenzo Tange trug bereits Ende der fünfziger Jahre mit der Arbeit an seinem Projekt für die Überbauung der Bucht von Tokio (siehe Seite 219) Wesentliches zur Diskussion über die künftige Stadtstruktur bei.

Zu Anfang des Jahres 1959 veröffentlichte Kiyonori Kikutake, einer der erfolgreichsten und progressivsten Repräsentanten des Metabolismus, sein Projekt »Turmstadt« (Abb. 42), ein Monat später folgte die »Schwimmende Stadt« (Abb. 43), bei der er mit künstlich geschaffenen Inseln aus schwimmenden Betonschalen Probleme der Meeresbesiedelung zu lösen suchte. Dieser Entwurf ist gewissermaßen die Umkehrung der Turmstadt. Kikutake hat dann auch beide Projekte unter der Bezeichnung »Unabara« vereinigt. Die Gemeinschaftseinrichtungen der schwimmenden Stadt sollen auf der Plattform über der Wasseroberfläche zusammengefaßt werden, wo auch Hubschrauber landen können. Die Wohneinheiten für je 3000 Menschen verteilen sich auf zylindrische Türme, die unter der künstlichen Insel ins Wasser hängen und über zentrale Rundschächte dem Sonnenlicht geöffnet sind. Als Nahverkehrsmittel würden U-Boote eingesetzt, die direkt die Wohnzylinder ansteuern.

Arata Isozaki, der als Mitarbeiter von Kenzo Tange an dessen Tokioplan beteiligt war, schlug 1962 eine Mastenbauweise für Wohnquartiere (Abb. 44) vor. Die Wohnungseinheiten sollen frei in der Luft an Kragarmen hängen, die — in ihrer Länge abgestuft — von unterschiedlich hohen Turmschäften aus nach vier Seiten vorspringen. Hier läßt sich übrigens die fruchtbare Auseinandersetzung mit der japanischen Architekturtradition, das Umschmelzen ihrer Substanz in eine moderne Formensprache, mit exemplarischer Deutlichkeit erkennen. Die Konstruktion von Isozakis Mastenbauten erinnert, und das sicher nicht zufällig, an die Holzkonstruktionen frühbuddhistischer Tempel und Pagoden (Abb. 45). In ganz verschiedenen Dimensionen liegt beiden eine übereinstimmende strukturelle Konzeption zugrunde.

Noriaki Kurokawa, der jüngste unter den Gründungsmitgliedern der Metabolistengruppe und wie Isozaki Schüler von Tange, geht bei seinem »Wandstadt«-Projekt von 1959 (Abb. 46) von riesigen geschwungenen Hausscheiben aus, die nach den Enden hin niedriger werden und weiträumig in ein horizontales Verkehrserschließungssystem eingefügt sind. 1960 machte Kurokawa mit der »Agrarstadt« (Abb. 47) einen bemerkenswerten Vorschlag, wie auch in landwirtschaftlichen Produktionsgebieten eine urbanistische Konzentration erreicht werden könnte. Seine Agrarstadt basiert auf stark durchbrochenen Gitterstrukturen mit 500×500 m Grundfläche, die vertikal in eine Produktionsebene, eine Gemeinschaftsebene und eine private Ebene gegliedert sind. Kurokawas kühnstes Projekt, mit dem er seinen internationalen Ruf endgültig festigte, ist zweifellos seine 1961 veröffentlichte »Helix-City« (Abb. 48): eine gigantische Raumstadt zum Wohnen und Arbeiten, mit helikoidalen Türmen, die als fächerartige Tragstrukturen in Leichtbauweise ausgeführte, individuelle Einheiten von Wohn-, Büro- und Geschäftshäusern aufnehmen. Die Schäfte der schraubenförmigen Türme enthalten alle notwendigen Installationen und vertikalen Verkehrselemente. Einbahnverkehrswege ziehen sich wie Arterien auf verschiedenen Ebenen durch die Superstruktur und verästeln sich in einem Netz von sekundären Verkehrswegen, wie auch die Türme selbst jeweils nach zehn Geschossen untereinander durch brückenartige Konnektoren verbunden sind. So könnte nach dem Willen ihres Erfinders eine Bewegungsstadt entstehen, »die dreidimensionales, organisches, vertikales Land schafft« — eine artifizielle Landschaft, die den dynamischen Entwicklungsprozeß der Natur mit den Mitteln der Technik nachvollzieht.

In der Praxis beschränkte sich die Aktivität der Metabolisten bisher nur auf Einzelbauten, zum Teil mit unterschiedlichen Ergebnissen, weil die realen Bauaufgaben oftmals zu Kompromissen zwangen. Immerhin wurde der Beweis erbracht, daß die metabolistischen Gestaltungstheorien auch beim einzelnen Gebäude sinnvoll anzuwenden sind, beispielsweise in der Trennung von fixierten und variablen Baugliedern oder in der Schaffung von multifunktional nutzbaren Raumeinheiten. Kikutakes Wohnbauten (Seite 32 und 38) oder sein Verwaltungsgebäude für den Izumo-Schrein (Seite 133) oder Kurokawas Freizeitzentrum in Yamagate (Seite 72) bieten dafür ebenso überzeugende Beispiele wie das Pressezentrum in Kofu (Seite 194) von Kenzo Tange. Mit seinem konstruktiven Gerüst aus sechzehn Stahlbetonzylindern und den dazwischengehängten versetzbaren Raumzellen kommt Tange der Vision einer metabolistischen Stadtstruktur am nächsten. Angesichts der Dringlichkeit, mit der die rapide Bevölkerungszunahme überall auf der Welt neue urbanistische Konzepte erzwingt, gebührt den Metabolisten das unbestreitbare Verdienst, mit ihren Projekten die Richtung gewiesen und die Dimensionen ausgemessen zu haben, in denen sich die Stadtplanung der Zukunft bewegen muß.

Norio Nishimura und Egon Tempel

1. A view of the landscape across living room and entrance platform. When, as shown here, the glass sliding doors disappear behind the wall panels, the interior is integrated with the outer platform. On the right are the sleeping bunks; on the left kitchenette and dining area.
2. Section A—B and plan.
3. Due to its column structure, the cottage is raised so far above the surrounding trees — conifer and deciduous — that these do not impede the wide view over the landscape in the south.

1. Blick durch den Wohnraum über die Eingangsplattform in die Landschaft. Wenn wie hier die verglasten Schiebetüren hinter den Wandscheiben verschwinden, bilden Innenraum und Außenplattform eine Einheit. Rechts der Schlafbereich, links Kochnische und Eßplatz.
2. Schnitt A-B und Grundriß.
3. Durch die Pfostenkonstruktion ist das an einem Südhang stehende Haus so weit über den umgebenden Mischwald emporgehoben, daß man über die Bäume hinweg einen weiten Blick in die Landschaft hat.

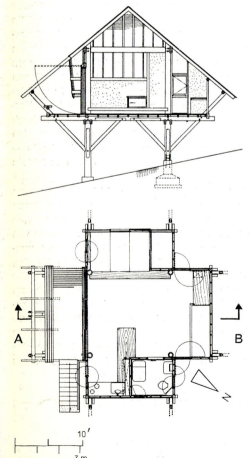

10'

3 m

Akio Yamamoto + Tsutomu Ikuta

Summer cottage in the Tateshina-Kogen mountains, 1964
Because of their scenic beauty and their comparatively short distance from Tokyo (120 miles), the Tateshina-Kogen mountains in central Japan are suitable for development as a holiday region. In view of the growing demand for holiday cottages, the architects have designed a type of house which can be produced in series. The length of the sub-structure columns can be adapted to the ground conditions, so that no earthworks are needed. The cottage has a single room of cruciform plan, and a pyramid-shaped roof. Fixtures and fittings are placed in three recesses. Kitchen, bathroom and W. C. are combined as a single installation unit in the north-east recess. The sleeping bunks are placed slightly above floor level in the open south-west recess which also contains a cupboard with sliding doors. From the north-west recess, which contains a sitting and working area, narrow, full-height side windows command a view of the landscape. On the south-east side, the place of the recess is taken by the entrance platform and terrace. Since, in these extensive woodlands, timber represents the cheapest building material, the structure consists entirely of round or sawn timber. Floors and roofs are boarded up, the walls are lined with plasterboard.

Sommerhaus in den Bergen von Tateshina-Kogen, 1964
Das Bergland von Tateshina-Kogen in Mitteljapan bietet wegen seiner landschaftlichen Schönheit und der mit 200 km relativ geringen Entfernung von Tokio günstige Voraussetzungen für die Entwicklung als Erholungsgebiet. Im Hinblick auf den wachsenden Bedarf an Ferienhäusern haben die Architekten einen serienmäßig produzierbaren Haustyp entworfen. Die Pfosten der Unterkonstruktion lassen sich in ihrer Länge dem Gelände anpassen, so daß eine Planierung nicht erforderlich ist. Das Einraum-Haus hat einen kreuzförmigen Grundriß und ein Pyramidendach. Die Möblierung ist auf drei Nischen verteilt. Küche, Bad und WC sind als Installationseinheit in der Nische auf der Nordostseite zusammengefaßt. Die Schlafstätte ist etwas erhöht über dem Fußboden in die offene Südwestnische eingebaut; an sie schließt ein Schrank mit Schiebetüren an. Von der Sitznische mit Arbeitsplatz auf der Nordwestseite hat man durch schmale raumhohe Seitenfenster Aussicht in die Landschaft. Auf der Südostseite tritt an die Stelle einer Nische die Eingangsplattform und Terrasse. Da Holz in dieser waldreichen Gegend der billigste Baustoff ist, besteht die Konstruktion durchweg aus Rund- und Kanthölzern. Boden und Dachschrägen sind mit Brettern verschalt, die Wände mit Gipsplatten verkleidet.

4. A view from the east. The four round timber columns supporting the house are anchored to their concrete foundations by means of steel flats. The roof is supported by timber struts which extrude from the columns like the branches of a tree. A single flight of stairs leads to the entrance platform.

5. Above the entrance platform, the roof is cut back to a higher level, sun protection being provided by the shutters above the sliding doors. The balustrade is also used as a bench.

4. Ansicht von Osten. Die vier Rundholzpfosten, auf denen das Haus steht, sind mit Stahllaschen in Betonfundamenten verankert. Das Dach lagert auf Streben auf, die wie die Äste eines Baumes aus den Pfosten herauswachsen. Eine einläufige Treppe führt zur Eingangsplattform hinauf.

5. Über der Eingangsplattform ist das Dach nicht so tief herabgezogen. Hier dienen die Klappläden vor den Schiebetüren als Sonnenschutz. Das Brüstungsgeländer wird zugleich als Bank verwendet.

6. With its tent roof structure — which remains fully visible — the living room seems spacious and airy. On the left, one of the narrow side windows next to the 'sitting room' recess; next to it the enclosed bathroom unit and the open kitchenette.

6. Der Wohnraum wirkt durch das Zeltdach, dessen Konstruktion sichtbar belassen wurde, weit und luftig. Links eines der schmalen Seitenfenster neben der Sitznische. Daneben die geschlossene Badezelle und die offene Kochnische.

1. The house is supported by four reinforced concrete wall slabs of identical cross-section but different height. Inserted between these 'walls' is the cross-wise reinforced floor slab whilst the gently pitched roof is placed on top of the walls. The low wing has a reinforced concrete framework with panel infilling.
2. Night view of the house from south-east. Access from the road to the main floor is over the roof of the low wing.

1. Das konstruktive Gerüst des Hauses besteht aus vier, im Querschnitt gleich großen, jedoch verschieden hohen Stahlbetonscheiben. Zwischen diese »Wände« ist die kreuzweise armierte Fußbodenplatte eingespannt; das flach geneigte Dach liegt auf den Scheiben auf. Das Sockelgeschoß ist als ausgefachtes Stahlbetonskelett konstruiert.
2. Nachtaufnahme von Südosten. Von der Straße aus führt der Zugang zum Hauptgeschoß über das Dach des unteren Baukörpers.

Kiyonori Kikutake

'Sky-House' at Tokyo, 1958

In designing his own house, Kikutake looked for a solution which could be adapted to the changes in family size over the years and would provide flexibility in space utilization. The house has a long single-storey wing at garden level, leaning against a rise in the ground on the east side. The flexibly designed rooms in this wing were originally used as an architectural studio and, later, as rooms for the growing children. The main floor, placed one storey above street level, is entered from the roof of the low wing. It contains a single large room which is sub-divided by an isolated cupboard wall into a sitting area and a dining and sleeping area. The kitchen, bathroom and W. C. units, which Kikutake calls 'Movenettes', are series-produced and can be replaced.

»Sky-House« in Tokio, 1958

Bei seinem eigenen Haus suchte Kikutake eine Lösung, die sowohl der im Lauf der Jahre wechselnden Familiengröße als auch den Ansprüchen an die Veränderbarkeit der Raumnutzung angepaßt werden konnte. Das Haus hat ein langgestrecktes, einstöckiges Sockelgeschoß auf Höhe des Gartens, das an eine Geländestufe auf der Ostseite angebaut ist. Die flexiblen Raumeinheiten dieses Traktes nahmen ursprünglich das Architekturbüro auf, später wurden dort die heranwachsenden Kinder untergebracht. Das Hauptgeschoß, das ein Stockwerk über Straßenniveau liegt, ist über das Dach des Sockelgeschosses zugänglich. Es enthält einen einzigen großen Raum, der durch eine frei aufgestellte Schrankwand in den Wohnteil und in den Eß- und Schlafbereich unterteilt wird. Die veränderbaren Aggregate von Küche, Bad und WC, die Kikutake »Move-nettes« nennt, bestehen aus industriell hergestellten Serienelementen.

3. Latticed, wooden sliding shutters on the outside of the surrounding gallery protect the main floor against the sun. Below the ceiling, which follows the pitch of the roof, the square-shaped room is entirely surrounded by a ribbon of high-level windows.

4. Plan of main floor, and section. Key: 1 living area, 2 sleeping area, 3 cupboard wall, 4 dining area, 5 replaceable kitchen unit, 6 replaceable bath and W.C. unit, 7 gallery, 8 stairs.

5. Living area, with the series-produced kitchen unit in the background. The curtains, which consist of wooden sticks held together by cotton, and the sliding shutters on the outside permit many variations of the room layout. The isolated cupboard wall on the left separates the living area from the dining and sleeping area.

3. Gitterartige Schiebeläden aus Holz an den Außenseiten der umlaufenden Galerie schützen das Hauptgeschoß vor Sonneneinstrahlung. Unter der Decke, die der Dachneigung folgt, umzieht ein hochliegendes Fensterband das ganze Raumquadrat.

4. Grundriß des Hauptgeschosses und Schnitt. Legende: 1 Wohnteil, 2 Schlafteil, 3 Schrankwand, 4 Eßplatz, 5 Auswechselbares Küchenelement, 6 Auswechselbares Element mit Bad und WC, 7 Galerie, 8 Treppe.

5. Blick über den Wohnteil zum serienmäßig hergestellten Küchenelement. Vorhänge aus Holzstabgewebe und die äußeren Schiebeläden ergeben veränderbare Raumgrenzen. Die frei stehende Schrankwand links trennt den Wohnteil vom Eß- und Schlafbereich.

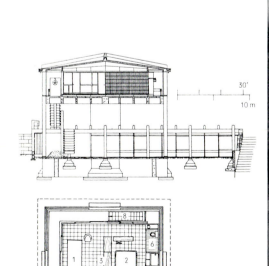

30'
10 m

1. View from the south. The cross-walls between the different cells rise above the flat roofs and, like the latter, project beyond the facades, so forming covered loggias in front of the living rooms and bedrooms.

1. Ansicht von Süden. Die Trennwände zwischen den einzelnen Zellen sind über die Flachdächer hochgeführt und wie diese vor die Fassaden gezogen, so daß sich vor den Wohn- und Schlafräumen überdachte Loggien ergeben.

Junzo Sakakura

'Cellular' house at Osaka-Tomigaoka, 1962

In order to obtain, on a narrow plot, a maximum of living space for four to six people at low cost and by simple construction, Sakakura developed a series of cellular units strung up along a straight central corridor. To match the rise of the ground, this central corridor has a number of steps so that the rooms are placed on four different levels. This has obviated the need for extensive earthworks. Owing to the differences in room heights, the projections and recesses of the facade, the alternation of window-less walls and large-size windows, and the variegation of the corridor width, the house has become extremely lively and differentiated. Terraces and bay-like patios seem to bring the exterior right into the house. The area module is governed by the Tatami mat (3 ft. 2 in. $\times$ 6 ft. 4 in.). 8 mats form the basic unit of a square room measuring 12 ft. 8 in. $\times$ 12 ft. 8 in. This module also determines the spacing of the bearing cross-walls which consist of light-weight concrete.

Einfamilienhaus aus Raumzellen in Osaka-Tomigaoka, 1962

Um auf dem schmalen Grundstück trotz größter Ökonomie und einfachster Bauweise möglichst viel Wohnfläche für 4 bis 6 Personen zu gewinnen, entwickelte Sakakura eine Folge von Raumzellen, die an einem gradlinigen Innenflur aufgereiht sind. Der Steigung des Geländes entsprechend, ist diese Hauptachse mehrfach abgetreppt, so daß sich die Räume auf vier verschiedene Ebenen verteilen. Dadurch konnten teure Erdbewegungen gespart werden, vor allem aber ergab sich durch die Stufung der Raumhöhen, durch die Vor- und Rücksprünge der Fassade, durch den Wechsel von geschlossenen Wandscheiben und großflächiger Verglasung und durch die Erweiterungen des Flurs ein höchst lebendiger, reich differenzierter Baukörper. Der Außenraum wird durch Terrassen und buchtartige Höfe in das Haus einbezogen. Die Flächenteilung geht von der Tatamimatte (0,95 x 1,90 m) aus: 8 Matten bilden die Grundeinheit eines quadratischen Raumes von 3,80 x 3,80 m. Dieses Maß bestimmt auch den Abstand der tragenden Zwischenwände aus Gasbeton.

2. In contrast to the rough-cast bearing walls which separate the cellular units, the non-bearing facade panels are lined with clinkers.

3. View from the bathroom level through the dining area towards living room and hall. The corridor, extending over four levels, is lit up through small high-level windows above the flat roofs. It is variegated by a floor-and-wall colour scheme and by glass sliding doors which lead to the different patios. Its width of 3 ft. 2 in. is also governed by the Tatami mat.

4,6. View from the living room towards the kitchen-cum-dining area which is open to the corridor (fig. 6), and a view in the opposite direction, towards the entrance. When the sliding doors are open, the pergola-covered patio is fully integrated with the living-cum-dining area.

5. Plan. Key: 1 entrance and porch, 2 corridor, 3 living room, 4 kitchen and dining area, 5 pergola-covered patio, 6 bathroom, 7 servant's room, 8 store room, 9. W. C., 10 children's rooms, separated by cupboard wall units, 11 master bedroom, 12 Tatami room.

2. Die nichttragenden Wandflächen in der Fassade sind im Gegensatz zu den verputzten Mauerscheiben der Zellentrennwände mit Klinkern verkleidet.

3. Blick von der Ebene des Badezimmers über den Eßbereich zum Wohnteil und Eingangsflur. Der vierfach abgetreppte Flur wird durch seitliche Oberlichtfenster über den Flachdächern belichtet. Farbwechsel in Bodenbelag und Wandfarbe sowie Glasschiebetüren zu den einbezogenen Höfen gliedern den Flur, dessen Breite mit 0,95 m ebenfalls dem Tatamiraster folgt.

4, 6. Blick vom Wohnraum in die zum Flur hin offene Küche mit dem Eßplatz (Abb. 6) und Blick in der Gegenrichtung zum Eingang. Der pergola-überdachte Hof kann durch Öffnen der Schiebetüren ganz in den Wohn-Eßbereich einbezogen werden.

5. Grundriß. Legende: 1 Eingang und Windfang, 2 Flur, 3 Wohnraum, 4 Küche und Eßplatz, 5 Pergola-überdachter Hof, 6 Bad, 7 Mädchenzimmer, 8 Abstellraum, 9 WC, 10 Kinderzimmer mit raumtrennender Schrankwand, 11 Elternschlafzimmer, 12 Tatamiraum.

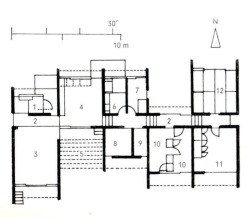

The Research Institute of Architecture (RIA)

KS house at Setagaya-Chitosehunabashi, Tokyo, 1964

This low-rise multi-patio house, spreading over about half the area of a quarter-acre plot, is occupied by an elderly couple and their daughter, a professional woman. As seen from the garden, larger units, nearly square in area and recognisable from the broad roof verges, alternate with smaller units which, in toto, take up no more than one third of the frontage; they are either annexes containing bathrooms, toilets, store rooms or the heating plant, or secluded patios to provide daylight for the adjacent main rooms. Functionally, the plan is divided into three areas: the self-contained dwelling areas of daughter and parents are separated from each other by the common living rooms in the centre of the house. Concentrated on the north side are a two-car garage, store rooms, utility patio, servant's room and service entrance. The reinforced concrete structure is partly left exposed and partly faced with a rich, differently textured cladding of various materials (clinkers, ceramic tiles, wood).

Wohnhaus KS in Setagaya-Chitosehunabashi, Tokio, 1964

Dieses eingeschossige Wohnhaus, das etwa die Hälfte eines rund 1000 m² großen Grundstücks einnimmt, wird von einem älteren Ehepaar und dessen berufstätiger Tochter bewohnt. Wie die Ansicht der Gartenseite zeigt, wechseln höhere, im Grundriß dem Quadrat angenäherte Raumzellen, erkenntlich an ihren kräftigen Dachgesimsen, mit niedrigeren, nur ein Drittel so breiten Sekundärräumen, die Bäder, Toiletten, Abstellkammern und Heizung aufnehmen oder als offene Innenhöfe die anschließenden Räume belichten. Funktionell gliedert sich der Grundriß in drei Zonen: Die separaten Wohnbereiche der Tochter und der Eltern werden durch die Gemeinschaftsräume in der Mitte des Hauses voneinander getrennt. Auf der Nordseite sind die Doppelgarage, Abstellräume, Wirtschaftshof, Mädchenzimmer und Serviceeingang zusammengefaßt. Das Haus ist in Stahlbeton ausgeführt, der teils schalungsrauh belassen, teils reich mit verschiedenen Materialien (Klinkern, Keramikplatten, Holz) in unterschiedlichen Texturen verkleidet ist.

1. South side (garden side). The roofs of the three living areas project above the terraces. These areas are separated by the projecting cells forming the secluded bathroom patios. The concrete walls still show the diagonal pattern of the shutter boards.

1. Die Gartenseite von Süden. Die Dächer der drei Wohnbereiche sind über die Terrassen vorgezogen, dazwischen liegen als geschlossene, vorspringende Zellen die Innenhöfe vor den Bädern. Die Stirnflächen ihrer Betonwände zeigen das Diagonalmuster der Bretterverschalung.

2. Plan. Key: 1 entrance patio, 2 porch, 3 inner patio, 4 living room, 5 dining room, 6 kitchen, 7 parents' bedroom, 8 Tatami room, 9 wooden terrace in traditional Japanese style, 10 garden terrace, 11 daughter's bed-sitting room, 12 guest room, 13 garage, 14 heating plant, 15 utility patio, 16 servant's room, 17 store room, 18 service entrance.

2. Grundriß. Legende: 1 Eingangshof, 2 Windfang, 3 Innenhof, 4 Wohnraum, 5 Eßzimmer, 6 Küche, 7 Elternschlafraum, 8 Tatamizimmer, 9 Holzterrasse im japanischen Stil, 10 Gartenterrasse, 11 Wohn-Schlafraum der Tochter, 12 Gastzimmer, 13 Garage, 14 Heizung, 15 Wirtschaftshof, 16 Mädchenzimmer, 17 Abstellraum, 18 Serviceeingang.

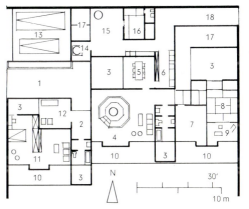

3. Towards the road, the house is completely enclosed by concrete walls, with the exception of the entrance patio which is spanned by concrete beams.
4. The centre of the house is formed by the large living room which is open on two sides. An octagonal low-level bench is the main feature of the interior.

5. Dining room with adjacent patio.
6. Glass curtain wall and sliding door of the bathroom face a completely secluded patio.

3. Zur Straße hin ist das Haus durch Betonscheiben vollkommen abgeschlossen, bis auf den Eingangshof, den Betonbalken überspannen.

4. Mittelpunkt des Hauses ist der große Wohnraum, der sich nach zwei Seiten öffnet. Eine vertieft eingebaute, achteckige Sitzbank bildet den Hauptakzent der Möblierung.
5. Das Eßzimmer mit dem dazugehörigen Innenhof.
6. Glaswand und Schiebetür der Badezimmer gehen auf einen ringsum geschlossenen Innenhof.

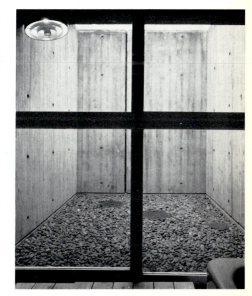

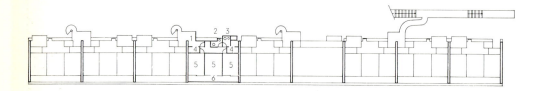

Kiyonori Kikutake

Apartment house at Asakawa-Yokohama, 1963-64
The narrow, oblong apartment house stands across a depression in the ground so that its central part has two storeys or at least an open ground floor. An approach road on the north side leads to the spiral or straight flights of stairs which provide access to two apartments on each landing. The apartments are separated by 1 ft. thick reinforced concrete cross-walls, 26 ft. 3 in. apart. On the lower floor are four apartments, on the upper floor nine; they are arranged in pairs with counter-symmetric, but otherwise identical layouts. On the south side, facing a loggia, are three Tatami rooms measuring 8 ft. 4 in. × 11 ft. 2 in. each of which can be opened up by sliding doors towards each other, towards the loggia, and towards the corridor. Adjacent to the two outer rooms are wardrobe closets; a kitchenette is adjoined to the room in the centre. Bathroom and W. C. are suspended from the rear facade in the form of pre-fabricated installation units measuring 7 ft. 6 in. × 5 ft. 9 in. which could, at any time, be replaced by improved variants that might come onto the market.

Apartmenthaus in Asakawa-Yokohama, 1963-64
Das schmale, langgezogene Apartmenthaus streckt sich quer über eine Geländevertiefung, so daß das Mittelstück teils zweigeschossig ausgebaut, teils als Freigeschoß offen gehalten werden konnte. Eine Erschließungsstraße führt auf der Nordseite zu den Wendel- bzw. geradläufigen Treppen, an deren Podest jeweils zwei Wohnungseingänge liegen. Jede Wohnungseinheit wird durch die im Abstand von 8 m stehenden tragenden Querwände aus 30 cm starkem Stahlbeton gebildet. Vier Einheiten sind im Erdgeschoß, neun im Obergeschoß untergebracht, alle mit dem gleichen Grundriß, jedoch paarweise spiegelbildlich. Auf der Südseite, die sich auf eine Loggia öffnet, liegen drei Tatamiräume von je 2,54 x 3,40 m, die untereinander, zur Loggia und zum Flur hin mit Schiebetüren geöffnet werden können. An die beiden äußeren Räume schließt sich je ein begehbarer Schrank an, während mit dem mittleren Raum die Kochnische in Verbindung steht. Bad und WC sind als vorfabrizierte Installationszelle von 2,30 x 1,70 m vor die Rückfassade gehängt; kommen neue, verbesserte Sanitäreinheiten auf den Markt, so kann die Zelle jederzeit ausgewechselt werden.

1. South side. The apartments are separated by load-bearing cross-walls, spaced at 26 ft. 3 in. intervals.
2. Plan. Key: 1 entrance, 2 installation unit with kitchenette, 3 bathroom and W. C., 4 wardrobe closet, 5 Tatami room, 6 loggia.

1. Ansicht von Süden. Zwischen den tragenden Querwänden, im Achsabstand von 8 m, liegt je eine Wohneinheit.
2. Grundriß. Legende: 1 Eingang, 2 Installationselement mit Kochnische, 3 Bad und WC, 4 Begehbarer Schrank, 5 Wohn-Schlafraum, 6 Loggia. 38

3. The north side is variegated by the replaceable suspended installation units. The supply pipes for kitchen and bathroom are left exposed in the open ground floor space.

4. In the two-storey part, each pair of top floor apartments is reached via spiral stairs. A platform several steps above ground level provides access to the lower floor apartments.

5. Nocturnal view from outside through the loggia railings into the three Tatami rooms which form the south side of each apartment. Visible in the background are the wardrobe closets with sliding doors adjoining the two outer rooms and the kitchenette adjoining the central room.

6. The sliding doors of the three Tatami rooms can be opened or closed at will so as to provide numerous varieties of space combinations and vistas. The rooms have a clear height of 8 ft. All the piping and wiring is contained in the longitudinal, cylindrical cavities of the 1 ft. high prefabricated ceiling units.

3. Die Nordseite erhält durch die angehängten, austauschbaren Installationselemente ein starkes Relief. Die Versorgungsleitungen von Küche und Bad stehen frei im offenen Untergeschoß.

4. Im zweigeschossigen Gebäudeteil werden je zwei Wohnungen des Obergeschosses über eine Wendeltreppe erschlossen. Die Erdgeschoßwohnungen liegen einige Stufen über dem Terrain und sind über ein Podest zugänglich.

5. Blick von außen durch das Stabgeländer der Loggien in die drei Tatamizimmer, die auf der Südseite jeder Wohneinheit liegen. In der Tiefe der äußeren Räume sind die begehbaren Schränke mit Schiebetüren zu erkennen, an den mittleren Raumabschnitt schließt sich die Kochnische an.

6. Durch Öffnen oder Schließen der Schiebetüren lassen sich in den Wohnräumen, die mit Tatamimatten ausgelegt sind, Durchblicke und Raumeindrücke vielfältig variieren. Die lichte Geschoßhöhe beträgt 2,40 m. Vorfabrizierte, 30 cm hohe Deckenelemente, die in der Längsrichtung mit kreisrunden Aussparungen versehen sind, nehmen sämtliche Leitungen auf.

The Research Institute of Architecture (RIA)

Actors' colony at the Shinseisaku Theatrical and Cultural Centre at Hatchiogi, 1964
The Shinseisaku Itinerant Theatre which, since 1951, has made it its business to acquaint workers, villagers and students with modern plays, has been given a home in a Tokyo suburb where, in contrast to conventional inner-urban centres of culture, theatrical art has a chance to resume its contact with nature, remote from the hectic life of the metropolis. The cluster of buildings is divided into three distinct parts. One of them is formed by a theatre for 500 spectators. The full-height windows of the foyer command a wide view of the landscape whilst the enormous concrete face of the rear wall, forming a monumental backdrop to an open-air stage, is deliberately designed as a counterpoint to the open landscape. The second part, a long two-storey wing containing the offices and all common amenities, forms the link with the residential buildings:— two rows of two-storey terrace houses adapted to the contour lines of the steep slope. The apartments, accessible from a gallery in the rear, have two or four beds with a total accommodation for 144 actors. Here, the cyclopic blocks of concrete with their deep cavities and widely overhung square balconies provide a deliberate contrast to the landscape. The fortress-like character of this architecture is further strengthened by the prismatic hoods above the small windows in the otherwise solid walls of exposed concrete.

Siedlung für Schauspieler im Shinseisaku-Theater- und Kulturzentrum in Hatchiogi, 1964
Das Shinseisaku-Wandertheater, das seit 1951 Arbeiter, Dorfbewohner und Studenten mit modernen Stücken bekanntmacht, erhielt in einem Vorort von Tokio eine Heimstätte, die — anders als die üblichen innerstädtischen Kulturzentren — abseits vom Großstadtgetriebe die Verbindung mit der Natur wiederherstellen soll. Der Komplex besteht aus drei Baugruppen: dem Theater für 500 Zuschauer, dessen Foyer sich mit raumhohen Fensterwänden zur Natur öffnet, während die Rückwand des Bühnenhauses, eine riesige Betonfläche, als Kontrapunkt zur offenen Landschaft gedacht ist: sie bildet die monumentale Kulisse einer Freilichtbühne. Ein langgestreckter, zweigeschossiger Trakt, der die Verwaltung und alle Gemeinschaftseinrichtungen enthält, leitet über zu den Wohnbauten. Ihre beiden Hauszeilen aus zweigeschossigen Reihenhäusern folgen der Biegung des steilen Hanges. Sie werden über Laubengänge auf der Bergseite erschlossen und bieten in Einheiten mit zwei und vier Betten Wohnraum für 144 Schauspieler. Mit ihren zyklopenhaft gefügten Blöcken, den starken Aushöhlungen und quaderförmigen Balkonvorsprüngen steht hier das Gebaute in ausgeprägtem Kontrast zur Natur. Prismatische Lichtluken in den geschlossenen Wandflächen aus rohem Beton verstärken noch den wehrhaften Charakter dieser Architektur.

1. View from the east. The terrace houses show a strong rhythm whilst the community centre (foreground, right) is held in a quieter vein. The latter stands along the flank of the spectators' forum of the open-air theatre which, at its lower end, adjoins the swimming pool.
2. Stairs connecting the lower row of houses (left) with the upper row. The exposed concrete walls with their random texture and colour shades and the coarse details are reminiscent of ancient battlements.

1. Ansicht von Osten. Die Wohnbauten zeigen eine kräftige Rhythmisierung der beiden Hauszeilen. Dagegen ist das Gemeinschaftsgebäude rechts vorn ruhiger gehalten. Es begrenzt die Zuschauerterrasse der Freilichtbühne auf der Längsseite, während das Schwimmbad sie nach unten abschließt.
2. Treppenaufgang von der unteren Hauszeile (links) zur oberen Häuserreihe. Die rohen Betonwände mit ihrer zufälligen Textur- und Farb-Schattierung und die groben Details erinnern an historische Wehrbauten.

3. The 'gorge' between the two rows of terrace houses. With its galleries and projecting roofs, the rear side of the lower houses has a deliberate horizontal emphasis whilst the main frontages facing the valley are accentuated by the cubic projections and cavities.

4. The facade design reflects the functions of the interiors: The projecting balconies form extensions of the living rooms whilst the small prismatic hoods, open at the bottom, serve as windows for the sleeping bunks.

5. Interior of a Type B 2 apartment for two people. The sleeping area, laid out with Tatami mats, also serves as an extension to the living room. A glass door and a sliding door connect with balcony and living room; the latter, in its turn, can be opened by a sliding door to the balcony.

6. In the apartments for four people, the upper bed has its own prismatic window for lighting and airing.

7. Plans of Types B 1 and A apartments.

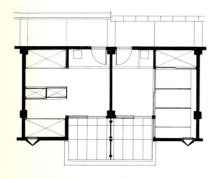

3. Durchblick zwischen den Hauszeilen. Die Bergseite ist durch die Laubengänge und die vorgezogenen Dächer betont horizontal gegliedert, während die Talseiten mehr blockhaft akzentuiert wurden.

4. Die Fassadengestaltung spiegelt die Funktion der Innenräume wider: Vorgezogene Balkone erweitern die Wohnräume; nach unten offene Prismen belichten die Schlafnischen.

5. Blick in ein Zweibett-Apartment vom Typ B 2. Der mit Tatamimatten ausgelegte Schlafteil ist zugleich erweiterter Wohnteil. Eine Glastür und eine Schiebetür verbinden ihn mit Balkon und Wohnraum, der sich seinerseits mit einer Schiebetür zum Balkon öffnen läßt.

6. Bei den Wohneinheiten für vier Personen hat auch das obere Bett ein eigenes Prismenfenster zur Belichtung und Belüftung.

7. Grundrisse der Wohnungstypen B 1 und A.

8. Site plan.
9. The theatre building, dominated by the stage tower, hugs the depression of the valley. An outer row of columns, supporting the heavily profiled ribbed roof, forms a colonnade.
10. The stage of the open-air theatre is placed a few steps above the spectators' forum. The high wall of exposed concrete forms an ideal backdrop.

8. Lageplan.
9. Das in die Talsenke geschmiegte Theatergebäude mit dem blockhaften Bühnenturm. Durch eine äußere Stützenreihe bildet das stark profilierte Rippendach einen Umgang.
10. Das Bühnenpodest der Freilichtbühne liegt einige Stufen über dem Zuschauerforum. Die hohe, rauhe Betonwand bildet eine ideale Kulisse.

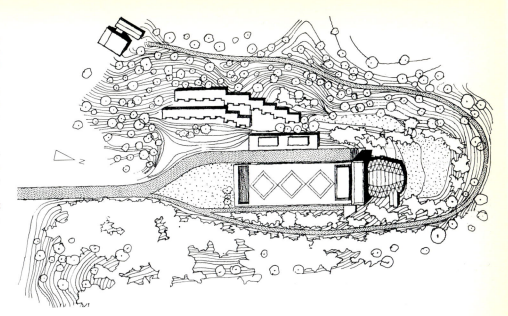

1. View from south-east. On the roof, a covered tennis court; on the right, lift turret and chimney.
2. General view from the south.
3. Facade detail. The structure is of reinforced concrete. Two intersecting wall diaphragms and the strongly built stairwell form an earthquake-proof core which is surrounded by an outer ring of articulated stanchions. The structural floors are supported by crosswise arranged main girders which are spaced at 11 ft. 6 in. intervals and protrude 8 in. beyond the facade. The curtain walls are formed by full-height, aluminium-framed glass sliding doors.

1. Ansicht von Südosten. Auf dem Dach ein gedeckter Tennisplatz, rechts Liftturm und Kamin.
2. Gesamtansicht von Süden.
3. Fassadendetail. Die Konstruktion besteht aus Stahlbeton, wobei zwei einander kreuzförmig durchdringende Wandscheiben in Verbindung mit dem steifen Treppenhauskern das erdbeben-sichere Zentrum bilden, das von einem Kranz äußerer Pendelstützen umgeben wird. Die Geschoßdecken ruhen auf kreuzweise im Abstand von 3,50 m angeordneten Unterzügen, die 20 cm vor die Fassade auskragen. Raumhohe Glasschiebetüren in Aluminiumrahmen bilden die Außenwände.

Eiji Hotta & Associates

Villa Bianca Apartment House at Tokyo, 1964
Due to the favourable position close to the town centre and the Meiji-Jingu Park, the land values at the Harajuku site in the Shibuya-ku district to the west of the town centre are very high. The private developer therefore required a compact multi-storey building which would permit a good utilization of the site. It contains 47 resident-owned luxury flats with three or four rooms, with a floor area ranging from 850 to 1400 sq. ft. The purchase price ranges from $ 22,500 to $ 62,500 per apartment. Each flat has a large or small loggia, so arranged that, vertically, the cavity of an open loggia alternates with a projecting bay on the next floor. In this way, and due to step-wise recession of the facades in the plan, the alveolate building offers a highly differentiated, lively appearance. Moreover, the ownership boundaries are thereby clearly defined. On the two lower floors are staff rooms, plant rooms for sanitary and electrical installations, as well as a low-level garage for the residents. The ground floor is left open except for the enclosed core containing the lifts and staircase. On the first floor are five flats of different size as well as an office with separate entrance. The second floor apartments conform to seven different plan types which are repeated on the fourth and sixth floor but are varied on the third and fifth floor.

Apartmenthaus Villa Bianca in Tokio, 1964
Die verkehrsmäßig günstige Lage, die Nähe des Stadtzentrums und die Nachbarschaft des Meiji-Jingu-Parks machen das Baugelände in Harajuku im westlich vom Zentrum gelegenen Stadtteil Shibuya-ku sehr teuer. Der private Bauträger verlangte deshalb eine relativ hohe Nutzung des Grundstücks durch eine kompakte, mehrgeschossige Bauweise. So enthält das Apartmenthaus 47 Luxus-Eigentumswohnungen von 78 bis 132 m² mit 3 oder 4 Zimmern. Der Kaufpreis lag bei 90 000 bis 250 000 DM pro Wohnung. Jede Wohneinheit hat eine größere oder kleinere Loggia, die von Geschoß zu Geschoß jeweils versetzt angeordnet wurde, d. h. einem vor die Gebäudefront vorspringenden Raumkubus entspricht im darüberliegenden Geschoß der eingekerbte Hohlraum einer Loggia. Dadurch und durch die Abtreppung der Fassaden entsteht ein reich differenziertes, lebendiges Erscheinungsbild des wabenartigen Baukörpers, und zudem ergibt sich eine klare Abgrenzung der Eigentumsbereiche. In den beiden Untergeschossen sind Personal- und technische Räume für Sanitär- und Elektroinstallation sowie eine Tiefgarage für die Hausbewohner untergebracht. Das Erdgeschoß ist als freies Stützengeschoß angelegt, in dem nur der Aufzugs- und Treppenkern als geschlossener Raumblock in Erscheinung tritt. Das 1. Obergeschoß enthält neben fünf Wohnungen verschiedener Größe ein Büro mit separatem Eingang. Die Wohnungen des 2. Obergeschosses bestehen aus sieben verschiedenen Grundrißtypen, die sich im 4. und 6. Obergeschoß wiederholen. Das 3. und 5. Obergeschoß variiert diese Typen.

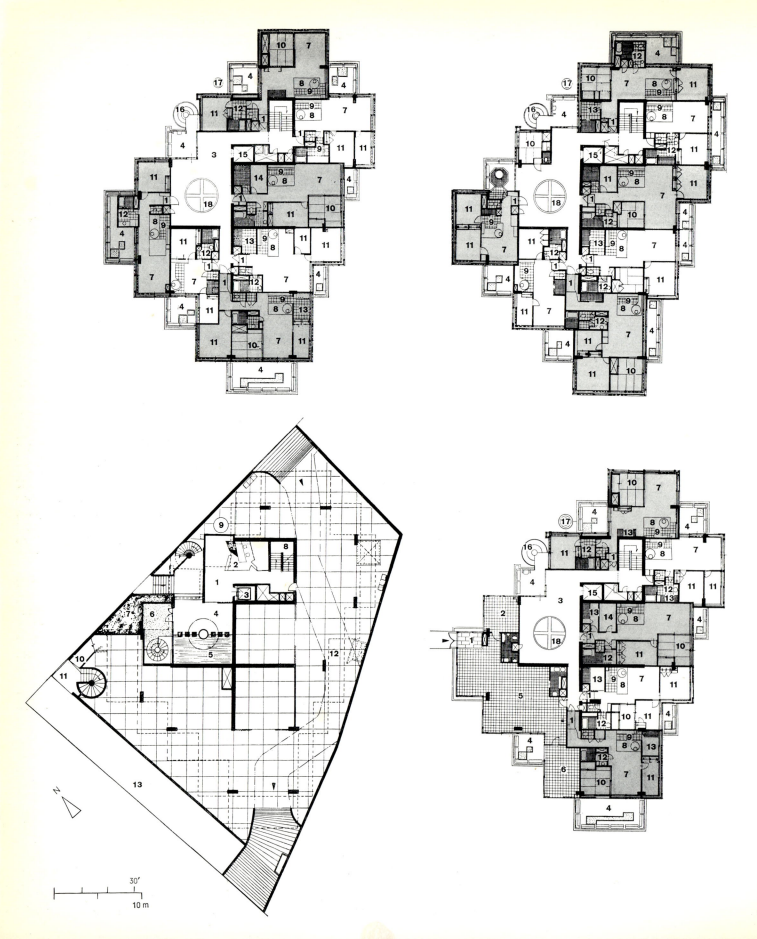

30'

10 m

4. Plans of second, fourth and sixth floor (top left), third and fifth floor (top right), ground floor (bottom left) and first floor (bottom right).
Key to ground floor plan: 1 lobby, 2 porter's lodge, 3 lift, 4 patio, 5 pond, 6 lobby, 7 rock garden, 8 stairwell, 9 chimney, 10 corridor leading to first floor office, 11 office entrance, 12 down ramp to garage, 13 road.
Key to upper floor plans: 1 entrance, 2 reception, 3 hall, 4 terrace, 5 office, 6 manager's office, 7 living room, 8 serving hatch, 9 kitchen, 10 Tatami room, 11 bedroom, 12 bathroom, 13 cupboards and service room, 14 luggage room, 15 lift, 16 fire escape, 17 chimney, 18 floor concourse.

4. Grundrisse des 2., 4. und 6. Obergeschosses (oben links), des 3. und 5. Obergeschosses (oben rechts), des Erdgeschosses (unten links) und des 1. Obergeschosses (unten rechts).
Legende zum Grundriß Erdgeschoß: 1 Eingangshalle, 2 Hausmeisterbüro, 3 Aufzug, 4 Atriumgarten, 5 Teich, 6 Halle, 7 Steingarten, 8 Treppenhaus, 9 Schornstein, 10 Gang zum Büro im ersten Stock, 11 Büroeingang, 12 Garagenabfahrt, 13 Straße.
Legende zu den Obergeschoßgrundrissen: 1 Eingang, 2 Empfang, 3 Halle, 4 Terrasse, 5 Büro, 6 Büro des Präsidenten, 7 Wohnraum, 8 Küchenblock, 9 Küche, 10 Tatamiraum, 11 Schlafzimmer, 12 Bad, 13 Schrank- und Wirtschaftsraum, 14 Kofferraum, 15 Aufzug, 16 Feuertreppe, 17 Schornstein, 18 Allgemeine Geschoßhalle.

5. The kitchens are integrated with the living room. The kitchen unit, protected by a ventilation hood, forms a table-high island in the room.
6. Terrace, seen from one of the living rooms. Each terrace has a small flower bed arrangement. To keep out the street noise, the outer wall is of the three-ply type, with a glass curtain of aluminium-framed sliding doors on the outside (Fig. 3), a lattice-work curtain in the middle (Fig. 6), and a paper-lined sliding wall panel on the inside.

5. Die Küchen sind im Wohnraum integriert. Der Küchenblock mit Wrasenfang steht als tischhohes Element frei im Raum.
6. Blick von einem Wohnraum auf die Terrasse, auf der wie in allen Wohnungen ein kleiner Außengarten eingerichtet ist. Um den Straßenlärm abzuhalten, ist die Außenwand dreischichtig ausgebildet: äußere Glaswand mit Aluminium-Schiebetüren (Abb. 3), Brüstungsgitter (Abb. 6) und Vorhang und innere, papierbespannte Schiebewand.

1. View from the air. Along the south side of the long, diaphragmatic block of flats extends a landscaped garden twice as wide as the block. On this side, too, is the main lobby, accessible from a footbridge.
2. Cross-section of all floors except the ground floor. The letters indicate the types of flats encountered on each floor.

1. Luftansicht. Auf der Südseite der langen Hochhausscheibe eine gärtnerisch gestaltete Grünzone von doppelter Hausbreite. Nach dieser Richtung ist auch die Haupteingangshalle orientiert, zu der ein gangwayartiger Steg führt.
2. Querschnitt durch das 1.—9. Wohngeschoß und Dachgeschoß (ohne Erdgeschoß) mit Angabe der in den einzelnen Stockwerken befindlichen Wohnungstypen.

Kunio Mayekawa & Associates

Block of flats at Harumi, Tokyo, 1956
The long and narrow block, which contains 170 flatlets and covers an area of 10,650 sq. ft., is part of the Harumi housing development close to some lower blocks. The first-floor flats are accessible, in pairs, from cylindrical stairwells of unusual design, placed outside the north facade, whilst the upper floors are served by the main stairs and lifts from the central lobby on the ground floor. Galleries and internal flights of stairs on the second, fifth and eighth floor also lead to the flats on the third, fourth, sixth, seventh and ninth floor. The plans of the 170 flatlets are of three basic types (A=452 sq. ft., B=345 sq. ft., C=452 sq. ft.).
Each of these units consists of living room and Japanese-type sleeping room with sliding partition, kitchen, Japanese bath (with a 2 ft. 4 in. high bath tub), W. C. and box room. Since, in accordance with ancient Japanese custom, the sleeping mats are rolled up in the morning and stowed away in a cupboard, the sleeping room can be jointly used with the living-room in the daytime. The weight of the building is supported by a steel framework with reinforced concrete cladding. As an anti-seismic measure, the columns are, on the two bottom floors, straddled so as to form wedge-shaped buttresses.

Apartmenthaus in Harumi, Tokio, 1956
Das langgestreckte Wohnhochhaus, das bei 990 m² überbauter Fläche 170 Kleinwohnungen enthält, steht im Neubaugebiet Harumi in der Nachbarschaft kleinerer Wohnbauten. Zur Erschliessung von jeweils zwei Wohnungen im 1. Obergeschoß dienen originelle Treppenhauszylinder, die vor die Nordfassade gesetzt wurden, während die Haupttreppe und die Aufzüge zu den übrigen Geschossen von der zentralen Eingangshalle im Erdgeschoß zugänglich sind. Über Laubengänge und interne Verbindungstreppen im 2., 5. und 8. Obergeschoß gelangt man auch zu den Wohnungen des 3., 4., 6., 7. und 9. Obergeschosses. Für die 170 Wohnungen wurden drei Grundrißtypen (A = 42 m², B = 32 m², C = 42 m²) entwickelt. Jede dieser Einheiten besteht aus Wohn- und Schlafraum mit Schiebewand, Küche, japanischem Bad (mit 70 cm hohem Badezuber), WC und Abstellraum. Da nach alter japanischer Sitte die Schlafmatten nach dem Aufstehen zusammengerollt und in einem Schrank verstaut werden, kann der Schlafraum tagsüber gemeinsam mit dem Wohnzimmer benutzt werden. Die großen Lasten des Gebäudes werden von einem Stahlskelett mit armierter Betonummantelung aufgenommen, dessen Stützen wegen der Erdbebengefahr in den beiden untersten Geschossen zu keilförmigen Strebepfeilern verstärkt wurden.

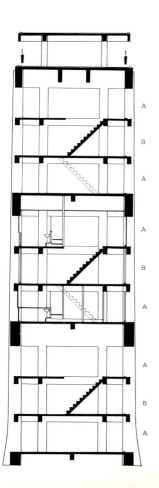

3. Plans of ground floor (bottom) with flats of Type C, first floor (centre) with flats of Type A, and third, sixth and ninth floor with flats of Type A.
4. Plans of Type A (102 flats with a floor area of 452 sq. ft. each) and Type B (51 flats with a floor area of 345 sq. ft. each). Key: 1 entrance, 2 dining area, 3 living room, 4 box room, 5 W. C., 6 bathroom, 7 kitchen, 8 sleeping room, 9 additional sleeping room, 10 balcony.

3. Grundrisse von Erdgeschoß (unten) mit Wohnungstyp C, 1. Obergeschoß (Mitte) mit Wohnungstyp A und 3., 6., 9. Obergeschoß mit Wohnungstyp A.
4. Grundrisse von Wohnungstyp A (102 Wohnungen mit je 42 m²) und Wohnungstyp B (51 Wohnungen mit je 32 m²). Legende: 1 Eingang, 2 Eßplatz, 3 Wohnraum, 4 Abstellraum, 5 WC, 6 Bad, 7 Küche, 8 Schlafraum, 9 Zusätzliche Schlafstelle, 10 Balkon.

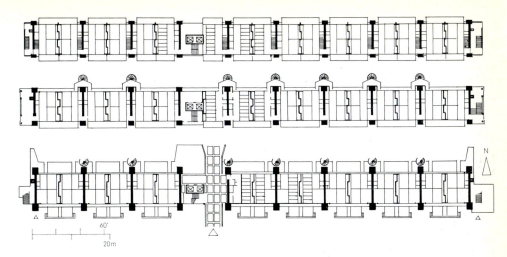

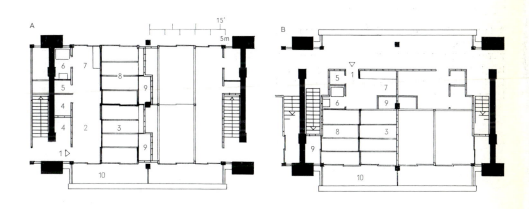

5. Le Corbusier's influence is apparent from the highly sculptured south facade with its balconies projecting between the columns, and from the fact that the flats extend through the whole depth of the building. This arrangement, which permits cross-ventilation, is one of the leading principles applied to Le Corbusier's 'Unités d'Habitation'. In the centre is the main stairwell.

5. Zwischen den Haupttragpfeilern auskragende Balkone geben der Südfront eine starke plastische Gliederung, die ebenso Le Corbusiers Einfluß erkennen läßt wie die Ausdehnung der Wohnungen durch die ganze Tiefe des Gebäudes, so daß Querlüftung möglich ist — eines der wichtigsten Prinzipien, die Le Corbusier seinen Unités d'Habitation zugrunde gelegt hat. In der Mitte das zentrale Treppenhaus.

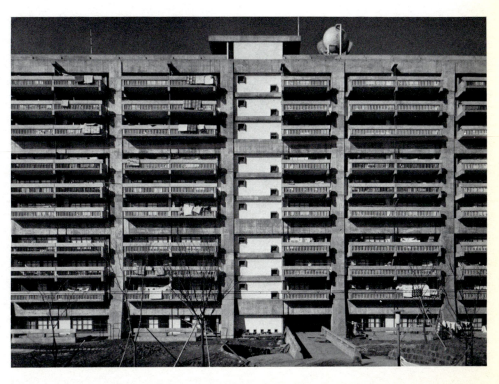

6. Interior of a Type A flat. Dining area, seen from the kitchen.

7. Type A flat. Behind the dining area (foreground, left) is the kitchen, next to it the sleeping room. In the foreground, right, is the living room, separated by a sliding door.

6. Innenansicht einer Wohnung vom Typ A. Blick von der Küche zum Eßplatz.

7. Wohnung Typ A. Hinter dem Eßplatz (links vorn) die Küche, daneben der Schlafraum. Rechts vorn der durch eine Schiebetür abgeteilte Wohnraum.

8. North side, seen from the street. Roofed balconies mark the gallery floors. The seven circular turrets provide access to the first-floor flats. In accordance with the regulations governing Japanese low-rent housing, the fire escapes at the two ends lead directly into the open, without a hall. Above ground floor level, the fire escapes are inside the building.

8. Die Nordseite von der Straße aus. Überdachte Balkons markieren die Laubenganggeschosse. Die sieben Rundtürme erschließen die Wohnungen im 1. Obergeschoß. Einer Vorschrift des sozialen Wohnungsbaus in Japan entsprechend münden die Nottreppen an den beiden Schmalseiten ohne Vorhalle direkt ins Freie. Vom 1. Obergeschoß an verlaufen sie innerhalb des Baukörpers.

1. A model of the re-development scheme, seen from the east. On the right, the planned cultural centre. The platform, rising 17 ft. 5 in. above the ground, is supported by reinforced concrete columns spaced at 30 ft.
2. General view of the model, seen from the south. The central part is completed; the remaining houses will be erected during the second stage. In the background and along the main road on the left extends the proposed cultural and shopping centre.
3. West-to-east section of the platform.

1. Modell von Osten. Rechts das künftige Kulturzentrum. Die 5,30 m hohe Plattform wird von Stahlbetonstützen im Abstand von 9,18 m getragen.
2. Modellansicht der Gesamtbebauung von Süden. Der mittlere Teil ist ausgeführt, als zweiter Bauabschnitt folgen die übrigen Wohnbauten. Den Abschluß bilden das Kultur- und das Geschäftszentrum (hinten) und der linke Randstreifen an der Hauptstraße.
3. Schnitt durch die Plattform in West-Ost-Richtung.

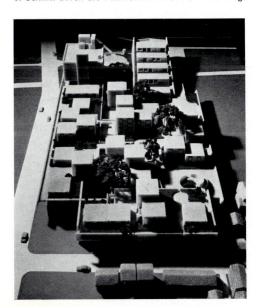

Masato Otaka

Urban development on a man-made platform at Sakaide, First stage, 1966-68

The re-development of a blighted residential district in the town centre was designed not only to create better housing conditions for the local inhabitants but also to overcome the parking difficulties which increasingly impaired the viability of the nearby shopping centre along the High Street. The re-development plans were primarily concentrated on an area of about 2½ acres, which is being re-developed in three stages. The first stage comprised an area of about 1 acre with 57 dwellings which have been erected on a man-made platform of reinforced concrete, rising 17 ft. 5 in. above the ground. The space below this platform serves for parking and traffic purposes. The two levels are connected by ramps and stairs. In accordance with the regulations for low-rent housing, the houses erected on the platform have up to four storeys, with flats of two different types. By adopting a staggered arrangement, a lively group has been created with broad and narrow paths and plazas embellished by greenery and even by trees which, rooted in the ground, grow through openings in the platform. In the final stage of the re-development, the houses will be supplemented by a cultural and shopping centre.

Siedlung auf einer künstlichen Ebene in Sakaide, 1. Bauabschnitt 1966-68

Die Sanierung des innerstädtischen Wohngebiets mußte nicht nur neuen Lebensraum für die Bewohner schaffen, sondern auch die Parknot beseitigen, die das Funktionieren des benachbarten Geschäftszentrums an der Hauptgeschäftsstraße immer mehr beeinträchtigte. Die Sanierungspläne konzentrierten sich zunächst auf ein Gebiet von annähernd 10 000 m², das in drei Bauetappen umgestaltet wird. Der erste Abschnitt umfaßte eine Fläche von 3750 m² mit 56 Wohnungen, die auf einem künstlichen Plateau aus Stahlbeton, 5,30 m über dem natürlichen Terrain, stehen. Der Raum unter der Plattform dient als Parkgeschoß und Verkehrsfläche. Beide Ebenen sind durch Rampen und Treppen verbunden. Die Wohnebene ist nach den Richtlinien des sozialen Wohnungsbaus mit ein- bis viergeschossigen Wohnhäusern überbaut, die zwei verschiedene Grundrißtypen aufweisen. Durch Versetzen der Bauten entstand eine lebendige Gruppe mit größeren und kleineren Wegen und Plätzen, Grünflächen und Bäumen, die durch Aussparungen in der Plattform von der Parkebene emporwachsen. Im Endausbau werden ein Kultur- und ein Geschäftszentrum die Wohnbauten ergänzen.

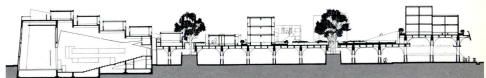

4. Plans at parking level (bottom), and plan of the platform, with the ground floor plan of the houses. Key: 1 shops, 2 parking area, 3 ramp, 4 spiral ramp, 5 plaza, 6 vestibule, 7 auditorium, 8 stage, 9 administration and cloakrooms, 10 patio, 11 space above auditorium, 12 children's playground, 13 platform with houses.

5. One of the roads on the platform. The road is paved with concrete flags; the sewers are embedded in the 5 ft. thick ribbed reinforced concrete deck.

6. A group of buildings with one, three and four storeys. Trees rooted in the natural ground grow through circular openings which, at the same time, serve to admit air and light to the parking area below.

7. The first stage of the re-development, seen in its urban setting from the north. The project was made possible by the acquisition, on the part of the local authorities, of numerous private properties with small houses.

4. Grundrisse der Parkebene (unten) und der Plattform mit dem Erdgeschoß der Wohnbauten. Legende: 1 Läden, 2 Parkfläche, 3 Rampe, 4 Spiralrampe, 5 Fußgängerbereich, 6 Foyer, 7 Auditorium, 8 Bühne, 9 Verwaltung und Garderoben, 10 Lichthof, 11 Luftraum über Auditorium, 12 Kinderspielplatz, 13 Plattform mit Wohnbauten.

5. Ein Weg in der Siedlung. Straßenbelag aus Betonplatten, Kanalisation in der 1,5 m hohen Bodenplatte (Stahlbetonrippendecke).

6. Eine Gebäudegruppe aus ein-, drei- und viergeschossigen Häusern. Bäume, die auf der unteren Ebene wurzeln, wachsen durch runde Öffnungen, die zugleich das Parkgeschoß belüften und belichten.

7. Die 1. Baustufe der Siedlung im Stadtbild, von Norden gesehen. Voraussetzung für das Projekt war der Erwerb zahlreicher Privatgrundstücke, auf denen Einfamilienhäuser standen, durch die Stadt.

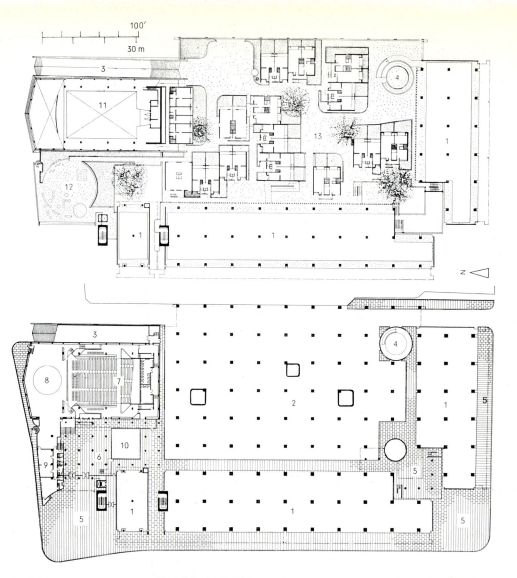

1. General view from the north, with main entrance and the ribbon of windows on the dormitory floor.
2. Detail of one of the gables. The diagonally boarded timber wall covers the small, low-level windows like a protective shield.
3. South-east corner with the open part of the lower floor, placed on columns.

1. Gesamtansicht von Norden mit dem Haupteingang und dem Fensterband des Schlafgeschosses.
2. Detail einer Giebelfront. Wie ein Schutzschild ist die diagonal verschalte Bretterwand über die tief liegenden Fensteröffnungen gezogen.
3. Südostecke mit dem zur Hälfte auf Stützen gestellten, offenen Untergeschoß.

Masako Hayashi

Ski-hut near Inawashiro in the Fukushima district, 1962

The southern slope of Mount Bandai in the North-Japanese district of Fukushima, some 140 miles from Tokyo, is a skiing area of nation-wide repute. This ski-hut, overlooking a plateau near the city of Inawashiro, commands a fine view of the lake of the same name. The site was selected so as to protect the hut against the violent blizzards and deep snow drifts. That is why the pitch of the saddle roof which covers the length of the building is placed parallel to the slope. The large gables have been given a north-south orientation, less exposed to the blizzards. On the valley side, the hut is placed on cruciform columns of 8 ft. height. On the up-hill side, the hut has a solid lower floor containing utility rooms, changing rooms and heating plant. The entrance floor with the living rooms is placed a few steps above the high ground. The hut is extended outwards by terraces and balconies outside dining room, lobby and ski room. The sleeping cabins, each containing four bunks on two tiers, are on the upper floor. Each cabin is 12 ft. 7 in. long and 8 ft. 4 in. wide. The attic contains store rooms. With the exception of the concrete base, the hut is erected in timber. It is equipped with running water and central heating.

Skihütte bei Inawashiro im Bezirk Fukushima, 1962

Der Südhang des Bandai-Berges im nordjapanischen Bezirk Fukushima, etwa 220 km von Tokio entfernt, ist nationales Skigebiet. Von der Skihütte aus, die über einer Hochebene bei der Stadt Inawashiro steht, hat man einen schönen Blick auf den Inawashirosee. Der Standort wurde so gewählt, daß die Hütte durch die heftigen Schneestürme und die hohen Schneeverwehungen nicht gefährdet werden kann. Deshalb verläuft die Neigung des Satteldaches, welches das Haus in seiner größten Ausdehnung überdeckt, parallel zum Hang. Die breiten Giebelflächen stehen in Nord-Süd-Richtung, die den Stürmen weniger ausgesetzt ist. Auf der Talseite wurde das Haus auf kreuzförmige, 2,40 m tiefe Stützen gestellt. Die bergseitige Hälfte ist als massives Untergeschoß ausgebaut, das Wirtschafts- und Umkleideräume und Heizung enthält. Das Eingangsgeschoß mit den Gemeinschaftsräumen liegt einige Stufen über dem Hanggelände. Terrassen und Balkone vor dem Speisesaal, der Eingangshalle und dem Ski-abstellraum erweitern die Nutzfläche nach außen. Die Schlafkabinen mit je vier Doppelstockbetten nehmen das 1. Obergeschoß ein. Jede Kabine ist 3,80 m lang und 2,50 m breit. Im Dachgeschoß sind Lagerräume untergebracht. Die Hütte ist mit Ausnahme des betonierten Sockelgeschosses in Holzbauweise errichtet. Sie ist mit fließendem Wasser und Zentralheizung ausgestattet.

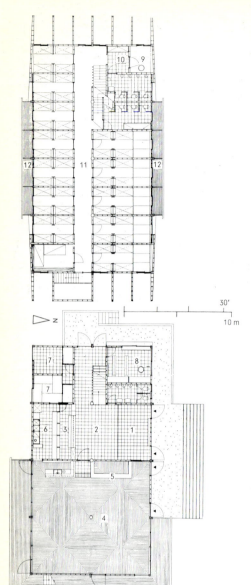

4. Plans of ground floor (entrance floor) and first floor. Key: 1 entrance (porch), 2 hall, 3 reception, 4 dining room, 5 kiosk, 6 hatch with meals elevator from the lower floor pantry, 7 office, 8 ski room, 9 linen room, 10 washroom, 11 corridor along the sleeping bunks, 12 balcony.
5. Corridor along the sleeping bunks on the upper floor. Even inside, the dominating features are exposed, round timber, raw deal boards and plywood panels.
6. Detail of north side with dining room corner.

4. Grundrisse von Erdgeschoß (Eingangsgeschoß) und 1. Obergeschoß. Legende: 1 Eingang (Windfang), 2 Eingangshalle, 3 Anmeldung, 4 Speisesaal, 5 Verkaufsstand, 6 Anrichte mit Speiseaufzug zur Küche im Untergeschoß, 7 Büro, 8 Skiabstellraum, 9 Bettwäsche, 10 Waschraum, 11 Flur, 12 Balkon.
5. Flur vor den Schlafkojen im 1. Obergeschoß. Auch im Inneren geschälte Rundhölzer, rohe Tannenbretter und Sperrholz als dominierende Materialien.
6. Ausschnitt aus der Nordseite mit Speisesaal.

1. Entrance side with drive. The only openings in the otherwise fully enclosed core of the spiral-shaped main building are the entrance and the games room windows. The windows of the banqueting hall in the low wing on the right face the entrance yard. The spiral stairs on the left lead to the restaurant terrace above the hotel wing.
2. Site plan.

1. Die Eingangsseite mit der Vorfahrt. Der weitgehend geschlossene Kern des spiralförmigen Hauptgebäudes ist nur durch den Eingang und die Fenster des Spielzimmers unterbrochen. Rechts im flachen Teil der zum Hof verglaste Festsaal. Der runde Treppenturm links führt auf die Restaurantterrasse über dem Gästeflügel.
2. Lageplan.

Ichiro Ebihara

Asama Motel near Karuizawa, 1964

The motel stands at an altitude of 3000 ft. at the National Highway from Tokyo to Nagano in a popular tourist area below the still active Asama Volcano. The group comprises a three-storey main building of spiral-shaped plan, a two-storey hotel wing, as well as external installations such as petrol station, garages and car parks. A circular courtyard on the north side forms the transition from the service area to the motel and also serves as entrance yard. Seen from the approach road, the buildings seem to be low since the lower floor is only visible on the valley side in the south. Because of the spiral-shaped plan, the premises of the main building appear to be of unlimited width and are capable of extension without break in continuity. On the entrance floor, reception hall, lobby and lounge with bar form a string of rooms along the spiral, which terminates in a banqueting hall. The top floor restaurant is linked with the main kitchen in the basement by two meal elevators. The top of the spiral is formed by a games room on the second floor. A cylindrical shaft in the centre of the spiral contains the cloakrooms. On each floor of the hotel wing are eight suites of different types, all with bathroom. The roof terrace forms an extension of the restaurant. The dominating materials are exposed concrete and brickwork.

Motel Asama bei Karuizawa, 1964

Das Motel steht in 1000 m Höhe an der Nationalstraße von Tokio nach Nagano in einem stark frequentierten Touristengebiet unterhalb des noch aktiven Vulkans Asama. Die Anlage umfaßt ein dreigeschossiges Hauptgebäude mit spiralförmigem Grundriß und einen zweigeschossigen Zimmerflügel, ferner Außenanlagen wie Tankstelle, Garagen und Parkplätze. Ein runder Platz auf der Nordseite bildet den Übergang von der Servicestation zum Motel und dient zugleich als Eingangsforum. Von der Zufahrt her wirkt der Komplex niedriger, weil ein Geschoß in den Hang versenkt wurde und nur auf der Südseite in Erscheinung tritt. Der spiralförmige Grundriß gibt dem Innenraum des Hauptgebäudes scheinbar unbegrenzte Weite und ermöglicht eine spätere kontinuierliche Vergrößerung. Im Eingangsgeschoß, wo innerhalb der Spirale Empfangshalle, Lobby und Lounge mit Bar hintereinanderliegen, schließt die Raumfolge mit dem Festsaal ab. Das Restaurant im 1. Obergeschoß ist mit der Hauptküche im Untergeschoß durch zwei Speisenaufzüge verbunden. Mit einem Spielzimmer im 2. Obergeschoß wird die Höhenentwicklung der Spirale abgeschlossen. Ein Zylinder in ihrem Zentrum enthält die sanitären Räume. Im Zimmerflügel liegen auf jedem Geschoß je 8 Apartments verschiedener Typen, alle mit Bad. Die Dachterrasse dient als Erweiterung des Restaurants. Als Materialien dominieren schalungsrauher Sichtbeton und Ziegelmauerwerk.

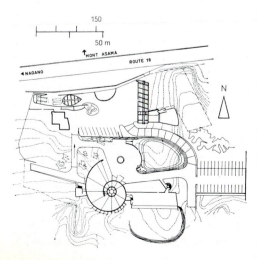

3. View from north-west. Seen from this side, the main building, gradually narrowing as it rises, has a fortress-like appearance.

4. The relatively low ceiling of the lounge on the entrance floor consists of diagonal wooden boards. Sliding doors give access to a terrace with low parapet. The stairs on the right lead to the restaurant.

5. First floor restaurant. The reinforced concrete beams, which are of different length, are supported on the reinforced concrete cylinder in the centre and on steel columns along the periphery. Below the overhanging roof are curved balconies with outdoor restaurant tables.

6. A view from the restaurant balcony onto the roof terace of the hotel wing, where each group of two rooms is flanked by screens.

3. Ansicht von Nordwesten. Von dieser Seite wirkt der Hauptbaukörper, der kontinuierlich ansteigt und dabei im Grundriß immer schmaler wird, wie eine Festung.

4. Die verhältnismäßig niedrige Lounge im Eingangsgeschoß mit diagonal verschalter Holzdecke. Schiebetüren führen auf eine Terrasse mit niedriger Brüstung. Rechts die Treppe zum Restaurant.

5. Das Restaurant im 1. Obergeschoß. Stahlbetonunterzüge verschiedener Länge sind auf dem Stahlbetonzylinder im Zentrum aufgelagert. Auf der Außenseite werden sie von Stahlstützen getragen. Unter dem Dachüberstand bogenartige Balkone mit Restauranttischen im Freien.

6. Blick von den Balkonen vor dem Restaurant auf die Dachterrasse über dem Gästeflügel, dessen Zimmer paarweise zwischen Sichtschutzwandscheiben liegen.

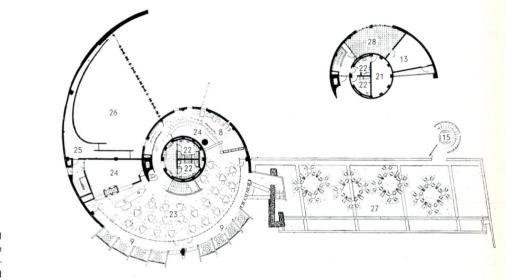

7. View from the south-west. By means of external stairs the terrace of the lounge is linked to the southern site. The balconies in front of the dining-room on the first floor are divided like lodges and project far beyond the façade. At right, the two-storey bedroom wing.

8. South elevation and plans. Bottom to top: Lower floor (built into the slope); entrance floor; first floor with restaurant and roof terrace; second floor with games room. Key: 1 drive, 2 entrance hall, 3 reception, 4 cloakroom, 5 office, 6 lobby, 7 lounge, 8 bar, 9 balcony, 10 administration, 11 banqueting hall, 12 stage, 13 stores, 14 hotel room, 15 spiral stairs leading to roof terrace, 16 lawn, 17 kitchen, 18 staff dining room, 19 bathrooms, 20 night porter, 21 heating plant and technical installations, 22 W. C., 23 restaurant, 24 pantry, 25 air-conditioning plant, 26 space above banqueting hall, 27 roof terrace, 28 games room.

7. Ansicht von Südwesten. Über eine Außentreppe ist die Terrasse der Lounge mit dem südlichen Gelände verbunden. Die Balkons vor dem Speisesaal im 1. Obergeschoß sind logenartig unterteilt und kragen weit vor das Gebäude vor. Rechts der zweigeschossige Gästeflügel.

8. Ansicht der Südseite und Grundrisse. Von unten nach oben: Untergeschoß (Hanggeschoß); Eingangsgeschoß; 1. Obergeschoß mit Restaurant und Dachterrasse; 2. Obergeschoß mit Spielzimmer. Legende: 1 Anfahrt, 2 Eingangshalle, 3 Empfang, 4 Garderobe, 5 Büro, 6 Lobby, 7 Lounge, 8 Bar, 9 Balkon, 10 Verwaltung, 11 Festsaal, 12 Bühne, 13 Depot, 14 Gästezimmer, 15 Wendeltreppe zur Dachterrasse, 16 Rasen, 17 Küche, 18 Personalspeiseraum, 19 Baderäume, 20 Nachtportier, 21 Heizung und technische Installation, 22 WC, 23 Restaurant, 24 Anrichte, 25 Klimaanlage, 26 Luftraum über dem Festsaal, 27 Dachterrasse, 28 Spielzimmer.

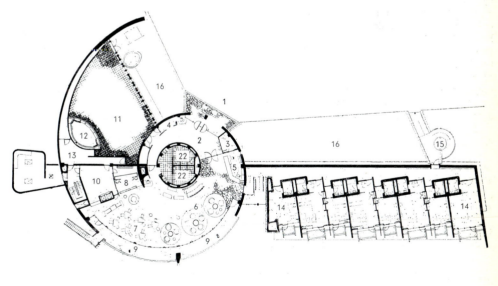

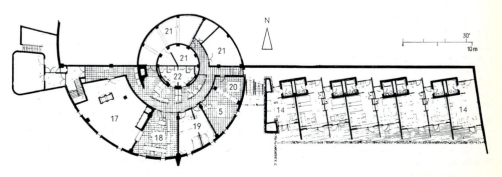

Noriaki Kurokawa & Associates

Honjima Hotel, 1964

The hotel stands on the main island of the Shioaki Archipelagos in the lake district of Seto National Park. The site on the front plateau of a hill commands a wide view across the sea and the old township in the south-east. The approach road, coming from the north-east, ends in a circular car park from which a flight of stairs leads up to the likewise circular entrance yard. Inserted into the circular walls surrounding this yard is the solid block of the staircase tower. The main entrance leads to the first floor lobby. In this building, the architect has tried to develop his idea of an 'architecture of passages'. The building is permeated by long corridors, ending in cross-passages. One of the latter, connected with the lobby by a flight of stairs, is inserted between the guest rooms and is, at ground floor level, projected like a pier far out onto the plateau. In shorter variants, e. g. as a pulpit-like projection, this cross-passage is repeated on the upper floors; it is meant to bring the building into closer contact with the landscape. A planned second cross-passage on the south-west side of the hotel will later be extended as a stairway path leading to the beach. The attempt to make the interior passages as variegated as possible has also influenced the staggered arrangement of the storeys both in the longitudinal section and in the cross-section. The guest rooms, governed by the module of the Tatami mat, are placed in the ground floor and first floor, whilst the lounges are on the second and third floor.

1. South-east side. The staggered arrangement of the storeys in the cross-section (Fig. 2) is matched by a corresponding stagger in the longitudinal section. Water spouts are cut into the broad parapets and provide deliberate accents in the facade. Their V-shape matches the diagonal pattern at the entrance side (Fig. 3). On the right, the solid block of the stairwell tower; to the left of it, the cross-passage with its long pier-like projection at ground floor level.
Construction: Reinforced concrete framework with exposed concrete faces inside and outside, crosswise reinforced waffle-type floors.
2. Cross-section.
3. North-east side of the building with the entrance yard. Prominent features are the horizontal bands dividing the terraced storeys and the V-shaped pattern of the timber board cladding of the stairwell tower.

Hotel Honjima, 1964

Das Hotel steht auf der Hauptinsel der Shioaki-Inselgruppe im Binnenseegebiet des Seto-Nationalparks. Vom Grundstück auf dem Plateau an der Vorderseite eines Bergrückens hat man einen weiten Blick auf das Meer und die alte Siedlung im Südosten. Die von Nordosten kommende Zufahrtsstraße mündet in einen runden Parkhof, von dem eine Treppe zum ebenfalls kreisförmigen Eingangshof hinaufführt. In den Mauerring um diesen Hof ist der Treppenturm als massiver Block hineingestellt. Durch den Haupteingang betritt man die Halle des 1. Obergeschosses. Der Architekt versuchte, bei diesem Bau seine Idee einer »Architektur der Passagen« weiterzuentwickeln. Der Baukörper wird von langen Innenfluren durchzogen, die auf Querspangen münden. Die eine, die über eine Treppe mit der Eingangshalle verbunden ist, schiebt sich zwischen die Gastzimmer und ragt im Erdgeschoß wie ein Steg weit auf das Plateau hinaus. Sie tritt in verkürzter Form, teilweise als kanzelartige Auskragung, auch in den oberen Geschossen auf und soll das Gebäude enger mit der Landschaft verzahnen. Die zweite Querspange wird später als Treppenweg auf der Südwestseite das Hotel mit dem Strand verbinden. Die Absicht, die Innenpassagen möglichst abwechslungsreich zu gestalten, hat auch die geschoßweise Versetzung der Etagen und die Abtreppung des Baukörpers beeinflußt. Die Gästezimmer, die nach dem Maß der Tatamimatte bemessen sind, liegen im Erdgeschoß und im 1. Obergeschoß, die Gemeinschaftsräume im 2. und 3. Obergeschoß.

1. Ansicht von Südosten. Als Entsprechung zur Abtreppung des Gebäudequerschnitts (Abb. 2) ist der Baukörper auch in der Längsrichtung abgestuft. Wasserspeier durchstoßen die breiten Gesimsbänder und bringen eine gewollte Spannung in die Fassade. Ihre V-Form korrespondiert mit dem Diagonalmuster an der Eingangsseite (Abb. 3). Rechts der geschlossene Block des Treppenhauses; links davon zeichnet sich die innere Querpassage ab mit dem weit vorspringenden Steg im Erdgeschoß.
Konstruktion: Stahlbetonskelett mit schalungsrauhen Betonsichtflächen innen und außen, kreuzweise armierte Kassettendecken.
2. Querschnitt.
3. Eingangshof und Schmalseite von Nordosten. Die Giebelbänder der abgetreppten Geschosse und die Vorderseite des Treppenturms mit V-förmiger Holzverschalung.

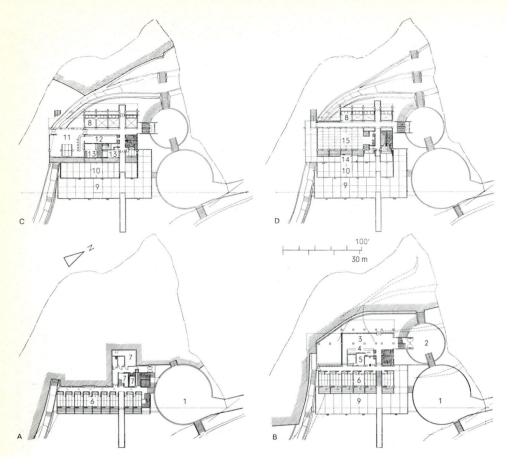

5. The banqueting hall on the third floor can be divided into smaller rooms by collapsible partitions.
6. Each hotel room has a sliding door, connecting with a loggia.
7. Whilst the cross-passage on the upper floors ends in a recess, the one on the ground floor has a pier-like projection.
8. The lounge in the rear of the lobby extends through three storeys in open connection with the longitudinal corridors.
9. In the rear, the columns and beams of the concrete framework — with crosswise intersections near the ends — are placed outside the facade.
10. On the first floor, the wooden wardrobes of the guest rooms protrude far into the corridor.

5. Der Festsaal im 3. Obergeschoß kann durch Faltwände in kleinere Räume unterteilt werden.
6. Jedes Gästezimmer läßt sich durch eine Schiebetür auf die vorgeschaltete Loggia öffnen.
7. Während die Querpassage in den oberen Geschossen als Einkerbung im Baukörper erscheint, springt sie im Erdgeschoß stegförmig vor.
8. Der zu den Längsfluren offene, durch drei Geschosse gehende Gesellschaftsraum auf der Hangseite der Eingangshalle.
9. Die Stützen und die sich an den Enden durchkreuzenden Balken des Betonskeletts stehen auf der Hangseite frei vor der Fassade.
10. Flur vor den Gästezimmern im 1. Obergeschoß, in den die Holzschränke der Zimmer weit hineinragen.

4. Plans of ground floor (A), first floor (B), second floor (C) and third floor (D). Key: 1 car park, 2 entrance yard, 3 lobby, 4 reception, 5 administration, 6 guest rooms (6 or 8 Tatami), 7 technical plant, 8 air space above lobby, 9 ground floor roof, 10 first floor roof, 11 dining room, 12 kitchen, 13 bathrooms, 14 second floor roof, 15 banqueting hall.

4. Grundrisse von Erdgeschoß (A), 1. Obergeschoß (B), 2. Obergeschoß (C) und 3. Obergeschoß (D). Legende: 1 Parkplatz, 2 Eingangshof, 3 Eingangshalle, 4 Empfang, 5 Verwaltung, 6 Gästezimmer (6 bzw. 8 Tatami), 7 Technische Räume, 8 Luftraum über Eingangshalle, 9 Dach Erdgeschoß, 10 Dach 1. Obergeschoß, 11 Speisesaal, 12 Küche, 13 Baderäume, 14 Dach 2. Obergeschoß, 15 Festsaal.

Kiyonori Kikutake

Tokoen Hotel at the holiday resort of Kaike in the Island of Honshu, 1963-64
The building represents the first stage of an ambitious project and is the core of a group of older one- and two-storey hotel buildings surrounding a central garden. The large windows of the two-storey lobby, which also forms a link with the older buildings, also face the park. The hotel storeys proper are raised above the surrounding houses so that they offer an unobstructed view over the coastal landscape. All the suites have the traditional Japanese features such as sliding walls, floor mats and wall recesses. As a secondary functional unit, stairwell and lift shaft are placed in a tower adjacent to the main building. This self-contained unit as well as the restaurant roof composed of hyperbolic-paraboloid shells reinforce the impression of rich, variegated plasticity already derived from the ramified framework construction. Internally as well as externally, the six main columns of reinforced concrete — placed outside the facade up to the third floor but further up inside — and the strong longitudinal beams below the roof storey are prominent features. From this framework, the pre-stressed reinforced concrete slabs of the hotel floors are suspended on steel cables. Cross-bracing has been achieved by adding satellite columns and cross-beams to the lower part of the main columns up to the third floor so that these columns form cruciform clusters.

Hotel Tokoen in Kaike Spa auf der Insel Honshu, 1963-64
Das Gebäude ist der erste Bauabschnitt einer groß angelegten Planung und Mittelpunkt eines Ensembles von älteren, ein- und zweigeschossigen Hotelbauten, die um einen zentralen Garten gruppiert sind. Mit ihrer großflächigen Verglasung öffnet sich die zweigeschossige Halle ebenfalls zum Park und bildet zugleich den Übergang zu den älteren Gästehäusern. Die eigentlichen Hotelgeschosse sind über die umliegende Bebauung emporgehoben, so daß der Blick ungehindert über die Küstenlandschaft schweifen kann. Alle Apartments wurden mit den traditionellen japanischen Wohnattributen wie Schiebewänden, Mattenfußböden und Wandnische ausgestattet. Als sekundäre Funktionseinheit ist das Treppenhaus und der Aufzugsschacht daneben turmartig an den Hauptbaukörper angefügt. Dieses selbständige Element und das Restaurantdach aus hyperbolisch-paraboloiden Schalen verstärken den Eindruck reicher, vielgliedriger Plastizität, den schon die verzweigte Skelettkonstruktion hervorruft. Innen wie außen treten die sechs Hauptstützen aus Stahlbeton, die bis zum 3. Obergeschoß herausgestellt und darüber in die Fassade einbezogen sind, und die mächtigen Längsträger unterhalb des Dachgeschosses als wichtige Gestaltungsmittel in Erscheinung. In dieses Gitterwerk wurden die vorgespannten Stahlbetonplatten der Hotelgeschosse an Stahlseilen eingehängt. Zur Queraussteifung sind die Hauptstützen bis zum 3. Obergeschoß durch Hilfsstützen mit Querbalken zu kreuzförmigen Stützenbündeln erweitert.

1. The hotel, here seen from the beach, overtowering the pinewoods along the wide sweep of the bay. From the 'Sky-lounge' restaurant on the roof, there is a comprehensive panorama of the Sea of Japan and the wooded hills of Honshu Island.
2. East side of the hotel, seen from the garden pond. Behind the horizontally orientated grid is the two-storey hotel lobby.

1. Blick vom Strand zum Hotel, das den Nadelwald an der weitgeschwungenen Bucht überragt. Vom Dachrestaurant, der »Sky-Lounge«, aus hat man eine umfassende Rundsicht auf das Japanische Meer und die bewaldeten Höhenzüge der Insel Honshu.
2. Ostansicht vom Teich des Hotelgartens aus. Hinter dem horizontal betonten Sprossenraster die zweigeschossige Hotelhalle.

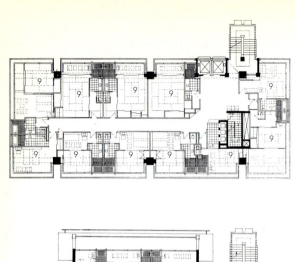

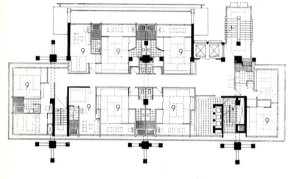

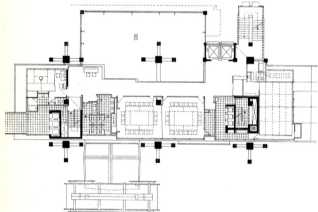

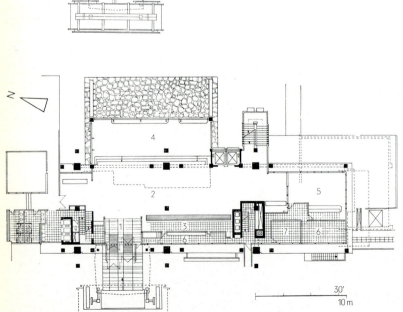

30'
10 m

3. Plans (bottom to top), of ground floor, first floor, second floor and fifth floor. Key: 1 main entrance, 2 lobby, 3 reception, 4 lounge, 5 restaurant, 6 offices, 7 telephone switchboard, 8 air space above lobby, 9 hotel rooms.
4. West side with main entrance. As the three lower floors are retracted, the main columns here remain just as exposed as in the open storey which is inserted so as to raise the guest room floors above.
5. Detail of one of the six column clusters. The main column in the centre and the three satellite columns are braced by longitudinal and cross-beams to guard against tornados and earthquakes.
6, 7. Views of the hotel lobby. The cruciform cluster of columns is both a structural element and a monumental feature. On the mezzanine above the reception are two conference rooms, connected by a gallery.
8. Japanese-type living room of one of the suites, commanding a view onto the sea. On the left, one step lower, is the Western-style bedroom which can be separated by a sliding partition. In the parapet below the non-openable windows are ventilation flaps.
9. Club room in Japanese style, surrounded by bands of high-level windows, with panel lighting in the ceiling. The sliding partitions consist of wooden latticework and transparent paper. The room can be further sub-divided down the centre.

3. Grundrisse von Erdgeschoß, 1. Obergeschoß, 2. Obergeschoß und 5. Obergeschoß (von unten nach oben). Legende: 1 Haupteingang, 2 Halle, 3 Empfang, 4 Lounge, 5 Restaurant, 6 Büroräume, 7 Telefonzentrale, 8 Luftraum über Eingangshalle, 9 Gästezimmer.
4. Westseite mit Haupteingang. Da die drei unteren Geschosse zurückgesetzt sind, werden die Hauptstützen hier ebenso sichtbar wie bei dem offenen Freigeschoß darüber, durch das die oberen Hoteletagen abgehoben sind.
5. Detail einer der sechs Gitterstützen. Der Hauptpfeiler in der Mitte und die drei Hilfsstützen sind zur Aussteifung gegen Wirbelstürme und Erdbeben durch Längs- und Querträger miteinander verbunden.
6, 7. Ausschnitte der Hotelhalle. Das kreuzförmige Stützenbündel ist konstruktives Element und Monumentalplastik zugleich. Über dem Empfang liegen im Zwischengeschoß zwei durch eine Galerie verbundene Konferenzräume.
8. Der japanische Wohnraum eines Apartments mit dem Blick auf das Meer. Nach links schließt sich, eine Stufe tiefer und durch eine Schiebewand abtrennbar, der westlich eingerichtete Schlafraum an. In der Brüstung unter den fest verglasten Fenstern Lüftungsschieber.
9. Klubraum im japanischen Stil mit umlaufendem Oberlichtband und Leuchtraster an der Decke. Die Schiebewände bestehen aus Holzgitterwerk und transparentem Papier. Der Raum kann in der Mitte nochmals unterteilt werden.

T. Amano

Golf Club House near Tokyo, 1961
The buildings designed by Amano reflect the design principles of his teacher, Frank Lloyd Wright. He knows how to combine the different elements of a building into a balanced composition and how to place the entire building in close relation to the surrounding landscape. The golf club house, one of the best examples of organic architecture in Japan, is a richly variegated three-level assembly of cubic and cylindrical shapes, seemingly forming an integral part of the slightly undulating ground. The liveliness of the external appearance is matched by the layout plan, which, with its numerous groups of rooms, reflects the functions of a high-class club house. Inside, wood is the dominating material. All the outer walls are white-washed in deliberate contrast with the well-kept lawns surrounding the house.

Golfklubhaus bei Tokio, 1961
In den Bauten des Architekten Amano sind die Gestaltungsprinzipien seines Lehrers Frank Lloyd Wright lebendig. Er versteht es, sowohl die einzelnen Elemente eines Gebäudes zu einer ausgewogenen Komposition zusammenzufügen als auch das ganze Bauwerk in enge Beziehung zur umgebenden Landschaft zu setzen. Das Golfklubhaus, eines der besten Beispiele organischer Architektur in Japan, ist ein auf drei Geschossen entwickeltes, reich gegliedertes Gebilde aus kubischen und zylindrischen Formen, das mit dem leicht gewellten Gelände zu verwachsen scheint. Der äußere Eindruck findet seine Entsprechung im lebendigen Grundrißbild, das mit seinen zahlreichen Raumgruppen die Funktionen eines anspruchsvollen Klubhauses widerspiegelt. Für den Innenausbau wurde vor allem Holz verwendet. Alle Außenmauern sind weiß gekalkt als Kontrast zu den gepflegten Rasenflächen, mit denen das Haus umgeben ist.

1. View from the west. Each unit of the building plastically reveals its own identity.
2. North side with staff entrance and pergola-covered utility yard.

1. Ansicht von Westen. Jede Raumeinheit des Baukörpers tritt plastisch hervor.
2. Die Nordseite mit Personaleingang und dem unter einer Pergola liegenden Wirtschaftshof.

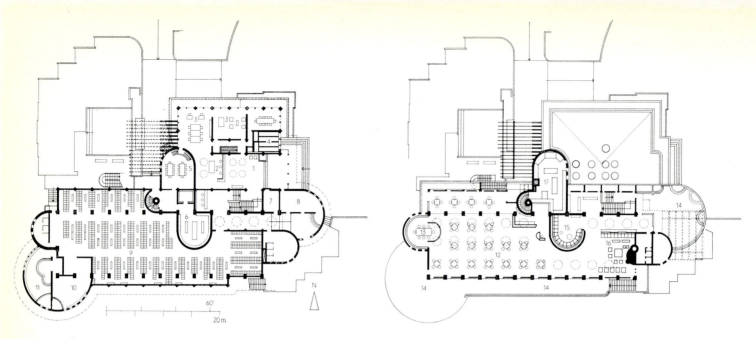

3. Plans of ground floor (left) and upper floor. Key: 1 lobby, 2 reception, 3 office, 4 Japanese-type room, 5 staff dining room, 6 stores, 7 golf professional, 8 caddies, 9 locker room for gentlemen, 10 changing room, 11 bathroom, 12 large restaurant, 13 small restaurant, 14 terrace, 15 lounge, 16 fire-side lounge, 17 kitchen.
4. Kitchen tower, seen from the east terrace facing the fire-side lounge. The top-light lanterns, which are surmounted by floodlights, are particularly conspicuous on the roof of the single-storey annex (right) which contains lobby and offices.

3. Grundrisse von Erdgeschoß (links) und Obergeschoß. Legende: 1 Eingangshalle, 2 Anmeldung, 3 Büro, 4 Japanischer Raum, 5 Personalspeiseraum, 6 Vorratsraum, 7 Golflehrer, 8 Balljungen, 9 Schrankraum für Herren, 10 Umkleideraum, 11 Baderaum, 12 Großes Restaurant, 13 Kleines Restaurant, 14 Terrasse, 15 Aufenthaltsraum, 16 Kaminraum, 17 Küche.
4. Blick von der Ostterrasse vor der Kaminhalle auf den Küchenturm. Das rechts sichtbare Dach des eingeschossigen Bauteils, in dem die Eingangshalle und die Verwaltungsräume liegen, zeigt besonders deutlich die Reihen der Oberlichtaufsätze, über denen für die künstliche Beleuchtung Strahler montiert sind.

5. Fire-side corner on the south side of the lounge. The continuous wooden ceiling seems to extend the room towards the staircase from which it is separated by latticework.

6. The dining room-cum-lounge on the upper floor is partly covered by a suspended ceiling. The curvature of this ceiling as well as the somewhat formalistic columns which, up to the band of high-level windows, give the appearance of heavy pillars — are also related to the external architecture. The top-lighting ensures an even spread of daylight throughout the large room.

7. The area in front of the brick-built fireplace has a paving of woodblocks.

8. Main stairs from lobby to upper floor. The columns end in a kind of capital.

5. Die Kaminecke an der Südseite des Gesellschaftsraums. Die durchgehende Holzdecke erweitert den Raum zum Treppenhaus hin, das durch ein Lattengitter abgegrenzt ist.

6. Über dem Speise- und Gesellschaftsraum im Obergeschoß ist eine abgehängte Decke einbezogen. Sie nimmt in ihrer geschwungenen Form ebenso Beziehungen zur Außenarchitektur auf wie die etwas formalistisch wirkenden Stützen, die bis zum Oberlichtband den Charakter schwerer Pfeiler haben. Die Oberlichter leuchten den großen Raum gleichmäßig aus.

7. Der Bereich vor dem gemauerten Kamin ist mit Hirnholzblöcken ausgelegt.

8. Haupttreppe von der Eingangshalle zum Obergeschoß.

Noriaki Kurokawa & Associates

'Hawaii Dreamland' leisure-time centre near Yamagata, 1967

The leisure-time centre is situated about 3 miles outside the town of Yamagata. Its informal design is reminiscent of an organic cell growth where the natural kinetic phenomena take place along circular paths. By emphasizing the seclusion towards the outer world, the attempt has been made to create, in the interior, an informal leisure-time world, centred on a sculptured courtyard with swimming pool and paddling pool, giant wheel, fish pond and rock garden. Following the thesis of metabolistic design, Kurokawa works with fixed and variable components. The catering premises are concentrated on the ground floor as a ribbon of rooms which is matched, on the opposite side, by a wing containing the administrative and technical premises. The changing and shower rooms form separate circular units placed between the columns. The isolated cylinders, partly overtowering the main building, contain stairs and toilets. The first floor premises form a continuous chain which is only broken by the entrance portal that extends through two storeys. They are used for a variety of purposes and are accessible from a ring of galleries connected to three staircase towers. The only firmly assigned major room on the upper floor is the bowling alley which occupies a straight section of the otherwise rather curviform group. A separate building in the shape of a truncated cone, connected by a foot-bridge with the upper floor of the main building, contains the traditional Japanese hot-water bath. The main building is a reinforced concrete structure. The bath-house pavilion has a steel framework with glass curtain walls on all sides.

Freizeitzentrum »Hawaii Dreamland« bei Yamagata, 1967

Das Freizeitzentrum liegt etwa 4 km außerhalb der Stadt Yamagata. Seine freie Form läßt an einen organischen Zellverband denken, in dem sich natürliche Bewegungsabläufe zirkulär vollziehen. Durch das Abschließen nach außen wird versucht, im Inneren eine ungezwungene Freizeitwelt zu schaffen, deren Zentrum der plastisch modellierte Hofraum mit Schwimmbecken und Kinderbassin, Riesenrad, Fischteich und Steingarten bildet. Im Sinne der metabolistischen Gestaltungslehre arbeitet Kurokawa mit fixierten und variablen Bauteilen. Die gastronomischen Räume sind im Erdgeschoß als bandartige Raumgruppe zusammengefaßt, der auf der gegen-überliegenden Seite ein Block aus Verwaltungs- und technischen Räumen entspricht. Die Umkleide- und Duschräume wurden als runde Raumeinheiten zwischen die Stützen gestellt. In die frei stehenden, zum Teil den Bau überragenden Zylinder sind Treppen und Toiletten eingebaut. Die Räume des ersten Obergeschosses bilden eine kontinuierliche Raumfolge, die nur durch das zweigeschossige Eingangsportal unterbrochen wird. Eine ringförmige Galerie, die über drei Treppentürme zugänglich ist, erschließt diese Räume, deren Nutzung variiert. Der einzige fixierte Großraum des Obergeschosses ist die Kegelbahn in einem geraden Teil-abschnitt der kurvenreichen Anlage. Ein frei stehendes, außerhalb des Ringbaus errichtetes und von diesem über einen Verbindungssteg im Obergeschoß erreichbares Gebäude in Form eines Kegelstumpfes enthält das traditionelle japanische Bad mit heißem Wasser. Das Haupt-gebäude ist in Stahlbeton ausgeführt; der Badepavillon besteht aus einem Stahlskelett.

1. Only some of the many rooms at the centre have outside windows. The main entrance leads through the two-storey entrance portal (left). The bath-house pavilion is connected with the main building by an enclosed footbridge. The sculptured appearance of the building is further emphasized by the isolated columns standing in front of the outer walls and by the curved parapet of the roof terrace.
2. With its seclusion emphasized still further by the surrounding boating moat, the 'leisure-time town' is reminiscent of a mediaeval stronghold. Its protective character is also enhanced by the high parapets of the roof terrace and the enclosed circular staircase towers. On the roof, a prome-nade zone with seats and resting places is sepa-rated by a railing from a Go-Cart track. In the foreground, outside the moat, is the bath-house pavilion.

1. Die vielfältigen Räume des Zentrums sind nur zum Teil nach außen geöffnet. Der Hauptzugang führt durch das doppelgeschossige Eingangsportal (links). Das Badehaus ist mit dem Hauptgebäude durch einen geschlossenen Steg verbunden. Die Plastizität des Baukörpers wird durch die frei ste-henden Säulen vor den Außenwänden und die ge-kurvte Brüstung der Dachterrasse noch betont.
2. Die Gesamtanlage erinnert in ihrer Abgeschlos-senheit, die durch den umlaufenden Wassergraben für Bootsfahrten noch betont wird, an eine mittel-alterliche Stadtbefestigung. Die hochgezogenen Brüstungen der Dachterrasse und die geschlosse-nen, runden Treppentürme unterstreichen ebenfalls den wehrhaften Charakter der »Freizeitstadt«. Auf dem Dach ist eine Promenadezone mit Sitz- und Ruheplätzen von der Go-Cart-Bahn durch ein Ge-länder abgetrennt. Im Vordergrund, außerhalb des Wassergrabens, das Badehaus.

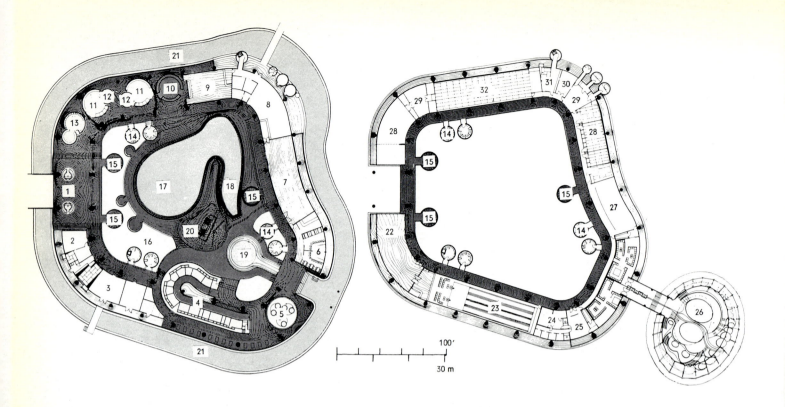

3. Plans of ground floor (left) and upper floor. Key: 1 entrance zone, 2 administration, 3 technical plant, 4 aquarium, 5 tea pavilion, 6 bar, 7 restaurant, 8 kitchen, 9 tea room, 10 public lounge, 11 changing room, 12 shower bath, 13 cloak room, 14 toilets, 15 staircase tower, 16 rock garden, 17 swimming pool, 18 paddling pool, 19 fishpond, 20 giant wheel, 21 boating moat, 22 games room, 23 bowling alley, 24 sauna bath, 25 rest room, 26 bath house, 27 public lounge, 28 conference and banqueting rooms, 29 hall, 30 chair store, 31 pantry, 32 large banqueting hall.

4. Inner courtyard, with the main entrance in the background. The pool is divided by a tongue-shaped peninsula into a swimming pool and a paddling pool. The inside of the main entrance is flanked by two staircase towers which contain the stairs leading to the upper floor.

5. The miniature 'giant wheel' stands on a raised platform between the paddling pool and the swimming pool. The footpaths between the different islands are covered with gravel. In the foreground the circular fishpond, on the left the aquarium.

3. Grundrisse von Erdgeschoß (links) und erstem Obergeschoß. Legende: 1 Eingangsbereich, 2 Verwaltung, 3 Technische Räume, 4 Aquarium, 5 Teepavillon, 6 Bar, 7 Restaurant, 8 Küche, 9 Teeraum, 10 Aufenthaltsraum, 11 Umkleideraum, 12 Dusche, 13 Garderobe, 14 WC, 15 Treppenturm, 16 Steingarten, 17 Schwimmbecken, 18 Kinderbassin, 19 Fischteich, 20 Riesenrad, 21 Wassergraben für Bootsfahrten, 22 Spielraum, 23 Kegelbahn, 24 Sauna, 25 Ruheraum, 26 Badehaus, 27 Aufenthaltsraum, 28 Konferenz- und Festsäle, 29 Halle, 30 Stuhllager, 31 Anrichte, 32 Großer Festsaal.

4. Blick über den Innenhof auf den Haupteingang. Das Bassin ist durch eine zungenförmige Halbinsel in Schwimmbecken und Kinderbecken geteilt. Die Innenseite des Haupteingangs wird von zwei Treppentürmen flankiert, die die Treppen zum Obergeschoß enthalten.

5. Das Miniatur-Riesenrad steht auf einer erhöhten Plattform zwischen Kinderbecken und Schwimmbad. Die Gehwege zwischen den einzelnen Inseln sind mit Kies bestreut. Im Vordergrund der runde Fischteich, links das Aquarium.

6. Courtyard, seen from the access gallery on the first floor. The gallery and the traffic zones on the ground floor are painted with striped bands in different colours, suggesting movements.

6. Blick von der Erschließungsgalerie im ersten Obergeschoß in den Innenhof. Die Galerie und die Verkehrszonen des Erdgeschosses sind mit streifenartigen Bändern in verschiedenen Farben bemalt, die Bewegungsabläufe suggerieren.

7. Rock garden at the entrance zone. From the path surrounding the swimming pool, cylindrical bays with benches project into the rock garden.
8. Entrance to the public lounge, situated between the changing rooms of the bath and the Tatami rooms. Some of the upper floor premises have windows facing the gallery. The stairs and installations towers are connected with the gallery by foot bridges.

7. Blick auf den Steingarten vor der Eingangszone. Vom Umgang um das Schwimmbecken ragen zylinderförmige Sitzerker in den Steingarten hinein.
8. Blick auf den Eingang zum Aufenthaltsraum zwischen den Umkleideräumen des Bades und den Tatamiräumen. Die Räume des ersten Obergeschosses sind teilweise zur Galerie hin verglast. Die Treppen und Installationstürme werden durch Stege mit der Galerie verbunden.

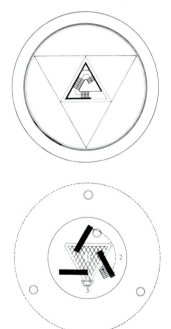

Plans of ground floor (bottom) and main platform.
Key: 1 pool of water, 2 paved entrance platform,
3 memorial plaque.

Grundrisse von Erdgeschoß (unten) und Aussichtsplattform. Legende: 1 Wasserbecken, 2 Gepflaster-
tes Eingangsplateau, 3 Gedenktafel.

Design office of the Kajima Building Society
Entwurfsabteilung der Baugesellschaft Kajima

Belvedere near Morioka, 1962

The belvedere stands on the top of Mount Iwayama, about 2 miles
to the east of Morioka, capital of North Japan. It has been erected
by the largest Building Society of the country as a memorial to their
founder who was born in this district. The plan repeats the triangular
shape of the mountain top. Inserted between three isolated wall
diaphragms of reinforced concrete and also serving as bracing is an
open flight of stairs which describes a polygonal spiral to the intermediate panorama platform at 22 ft. 2 in. level before continuing to
the widely overhung main platform of 85 ft. diameter which has a
bent rim reminiscent of the brim of a hat. A circular area around the
1 ft. deep pool of water at the foot of the tower is paved with granite.

Aussichtsturm bei Morioka, 1962

Der Aussichtsturm steht auf dem Gipfel des Iwayama, etwa 3 km östlich
von Morioka, der Hauptstadt Nord-Japans. Er wurde von der größten
Baugesellschaft des Landes als Denkmal für ihren Firmengründer
errichtet, der in dieser Gegend geboren ist. Der Grundriß nimmt die
Dreiecksform des Gipfelplateaus auf. Zwischen drei isoliert stehenden
Wandscheiben aus Stahlbeton wurde, zugleich als Queraussteifung,
eine offene Treppe eingebaut, die in einer polygonal gebrochenen Spirale zur Aussichtskanzel in 6,75 m Höhe und weiter zur stark auskragenden, wie eine Hutkrempe aufgebogenen Hauptplattform mit 26 m
Durchmesser hinaufführt. Am Fuß des Turmes ist um das etwa 30 cm
hohe Wasserbecken herum eine Kreisfläche mit Granit gepflastert.

Kenzo Tange

Olympic Sports Halls at Tokyo, 1963-64

The group of buildings consists of two sports halls of different size, developed from closely related basic shapes — circle and elipse —, and a single-storey wing by which the halls are linked scenically and functionally. Access is from two entrances: — the Harajuka Entrance on the north-east side of the ground (from Harajuka station) and the Shibuya Entrance, common to both halls, in the centre of the site (bearing the name of the urban district). The dominating building is that of the main hall which contains one swimming pool of 164 ft. length and one for divers. This hall, which can also be used as an ice rink, has 15,000 seats (12,546 permanent seats and 2,454 removable seats). The smaller hall which, during the 1964 Olympics, was used for basket-ball events, has 4,000 seats. This hall can also be used for other sports, e. g. boxing, in which case the 3,391 permanent seats can be supplemented by 1,980 removable seats. In choosing a suitable roof design, it was decided to use an economically favourable concave type of suspension roof which, compared with a convex cupola roof, permits considerable savings in heating and air-conditioning and provides better acoustics. Tange's basic idea was to create for both halls an 'open design', i. e. to find space concepts where the spectator does not get claustrophobia but is spontaneously aware, from every seat, of the openness of his environment.

Olympia-Sporthallen in Tokio, 1963-64

Der Komplex besteht aus zwei Sporthallen unterschiedlicher Größe, die aus verwandten Grundformen — Kreis und Ellipse — entwickelt sind, und einem eingeschossigen Verbindungsgebäude, das die Hallen organisatorisch und städtebaulich zusammenbindet. Die Erschließung erfolgt über zwei Eingänge: den Harajuka-Eingang auf der Nordostseite des Geländes (von der Harajuka-Station aus) und den für beide Hallen gemeinsamen Shibuya-Eingang im Zentrum des Grundstücks (nach dem Stadtbezirk Shibuya, in dem die Anlage steht). Das dominierende Bauwerk ist die Schwimmsporthalle, die ein Schwimmbecken von 50 m Länge und ein Sprungbecken enthält. Sie hat 15 000 Sitzplätze (12 546 feste Sitzplätze, 2 454 bewegliche) und kann auch als Eislaufhalle verwendet werden. Die kleine Halle, in der während der Olympiade 1964 das Korbballturnier stattfand, hat 4 000 Sitzplätze. Sie läßt sich auch für andere Sportarten, z. B. Boxen, verwenden; in diesem Fall können die 3 391 festen Sitzplätze durch 1 980 bewegliche Sitzplätze ergänzt werden. Bei der Wahl einer geeigneten Dachform fiel die Entscheidung zugunsten der ökonomisch günstigen Konkav-Hängekonstruktion, die im Gegensatz zu einer konvexen Kuppel bedeutende Einsparungen für Heizung und Klimaanlage möglich macht und außerdem eine bessere Akustik aufweist. Tanges Grundidee war es, für beide Hallen eine »offene Form« zu schaffen, das heißt Raumkonzeptionen zu finden, die nicht das bedrückende Gefühl völliger Eingeschlossenheit aufkommen lassen — also eine Form, bei der Offenheit nicht das Produkt von Bewegungsabläufen ist, sondern von jedem einzelnen Zuschauerplatz aus spontan erlebt werden kann.

1. Aerial photograph of the two halls, linked by the single-storey wing.
2. Cross-section of the swimming pool. Key: 1 main cables, 2 dual-curvature wire-net structure, covered with 2 in. thick steel sheeting, 3 top-light lantern, 4 arc-shaped main girder serving as an abutment for the wire-net structure, 5 circular gallery giving access to the tiers, 6 inner courtyard, 7 concourse on the roof of the connecting wing.
3. The two halls, seen from the east. In front of the swimming pool (foreground), a ramp — supported by a high retaining wall along the road — leads to the roof concourse of the single-storey wing linking the two halls. The two main cables from which the roof is suspended are, like those of a suspension bridge, suspended from pylons and anchored in concrete foundations. Visible on either side of the roof are the overhung, convex main girders which support the concavely suspended secondary cables carrying the roof.

1. Luftansicht der beiden Hallen mit dem eingeschossigen Verbindungsgebäude.
2. Querschnitt durch die Schwimmsporthalle. Legende: 1 Hauptkabel, 2 Doppelt gekrümmte Seilnetzkonstruktion, abgedeckt mit 4–5 mm starken Stahlplatten, 3 Aufsatz zur Belichtung, 4 Bogenförmiger Längsgurt als Widerlager der Seilnetzkonstruktion, 5 Verteilerring zur Erschließung der Zuschauerränge, 6 Innenhof, 7 Dachpromenade des Verbindungsgebäudes.
3. Die beiden Hallen von Osten. Vor der Schwimmhalle (vorn) führt eine Rampe, die zur Straße mit einer hohen Mauer abgestützt ist, auf die Dachpromenade über dem eingeschossigen Verbindungsgebäude zwischen den beiden Hallen. Die beiden Hauptkabel des Hängedaches sind wie bei einer Hängebrücke zwischen Pylonen gespannt und in Betonfundamenten verankert. Links und rechts sind am Auslauf des Daches die auskragenden, konvexen Längsträger zu erkennen, an denen die konkav durchhängenden Tragkabel der Dachhaut befestigt sind.

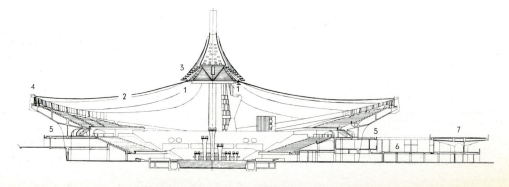

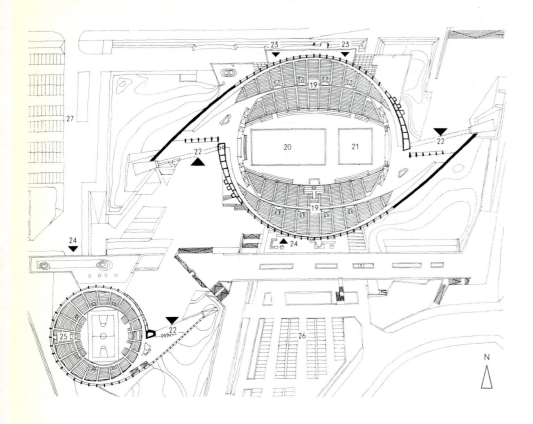

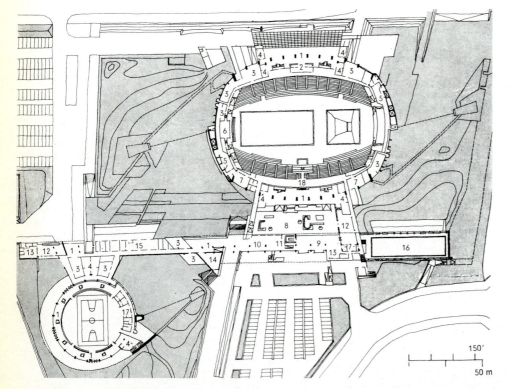

4. Plans of ground floor (bottom) and upper floor (entrance level). Key: 1 foyer, 2 snack bar, 3 stores, 4 cloak rooms, 5 air-conditioning plant, 6 control room, indicator boards, 7 machinery, 8 inner courtyard, 9 dining hall, 10 vestibule, 11 bar, 12 cafeteria, 13 kitchen, 14 conference room, 15 offices, 16 training pool, 17 sportsmen and referees, 18 'VIP' Lounge, 19 15,000 seats, 20 main swimming pool, 21 diving pool, 22 entrances for spectators, 23 press entrance (ground floor), 24 entrance for 'VIP's and referees, 25 4,000 seats, 26 car park for 120 cars, 27 car park for 110 cars.

4. Grundrisse von Erdgeschoß (unten) und Obergeschoß (Eingangsniveau). Legende: 1 Eingangshalle, 2 Snackbar, 3 Lagerraum, 4 Waschräume und WC, 5 Klimatechnik, 6 Kontrollraum, Anzeigentafel, 7 Maschinenraum, 8 Innenhof, 9 Speisesaal, 10 Vorhalle, 11 Bar, 12 Cafeteria, 13 Küche, 14 Konferenzraum, 15 Büros, 16 Trainingsbecken, 17 Sportler, Kampfrichter, 18 Raum für Ehrengäste, 19 15000 Sitzplätze, 20 Schwimmbecken, 21 Sprungbecken, 22 Eingänge für Zuschauer, 23 Im Erdgeschoß Presseeingang, 24 Eingang für Ehrengäste und Kampfrichter, 25 4000 Sitzplätze, 26 120 Parkplätze, 27 110 Parkplätze.

5. The roof of the swimming pool is suspended from the two longitudinal steel cables of 13 in. diameter which are supported by pylons and anchored in concrete foundations, and from the two convex main girders running parallel to the top rows of seats. The main girders are braced by stiff cross-beams which carry the cables for the pre-tensioning of the entire roof structure. The two main cables, each of them carrying one half of the roof, leave a broad skylight ribbon between them. The galleries behind the top tiers and at medium level receive direct daylight. The foundation is provided by the reinforced concrete substructure which is subjected to compressive stresses only.

6. The reinforced concrete diving towers are 10, 16, 32 and 48 ft. high. The curved design matching the outline of the suspended roof also governs the details.

7. Structural principle applied to the swimming pool building.

5. Das Dach der Schwimmhalle ist zwischen den beiden in Längsrichtung über Pylone geführten und in Zugfundamenten verankerten Stahlkabeln von 33 cm Durchmesser und den beiden konvexen Längsgurten, die parallel zu den obersten Sitzreihen verlaufen, aufgehängt. Starrquerträger, zwischen denen die Seile zur Vorspannung der gesamten Dachkonstruktion angeordnet sind, steifen die Längsträger aus. Zwischen den Hauptkabeln, an denen je eine Dachhälfte hängt, entsteht ein breites Lichtband.
Die Umgänge hinter den obersten Rängen und am Mittelgang werden von außen belichtet. Das Fundament bildet der nur auf Druck beanspruchte Unterbau aus Stahlbeton.

6. Die Sprungtürme aus Stahlbeton sind 3, 5, 10 und 15 m hoch. Die gekurvte Linie, die sich aus der hängenden Dachform ergab, ist auch für die Details bestimmend.

7. Konstruktionsschema der Schwimmsporthalle.

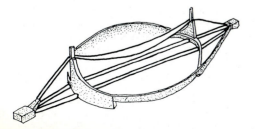
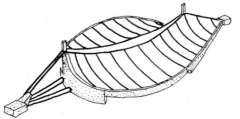
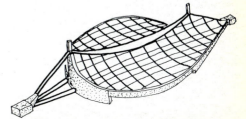

8. A broad concourse at entrance level divides the upper from the lower tiers. The full-height windows along this concourse and the upper concourse make the hall appear open and bright.

9. A view of the inner courtyard between the swimming pool and the single-storey wing. The latter contains offices, a large dining hall and a training pool; its roof serves as a concourse between the two halls. The courtyard is conceived as an outdoor extension of the dining hall. Its fixtures consist of bowl-shaped seats on concrete stems. The concrete cones serve to admit air and light to the changing rooms and lavatories on the lower floor.

8. Ein breiter Umgang auf Eingangsniveau teilt die Zuschauertribünen in einen oberen und einen unteren Bereich. Durch die Glaswände dieses Mittelgangs und des Umgangs hinter dem oberen Rang ist die Halle nach außen geöffnet und erhält viel Tageslicht.

9. Blick in den Innenhof zwischen der Schwimmhalle und dem eingeschossigen Verbindungsbau, dessen Dachpromenade für Fußgänger als Kommunikationszone zwischen Schwimm- und Sporthalle dient. Im Verbindungsbau selbst sind Verwaltungsräume, ein großer Speisesaal und ein Trainingsbecken untergebracht. Der Innenhof ist als räumliche Erweiterung des Speisesaals gedacht. Seine Möblierung besteht aus Sitzschalen auf Betonpodesten. Die Betonkegel belichten und belüften die Umkleide- und Waschräume im Untergeschoß.

10. A view from south-west. The artificial earth mounds forming part of the landscaping match the curvatures of the buildings. The design of the smaller hall in the foreground is similar to that of the large swimming pool building in the background: The substructure consists of a helical concrete ring. Tensioned between the end of this ring and the top of the pylon is a likewise helical steel cable which supports the secondary cables carrying the roof. Both halls are roofed with weld-assembled steel sheeting.

11. Structural principle applied to the smaller hall.
12. The helical main cable of the smaller hall is anchored to the pylon by means of spacers. Below the extruding roof is one of the entrances.

10. Ansicht von Südwesten. Bei der Gestaltung des Freiraums wurden Erdhügel aufgeschüttet, die den bewegten Gebäudeformen entsprechen. Vorn die kleine Halle. Ihre Konstruktion ist ähnlich wie bei der großen Schwimmhalle rechts hinten: Der Unterbau besteht aus einem spiralförmigen Betonring. Zwischen dem Ende des Rings und der Spitze des Pylons ist ebenfalls spiralförmig ein Stahlkabel gespannt, an dem die Tragkabel für die Dachhaut ansetzen. Beide Hallen sind mit verschweißten Stahlplatten abgedeckt.
11. Konstruktionsschema der kleinen Halle.
12. Das spiralförmige Hauptkabel der kleinen Halle ist mit Abstandhaltern am Pylon verankert. Unter dem nach außen laufenden Hallendach einer der Eingänge.

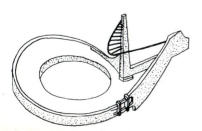

1. In the large oval of the Komazawa Olympia Park, the stadium, sports hall and volley-ball hall (top right, with bright roof) form a triangle which is intersected by a main road. The main axis of the raised entrance forum is marked by the volley-ball hall and the Olympia Tower.

1. In dem großen Oval des Komazawa-Olympiaparks bilden Stadion, Sporthalle und Volleyballhalle (rechts oben mit hellem Dach) ein Dreieck, das von einer quer verlaufenden Hauptverkehrsstraße geschnitten wird. In der Hauptachse der um eine Etage angehobenen Erschließungsplattform stehen sich Volleyballhalle und Olympiaturm gegenüber.

Yoshinobu Ashihara & Associates

Sports Hall at the Komazawa Olympia Park, Tokyo, 1964

The overall planning of the Komazawa Sports Park for the 1964 Olympics was in the hands of Eika Takayama. In collaboration with the architect of the sports hall (Yoshinobu Ashihara) and with the planner of the stadium (Masachika Murata, see page 88), it was first of all necessary to clarify the scenic relationship between these two dominating buildings. It was decided to provide a joint entrance forum, forming a central piazza between the two venues. To avoid disturbing the architectural integrity, no greenery was provided. The forum was placed on a higher level than the approach roads and is accessible by flights of stairs from the car park at Komazawa Avenue, the main traffic artery intersecting the grounds from east to west. The long sides of the piazza are extended as two wide footbridges across the road to the sports grounds in the southern part of the Olympia Park. In this way, integrity was preserved and the volley-ball hall (designed by Matsuda and Hisata) included in the group, forming the apex of a triangle on the south side of the entrance forum. At the northern end of the forum, standing in a pool of water, is the 164 ft. high Olympia Tower. This multi-purpose edifice serves as a belvedere, as a control centre for television, radio and telephone, as a water reservoir of 50 tons capacity and as an observation tower for traffic and parking control purposes.

The sports hall, with accommodation for 4,000 spectators, forming the western corner of the triangle, has been placed one storey below piazza level. It has a square plan and is surrounded by a circular yard of 354 ft. diameter. The interior is large enough for two basket-ball games to take place simultaneously. Spectators enter the hall from the central piazza where the main entrance forms a transverse axis with the entrances to the stadium on the opposite side. There is a service entrance via a ramp from a side street, and separate underground entrances are provided for contestants and officials. The octagonal roof of the hall consists of hyperbolic-paraboloid shells suspended from four main girders. The roofing is formed by reinforced concrete slabs with asphalt coating. The main structure of the hall is of steel. The main girders, which span the hall cross-wise and are anchored deep in the ground, are embedded in reinforced concrete. The ceiling is acoustically treated whilst all other surfaces have been left in exposed concrete.

Sporthalle im Komazawa-Olympiapark in Tokio, 1964

Die Gesamtplanung des Komazawa-Sportparks für die Olympiade 1964 lag in den Händen von Eika Takayama. In gemeinsamer Arbeit mit dem Erbauer der Sporthalle, Yoshinobu Ashihara, und Masachika Murata, der die Planung des Stadions (siehe S. 88) übernommen hatte, wurde zunächst die städtebauliche Beziehung zwischen diesen beiden wichtigsten Bauten geklärt. Man einigte sich darauf, zwischen den Sportstätten einen zentralen Platz als gemeinsames Eingangsforum anzulegen. Um den architektonischen Zusammenhang nicht zu stören, wurde auf eine Bepflanzung verzichtet. Der Platz liegt eine Ebene höher als die Zufahrtsstraßen und öffnet sich über eine Treppenanlage zu den Parkplätzen an der Komazawa Avenue, die als Hauptverkehrsader das Gelände von Osten nach Westen durchschneidet. An den Längsseiten des Platzes führen zwei breite Fußgängerbrücken über die Querstraße hinweg zu den Sportanlagen im Südteil des Olympiaparks. Auf diese Weise wurde der räumliche Zusammenhang gewahrt und die Volleyballhalle von Matsuda und Hisata in die städtebauliche Komposition einbezogen: Als Spitze eines Dreiecks begrenzt sie das Eingangsforum im Süden. Den nördlichen Abschluß bildet ein Wasserbecken, in dem der 50 m hohe Olympiaturm steht. Er ist als Aussichtsturm zugänglich, außerdem nimmt er die Kontrollzentren für Fernsehen, Funk und Telefon sowie einen Wasserbehälter von 50 t auf. Auch der Autoverkehr und die Belegung der Parkplätze wird von hier aus überwacht.

Die Sporthalle für 4000 Personen, die den westlichen Punkt des Dreiecks bildet, wurde um ein Geschoß unter das Platzniveau abgesenkt. Sie hat einen quadratischen Grundriß und wird von einem ringförmigen Hof mit 108 m Durchmesser umschlossen. Das Spielfeld in der Halle ist so groß bemessen, daß gleichzeitig zwei Basketballspiele veranstaltet werden können. Die Zuschauer betreten die Halle vom zentralen Platz her, wo der Haupteingang mit den Zugängen zum gegenüberliegenden Stadion eine Querachse bildet. Als Serviceeingang dient eine Rampe an einer Nebenstraße, während für Sportler und Funktionäre separate, unterirdische Eingänge angelegt sind. Das achteckige Dach der Halle besteht aus HP-Schalen, die zwischen vier Hauptträgern aufgehängt wurden. Die Dachhaut wird von Stahlbetonplatten mit Asphaltaufguß gebildet. Der konstruktive Aufbau der Halle ist aus Stahl. Die kreuzweise die Halle überspannenden Hauptträger, deren Fundamente tief in der Erde verankert sind, wurden mit Stahlbeton ummantelt. Die Innendecke ist mit Akustikplatten verkleidet, während alle übrigen Sichtflächen aus schalungsrauhem Beton bestehen.

2. Section, and plans at arena level (left) and main entrance level (piazza level).
3. The sports hall is placed in a circular pit. The octagonal roof is divided into four sectors by four concrete-embedded steel girders.
4. By placing the hall a storey lower than the piazza, and due to the elegant design of the hyperbolic-paraboloid roof shells, the visual intrusion of the building is greatly reduced. The lively pattern of the forum pavement is in keeping with the vivid lines of the roof edges. The pool of water surrounding the stone basin with the Olympic Flame and the Olympic Tower is placed a few steps below piazza level.

2. Schnitt und Hallengrundrisse auf dem Niveau des Spielfelds (links) und auf Höhe des Haupteingangs (Platzniveau).
3. Die Sporthalle steht in einer kreisförmigen Versenkung. Vier Stahlträger mit Betonummantelung unterteilen das achteckige Hallendach in vier Sektoren.
4. Durch das Absenken der Halle um ein Geschoß unter das Platzniveau und durch die elegante Form der HP-Schalen wird die Baumasse stark reduziert. Das lebhafte Plattenmuster der Platzfläche korrespondiert mit dem bewegten Linienspiel der Dachkanten. Die Wasserfläche, in der das Steinbecken mit der olympischen Flamme und der Olympiaturm stehen, liegt einige Stufen unter der Platzfläche.

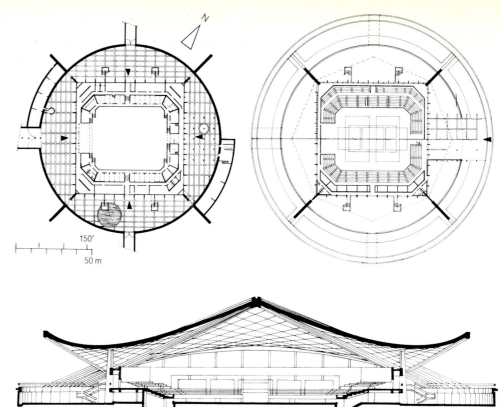

150'
50 m

100'
30 m

5. Interior of the hall. On the extreme right are the control cabins. The isolated lighting units are freely suspended from steel ropes, and can be raised or lowered at will. Above the continuous ribbons of light are inspection galleries. The seating accommodation can be increased by demountable rows of seats.

6. The circular low-level courtyard is surrounded by a retaining wall of clinkers and is linked by ramps with the entrance level. Pools of water recall the traditional Japanese garden.

5. Blick in die Halle. Ganz rechts die Kontrollkabinen. Die Beleuchtung hängt an Stahlseilen frei im Raum und läßt sich in der Höhe regulieren. Die Leuchtbänder sind als begehbare Galerien ausgebildet. Die Anzahl der Plätze kann durch demontable Tribünen erweitert werden.

6. Eine Stützmauer aus Klinkern faßt den versenkten ringförmigen Hof ein, der durch Rampen mit der Zufahrtsebene verbunden ist. Wasserbecken erinnern an den traditionellen japanischen Garten.

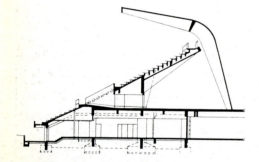

Masachika Murata & Associates

Olympic Stadium at the Komazawa Sports Park, Tokyo, 1962-64
The stadium, which was used for football events during the 1964 Olympics, has 20,639 seats which are mostly arranged on the long sides (34 rows at the mid-point, compared with 14 rows at the mid-point of the short sides) and command excellent visibility. On the west side, facing the entrance forum (cf. page 84), six overhanging roof shells serve as rain and sun protection for the seats of invited guests and for the eight prefabricated aluminium cabins assigned to press, radio and television reporters. With its alternation of solid surfaces and open cavities, the stadium as seen from the entrance forum has a markedly sculptural appearance. The entrances for spectators are at medium level — which is identical with the piazza level — and are so designed that the fully occupied stadium can be cleared within seven minutes. For purposes of reinforcement and seismic protection, the main girders of the reinforced concrete structure of the grandstand — which has an overhang of up to 30 ft. — are strengthened with corrugated concrete diaphragms. Prefabricated rows of seats, L-shaped in profile, are mounted between the cantilevered columns. The overhanging roof shells have restrained supports in the ground and at the tops of the main girders, and support each other by articulations.

Olympiastadion im Komazawa-Sportpark in Tokio, 1962-64
Das Stadion, in dem während der Olympiade 1964 das Fußballturnier veranstaltet wurde, hat 20 639 Sitzplätze, die zum größten Teil an den Längsseiten angeordnet sind (in der Querachse 34 Sitzreihen, in der Längsachse 14 Sitzreihen) und sehr gute Sichtverhältnisse bieten. Auf der Westseite, zur Erschließungsplattform hin (siehe Seite 84), schützen sechs schalenförmige Kragdächer die Ehrenplätze vor Regen und Sonne. Sie überdecken auch die acht vorfabrizierten Aluminiumkabinen für die Presse-, Funk- und Fernsehreporter. Durch den Wechsel von geschlossenen Flächen und offenen Hohlräumen verleihen sie der Ansicht vom Zugangsforum aus eine starke plastische Gliederung. Die Eingänge für die Zuschauer liegen in mittlerer Höhe auf dem Niveau des großen Platzes und sind so bemessen, daß das vollbesetzte Stadion in maximal sieben Minuten geräumt werden kann. Die Hauptbalken der bis zu 9 m auskragenden Tribünenkonstruktion aus Stahlbeton wurden zur Aussteifung und wegen der Erdbebengefahr mit gefalteten Betonscheiben verstärkt. Zwischen den Kragstützen sind vorgefertigte Sitzbänke mit L-Profil montiert. Die Kragdächer sind im Boden und an den höchsten Punkten der Hauptträger eingespannt und gegenseitig durch Gelenkverbindungen abgestützt.

1. The roof shells of the grandstand seem to grow out of the entrance piazza like fan-shaped plants.
2. Section of grandstand.
3. The concrete faces on the underside of the grandstands are corrugated so as to provide cross-bracing. The concourse gives access to the ground-level entrances of the grandstand.
4. The shell roofs covering the grandstand protect the seats for invited guests and the reporters' cabins.
5. The ribbed concrete beams of the roof shells bifurcate above the grandstand. The roof is additionally supported by a V-shaped pattern of secondary beams.

1. Ansicht der Haupttribüne mit den aus der Platzfläche der Eingangsplattform fächerförmig herauswachsenden Dachschalen.
2. Schnitt durch die Haupttribüne.
3. Die Betonflächen auf der Unterseite der Tribünen sind zur Querausteifung aufgefaltet. Im Umgang die ebenerdigen Tribüneneingänge.
4. Die Schalendächer über der Haupttribüne schützen die Ehrenplätze und die Reporterkabinen.
5. Die Betonrippenträger der Dachschalen verzweigen sich gabelförmig über den Tribünen. Die Dachplatte wird zusätzlich durch einen V-förmig geknickten Sekundärunterzug unterstützt.

Sachio Otani, Masao Tanaka, Koichi Fujita

Children's village at Nara-Machi, Kohoku District, 1967
On the basis of a landscaping project by Isamu Noguchi, a wooded dell has been remodelled into a playground with a number of different attractions, designed to satisfy the children's urge for play and to enrich their imagination: an open-air stage, a roller skating rink, a 'cave-man colony', a jungle landscape, sand pits with slides, etc. On a raised, levelled platform near the entrance to this area stands a 'village' with triangular roof shells which provide protection against the sun. In accordance with a triangular module, the village square is sub-divided into triangular, hexagonal or circular sections which, partly raised or lowered, form a lively pattern. The centre is formed by a mushroom-shaped mound, perforated by tunnels. Close to it, two rest rooms were created simply by enclosing two hexagonal bays with glass walls. The round columns and pre-tensioned roof girders are of steel whilst the roof shells, forming an isosceles triangle in the plan, consist of steel sheeting with stiffening ribs.

Kinderland in Nara-Machi im Bezirk Kohoku, 1967
Über das Spielplatzgelände in einer waldreichen Talsenke wurden nach dem Gartenplan von Isamu Noguchi verschiedene Anlagen verteilt, die den Spieltrieb der Kinder befriedigen und ihre Phantasie bereichern sollen: eine Freilichtbühne, eine Rollschuhbahn, eine Höhlenmen-schensiedlung, eine Dschungellandschaft, Sandplätze mit Rutschen usw. Am Eingang zu diesem Spielareal steht auf einer erhöhten, planierten Fläche ein »Dorf«, dessen dreieckige Dach-schalen vor der Sonne schützen. Der Dorfplatz wurde mit einem Dreieckraster in dreieckige, sechseckige oder runde Sektionen aufgeteilt, die, zum Teil vertieft oder erhöht, die Fläche beleben. Den Mittelpunkt bildet ein pilzförmiger Hügel, der von Tunneln durchzogen wird. In seiner Nähe entstanden zwei Ruheräume, einfach dadurch, daß zwei Sechseckfelder mit Glaswänden umschlossen wurden. Die Rundsäulen und die vorgespannten Dachträger sind aus Stahl; die Dachschalen, die im Grundriß ein gleichschenkliges Dreieck bilden, bestehen aus Stahlblech mit Versteifungsrippen.

1. General view from north-west. The site in the foreground provides space for future extensions of the 'village'.

1. Gesamtansicht von Nordwesten. Auf dem Ge-lände im Vordergrund kann sich das Dorf weiter ausdehnen.

2. Isolated triangular areas between the sandy paths of the 'village square' are paved with clinkers. The one shown here contains the footbath basin which has three taps embedded in inclined concrete blocks. The roof is here left open. On the right the paddling pool.

3. The undulating shape of the roofs matches that of the landscape. In the foreground is one of the glass-walled rest rooms. The cross-beams carrying the roof shells are screwed to ring-shaped column heads.

4. Plan. Key: 1 low-level access road, 2 underground lavatories for girls and boys, 3 climbing mound, 4 rest house, 5 washing facilities, 6 footbath basin, 7 paddling pool.

2. Zwischen den Sandwegen des Dorfplatzes sind einzelne Flächen mit dreieckigen Klinkern befestigt, hier das Dreiecksfeld der vertieften Fußwaschanlage, deren Zapfstellen in drei schräge Betonblöcke eingelassen wurden. Darüber ist das Dach ausgespart. Rechts das Planschbecken.

3. Die bewegte Dachform korrespondiert mit der Hügellandschaft. Im Vordergrund einer der verglasten Ruheräume. Die Querträger, auf denen die Dachschalen ruhen, werden an kranzförmigen Säulenköpfen verschraubt.

4. Lageplan. Legende: 1 Vertiefter Zugangsweg, 2 Unterirdische Toiletten für Mädchen und Jungen, 3 Kletterhügel, 4 Ruheraum, 5 Waschgelegenheit, 6 Fußwaschbecken, 7 Planschbecken.

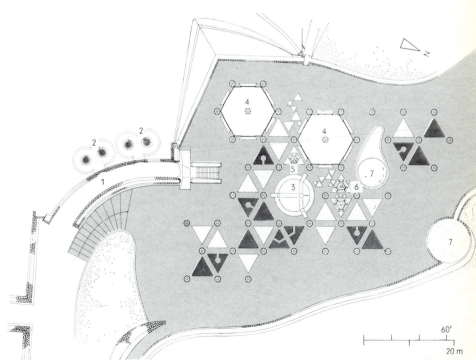

60'
20 m

1. View from the south-east, from one of the camping sites. The shape of the roof takes up the weightlessness of the surrounding tents. The contrast with the park landscape is emphasized by the white paint. The lower floor is erected in solid reinforced concrete. Lower floor and terrace floor are paved with stone flags. Concrete has also been used for the parapets of the terrace floor, for those of the upper floor which also serve as cross-bracing, as well as for the main columns and cantilevered beams. The tent roof itself is a steel structure. Both the inside and the outside of the building are painted white.
2. A view from the east. The landscape provides a fine backdrop for the open-air theatre stage at the lakeside. The spectators sit on grass steps cut into the slope.
3. A view at night. In the artificial light, the 'floating' effect of the upper floor is even stronger. Point lamps mark the path from the stage to the staircase.

1. Ansicht von Südosten, von einem der Camping-plätze aus. Die Form des Daches nimmt die Leichtigkeit der Zelte auf. Durch den weißen Anstrich wird der Kontrast zur Parklandschaft noch gesteigert. Das Untergeschoß ist in Stahlbeton-Massivbauweise ausgeführt. Die Brüstungen des Terrassengeschosses bestehen ebenfalls aus Beton. Der Boden des Untergeschosses und der Terrassen ist mit Steinplatten belegt. Auch das im Obergeschoß umlaufende Brüstungsband, das zur Queraussteifung dient, besteht wie die Hauptstützen und die Kragbalken aus Beton. Das Zeltdach ist als Stahlkonstruktion ausgeführt. Der Bau wurde innen und außen weiß gestrichen.
2. Ansicht von Osten. Die Landschaft als Kulisse für die Theaterbühne am See. Zuschauerplätze auf Rasenstufen am Hang.
3. Nachtansicht. Im Kunstlicht wird das »Schweben« des Obergeschosses noch stärker betont. Punktleuchten markieren den Weg vom Bühnenpodest zum Treppenhaus.

Noriaki Kurokawa & Associates

Assembly Square and Central Lodge of Camping Area National Children's Land near Yokohama, 1964-65

The central lodge of a large camping site, nestling in an undulating park landscape, serves as a training centre for youth leaders and as a community centre for the surrounding camping sites. Prompted by the position on the lakeside slope and by the desire to use the woods as a 'backdrop', the architects have divided the building into three parts, viz. a solid sub-structure, an open storey with terraces, and a cantilevered top floor. The lower floor is divided by a passage into two parts. This passage — an architectural motif which plays an important part in Kurokawa's work — widens at the centre into a square piazza open to the sky, surrounding a spiral flight of stairs. Around this piazza lie the community rooms. From the lower floor, external stairs and the central internal stairs lead to the open floor at main access level. This terrace floor is divided into a southern and northern half by the open space above the lower-floor passage. The top floor with its characteristic tent roof is supported by four columns. It contains dormitories and play rooms and is reached via the spiral stairs.

Versammlungsgebäude und Gemeinschaftszentrum im Jugend-Nationalpark bei Yokohama, 1964-65

Das Gemeinschaftsgebäude eines großen Zeltgeländes, das mitten in einer hügeligen Parklandschaft liegt, dient einmal als Ausbildungszentrum für Jugendleiter, zum anderen ist es Mittelpunkt der umliegenden Campingplätze. Durch die Hanglage oberhalb eines Sees und aus dem Bedürfnis heraus, den Wald im Hintergrund als Kulisse zu erhalten, ergab sich eine Dreiteilung in massiven Unterbau, offenes Terrassengeschoß und darüber auskragendes Obergeschoß. Das Untergeschoß wird durch eine Passage in zwei Teile getrennt. Diese Passage — ein architektonisches Motiv, das im Oeuvre Kurokawas eine wichtige Rolle spielt — weitet sich im Zentrum zu einem quadratischen, nach oben offenen Raum, in dessen Mitte eine Wendeltreppe plaziert ist. Um diesen Zentralraum sind die Gemeinschaftsräume gruppiert. Vom Untergeschoß führen Freitreppen und die zentrale Innentreppe zum Freigeschoß auf Zufahrtsniveau. Dieses Terrassengeschoß wird durch den offenen Schacht über der Passage des Untergeschosses in eine südliche und eine nördliche Hälfte geteilt. Das Obergeschoß mit seinem charakteristischen Zeltdach ruht auf vier Stützen. Es enthält Schlaf- und Spielräume und wird über die Wendeltreppe erschlossen.

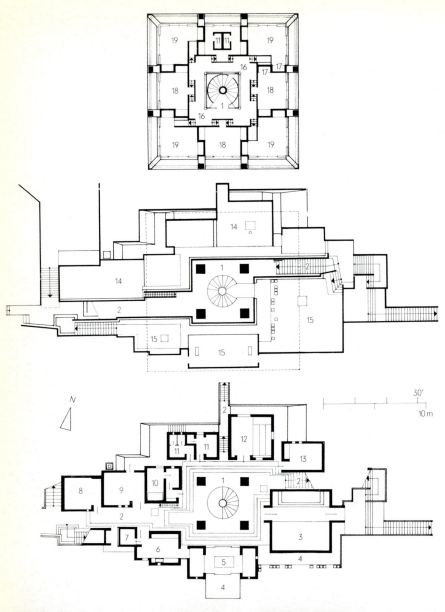

4. Plans of (bottom to top) lower floor, terrace floor and upper floor. Key to plans: 1 staircase hall, 2 passage, 3 meeting room, 4 outdoor seats, 5 dining hall, 6 kitchen, 7 kitchen stores, 8 machinery, 9 heating plant, 10 bathroom, 11 W. C., 12 administration, 13 stores room, 14 north terrace, 15 south terrace, 16 inside gallery, 17 lockers, 18 dormitory, 19 play room.

5. A view along the passage with the spiral stairs in the centre. The steps are suspended from steel tubes. The bearing structure of the upper floor seems to grow out of the staircase hall. The stairs on the right lead to the south terrace.

6. The passage is enlivened by steps. The narrow flight of stairs leads to the north terrace on the open terrace floor.

7. All the rooms adjoining the central staircase hall are a few steps above the level of that hall.

4. Grundrisse von Untergeschoß, offenem Terrassengeschoß und Obergeschoß (von unten nach oben). Legende zu den Plänen: 1 Treppenhalle, 2 Passage, 3 Versammlungsraum, 4 Freisitzplatz, 5 Speisesaal, 6 Küche, 7 Küchenvorräte, 8 Maschinenraum, 9 Heizung, 10 Baderaum, 11 WC, 12 Verwaltung, 13 Lagerraum, 14 Nordterrasse, 15 Südterrasse, 16 Innengalerie, 17 Schränke, 18 Schlafraum, 19 Spielraum.

5. Blick durch die Passage auf die Wendeltreppe im Zentrum. Ihre Stufen sind an Stahlrohren aufgehängt. Die Tragkonstruktion des Obergeschosses wächst aus der Treppenhalle heraus. Rechts die Treppe zur Südterrasse.

6. Die Passage ist durch Stufen reich differenziert. Die schmale Treppe verbindet sie mit der Nordterrasse im offenen Zwischengeschoß.

7. Alle an die zentrale Treppenhalle anschließenden Räume liegen einige Stufen über dem Hallenniveau.

8. View from the north. The service road closely adjoins the building at terrace floor level.

9. The south terrace narrows down for the stairs at the western end.

10. The tent-like roof governs the general appearance of the upper floor which is divided by low cupboards into individual cells.

8. Ansicht von Norden. Die Zufahrtstraße liegt dicht vor dem Gebäude, auf gleicher Höhe wie das Terrassengeschoß.

9. Blick über die Südterrasse, die sich zur Westtreppe hin verengt.

10. Das zeltartige Dach bestimmt den Raumeindruck des Obergeschosses, das durch niedrige Schränke in einzelne Raumzellen unterteilt wird.

1. A view across the playing field to the cabins on the slope. The problem of adapting the cabins to the slope is elegantly solved by the trefoil-shaped base of concrete diaphragms. One of the cabins has a tent roof. But for its two storeys, the main hall (left) has the same shape as the dormitory cabins.
2. Section of a typical cabin.

1. Blick über den Sportplatz auf die Kabinen am Hang. Der dreistrahlige Grundriß der Sockelscheiben ermöglicht die problemlose Anpassung an die Hangneigung. Eine der Kabinen ist mit einem Zeltdach überspannt. Das Gemeinschaftsgebäude links folgt in der Form den Wohnkabinen, ist aber zweigeschossig ausgebaut.
2. Schnitt durch eine Wohnkabine.

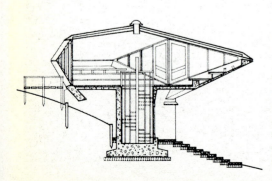

Kiyonori Kikutake

School Campus near Yokohama, 1967
The school campus occupies the eastern slope of a dell in the wooded hills of the Kohoku district. Each of the informally placed cabins serves to provide lodging and group lesson accommodation for 15 children. The main hall at the foot of the slope, which has a floor area of 5600 sq. ft., is the largest of the buildings and serves as an assembly and dining hall. At the bottom of the valley are a playing field and a swimming pool. The smaller cabins, covering an area of 807 sq. ft. each, are so arranged on the slope that all of them have an unobstructed view. Their horizontal distance is at least 50 ft., the difference in altitude at least 16 ft. The cabin plan shows a cluster of three interlinked pentagons. These rise towards the sides so that there are, inside the cabin, two breaks in level which the children can use as benches. The shape of the rhomboid window openings on three sides matches that of the cabin section. The steel-sheet roofed timber structure of the cabins stands on a trefoil-shaped sub-structure of reinforced concrete diaphragms. A two-storey bathing cabin and two changing cabins near the swimming pool are built to the same design.

Landschulheim bei Yokohama, 1967
Auf einem Osthang in einer Mulde der waldreichen Hügellandschaft des Bezirks Kohoku entstand eine locker gruppierte Landschule, in deren Wohnkabinen je 15 Kinder untergebracht und in Gruppen unterrichtet werden können. Die Hauptkabine am Fuß des Hanges, die mit 521 m² das größte Gebäude der Anlage ist, dient als Versammlungs- und Speisesaal. Im Talgrund liegen Sportplatz und Schwimmbecken. Die kleinen Wohnkabinen mit je 75 m² sind so über den Hang verteilt, daß alle freie Aussicht haben. Der horizontale Abstand beträgt mindestens 15 m, der Höhenunterschied 5 m. Im Grundriß zeigen die Kabinen drei miteinander verbundene Fünfecke, die nach den Außenseiten ansteigen. So entstehen im Raum zwei Höhenstufen, auf denen die Kinder sitzen können. Die rhombischen Fensteröffnungen an drei Seiten folgen dem Querschnitt der Kabinen, deren dreistrahliger Unterbau aus Stahlbetonscheiben einen mit Stahlplatten gedeckten Holzaufbau trägt. Eine zweigeschossige Badekabine und zwei Umkleidekabinen für das Freibad, alle im gleichen System, vervollständigen das Raumprogramm.

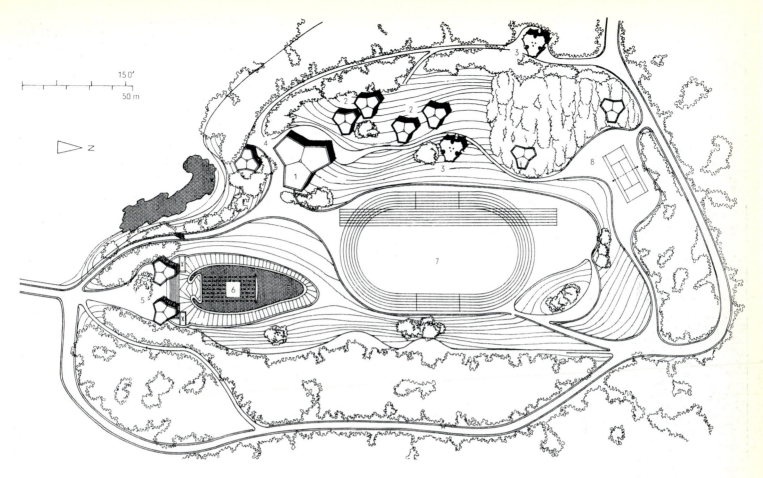

3. Site plan. Key: 1 main hall, 2 lodging cabins, 3 lodging cabin with tent roof, 4 bathing cabin, 5 changing room cabins, 6 swimming pool, 7 playing field, 8 tennis court.
4. The changing room cabins at the swimming pool (on the right for girls, on the left for boys) have two storeys. On the lower floor are the lavatories, on the upper floor the changing cabins.

3. Lageplan. Legende: 1 Hauptgebäude, 2 Wohnkabinen, 3 Wohnkabinen mit Zeltdach, 4 Badekabine, 5 Umkleidekabinen, 6 Freibad, 7 Sportplatz, 8 Tennisplatz.
4. Die Umkleidekabinen am Schwimmbad, für Mädchen rechts, für Jungen links, haben zwei Etagen. Im Untergeschoß liegen die WCs, im Obergeschoß die Umkleideräume.

5. Owing to the inclined floors and roofs, the volume of the cabins is greatly reduced. In this way, they blend well with the landscape and do not obstruct the views from adjacent cabins.

6. The lower floor of each cabin is equipped with two replaceable cells containing the sanitary installations.

7. Access to the cabins is from below, from centrally placed spiral stairs contained in a cylindrical core. Some of the cabins also have a direct gangway access from outside (cf. Fig. 5).

8. Plans of lower floor and main floor of a typical cabin.

5. Durch die schrägen Boden- und Dachflächen wird die Baumasse der Kabinen stark reduziert. Auf diese Weise ordnen sie sich gut in die Landschaft ein und lassen den Nachbarkabinen größere Durchblicke in die Umgebung frei.

6. Jede Kabine ist im Untergeschoß mit zwei Installationszellen ausgestattet, in denen die Sanitärräume untergebracht sind. Die Zellen sind auswechselbar.

7. Die Kabinen werden von unten durch zentrale Wendeltreppen in einem zylinderförmigen Kern erschlossen. Manche sind auch über einen Steg direkt mit der Außenwelt verbunden (siehe Abb. 5).

8. Grundrisse von Sockelgeschoß und Hauptgeschoß einer Wohnkabine.

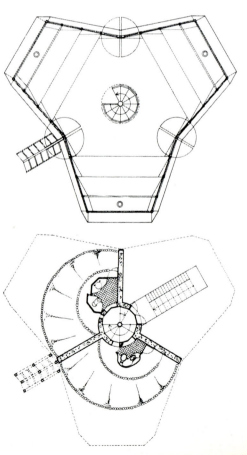

Hiroshi Hara, Research Studio for Architecture and Space

Keisho Kindergarten at Machida City, 1967-68
In the course of his research on the structure of space and, in particular, of the space-enclosing wall as related to the wall openings and lighting arrangements, Hiroshi Hara arrived at new concepts of space and thus also at a new external shape of his buildings. Ramps, inclined walls and roofs, roof superstructures and a generous use of relief effects on certain parts of the walls result in a highly plastic treatment of his buildings. The interiors are characterized by inclined skylight shafts and small, embrasure-like side windows on different levels. But other functional considerations too, have been fully taken into account. For instance, the room of the kindergarten supervisor projects like a platform from the front of the building so that he is able to keep an eye on the playground as well as the roof terrace and the nurseries on the ground floor. Also characteristic are numerous vertical links in the form of stairs or ramps which penetrate the building at a variety of points, forming a ubiquitous traffic network.

Keisho-Kindergarten in Machida City, 1967-68
Durch seine Untersuchungen über die Struktur des Raumes und besonders der raumabschließenden Wand im Zusammenhang mit den Wandöffnungen und der Lichtführung kam Hiroshi Hara zu neuen Raumformen und damit auch zu einer neuen äußeren Form seiner Bauten. Rampen, Wand- und Dachschrägen, Dachaufbauten und die kräftige Reliefierung einzelner Wandpartien ergeben eine starke plastische Durchgliederung der Baukörper. Für die Innenräume sind schräggezogene Oberlichtschächte und kleine, schießschartenähnliche Seitenfenster in verschiedenen Höhen charakteristisch. Aber auch andere funktionale Überlegungen sind voll berücksichtigt, so zum Beispiel wenn beim Keisho-Kindergarten das Zimmer des Kindergartenleiters wie eine Kanzel über die Gebäudefront hinausragt, damit von hier aus sowohl der Spielhof als auch die Dachterrasse und die Spielzimmer im Erdgeschoß zu übersehen sind. Eine weitere Eigenart sind die zahlreichen Vertikalverbindungen, die den Baukörper als Treppen oder Rampen an den verschiedensten Stellen durchdringen und ein vielfältiges Wegenetz ergeben.

1. General view from south-west. Placed on the projecting platform is the room of the kindergarten supervisor.
2. North elevation.

1. Gesamtansicht von Südwesten. In der vorspringenden Kanzel das Zimmer des Kindergartenleiters.
2. Ansicht der Nordseite.

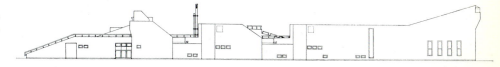

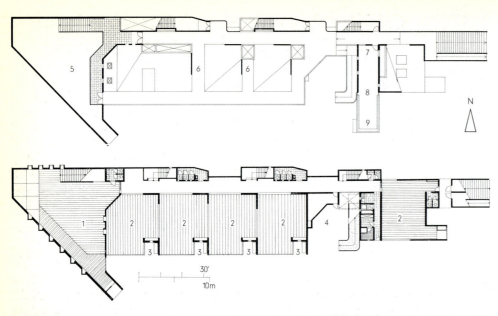

30'
10m

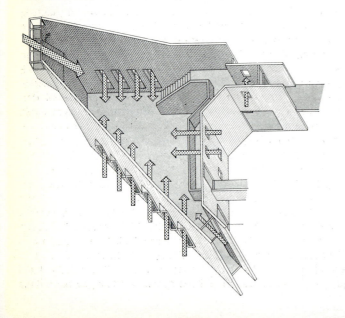

3. Plan of ground floor (bottom) and upper floor. Key: 1 group playroom, 2 nurseries, 3 footwash basin, 4 patio, 5 air space above group playroom, 6 roof terrace with skylight shafts above the nurseries, 7 office, 8 first-aid post, 9 kindergarten supervisor.

4. A view from the roof of the group playroom on the inclined roof and the skylight shafts above the nursery wing. In the background, the annexe with the offices and first-aid post. On the right, in dark, the platform carrying the room of the kindergarten supervisor.

5. Diagram of lighting arrangements for the group playroom (compare with the interiors Figs. 7 and 8). A refined system, consisting of a rectangular pattern of differently sized lighting channels.

3. Grundriß von Erdgeschoß (unten) und Obergeschoß. Legende: 1 Gruppen-Spielraum, 2 Spielzimmer, 3 Fußwaschbecken, 4 Innengarten, 5 Luftraum über dem Gruppen-Spielraum, 6 Dachterrasse mit Lichtschächten über den Spielzimmern, 7 Büro, 8 Erste-Hilfe-Station, 9 Kindergartenleiter.

4. Blick vom Dach über dem Gruppen-Spielraum auf die Dachschräge und die Oberlichtschächte über dem Trakt mit den Spielzimmern. Im Hintergrund der ausgebaute Querriegel mit der Verwaltung und dem Erste-Hilfe-Raum. Rechts im dunklen, kanzelartigen Vorsprung das Zimmer des Kindergartenleiters.

5. Belichtungsdiagramm des Gruppen-Spielraums (vergleiche dazu die Innenraumaufnahmen Abb. 7 und 8). Ein ausgeklügeltes System aus verschieden dimensionierten, rechtwinklig aufeinander bezogenen Lichtöffnungen.

6. The longitudinal corridor in the ground floor is in open conection with the nurseries and is lit-up through the skylight shafts in the roof terrace. Ceiling, walls and floors are held in striped colour patterns.

7,8. The group playroom extends through two storeys. It receives daylight mainly through a high-level window below the inclined ceiling whilst the light from the side enters through deep-slotted windows with chamfered ledges. Access to the roof terrace is provided by stairs and galleries on the east side.

6. Der Längsflur im Erdgeschoß ist zu den Spiel-zimmern hin offen; er wird über die Lichtschächte in der Dachterrasse mit belichtet. Decke, Wände und Fußböden sind mit farbigen Streifen abgesetzt.

7,8. Der Gruppen-Spielraum ist zwei Geschosse hoch. Er bekommt sein Hauptlicht durch ein hoch-liegendes Fenster unter der Schrägdecke, während das Seitenlicht durch tiefe Fensterschlitze mit abgeschrägten Simsen kommt. Treppe und Galerie auf der Ostseite erschließen die Dachterrasse.

Kenji Mitsuyoshi

Primary School at Nanayama in the Island of Kyushu, 1961-62
In a village where most of the villagers live on farming, a school of a standard of architectural design and equipment equivalent to urban schools was needed, in order to reduce the gap in the standard of education which is one of the reasons for the flight from the land. The new school consists of two parallel wings with twelve standard classrooms and three special classrooms. Along each wing, protected by overhanging roofs, run open galleries with short transverse spur corridors, each giving access to two classrooms. The roof consists of hyperbolic-paraboloid shells so that the classrooms have top lighting from three sides. The short western side of the oblong courtyard between the two wings is taken up by an annexe with lavatories and lockers. The administration building, a column-supported extension of the north wing, is distinguished from the classrooms by its flat roof and long ribbons of windows or parapets. The open ground floor is at the same level as the entrance yard which is connected by open stairs with the level of the school yard proper. Two mushroom-shaped roof shells form a portal at the top landing of the stairs and protect, at the same time, the cross-passage between the two classroom wings. The buildings have a reinforced concrete framework structure; the hyperbolic-paraboloid shells are rough-cast on the inside and have a copper roofing on the outside.

Volksschule in Nanayama auf der Insel Kyushu, 1961-62
In dem industriearmen Dorf, dessen Bewohner hauptsächlich von der Landwirtschaft leben, sollte eine Schule gebaut werden, die in der architektonischen Gestaltung und in der Ausstattung städtischen Schulen gleichwertig ist. Auf diese Weise wollte man dem Bildungsgefälle entgegenwirken, das unter den Gründen für die Landflucht eine wichtige Rolle spielt. Die neue Schule besteht aus zwei parallelen Klassentrakten mit 12 Normal- und 3 Spezialklassen. Von den offenen Korridoren, die — von einer Kragplatte überdeckt — an den Klassentrakten entlanglaufen, zweigen Stichflure ab, an denen jeweils paarweise die Klassenräume liegen. Ihre Dächer bestehen aus HP-Schalen, so daß die Klassen von drei Seiten Oberlicht bekommen. Der langgestreckte Hof zwischen den beiden Flügeln wird auf der westlichen Schmalseite von einem querstehenden Nebengebäude mit Toiletten und Schränken begrenzt. Die Verwaltung, die in der Verlängerung des nördlichen Klassenflügels auf Stützen steht, unterscheidet sich von den Klassen durch das Flachdach und die langen Fenster- bzw. Brüstungsbänder. Das offene Stützengeschoß ist niveaugleich mit dem Eingangshof, von dem aus eine Freitreppe auf die Ebene des eigentlichen Schulhofes hinaufführt. Zwei pilzförmige Dachschalen stehen als Portal am oberen Treppenpodest, zugleich überdecken sie die Querverbindung zwischen den beiden Klassentrakten. Die Bauten wurden in Stahlbeton-Skelettbauweise ausgeführt; die HP-Schalen sind innen verputzt und außen mit Kupfer verkleidet.

1. View from north-west. The classroom wings are placed on the lower part of the slope. The administration building is in the background, left. Built into its partly open ground floor are the lavatories for the playground on the left.

1. Ansicht von Nordwesten. Die Klassenräume stehen auf dem auslaufenden Hügelgelände, links hinten die Verwaltung. In das darunterliegende, teilweise offene Stützengeschoß sind die Toiletten für den links an die Anlage anschließenden Schulspielhof eingebaut.

2. Plan. Key: 1 entrance yard, 2 covered galleries, 3 school yard, 4 spur corridor, 5 standard classroom, Type A, 6 teaching implements, 7 standard classroom, Type B, 8 domestic science, 9 music studio, 10 headmaster, 11 masters' common room, 12 caretaker, 13 medical officer, 14 music room, 15 library, 16 hall, 17 annexe with lavatories.
3. A broad flight of open stairs connects the entrance yard with the school yard proper. The access to the upper courtyard is spanned by a portal of mushroom-shaped roof shells.

2. Grundriß. Legende: 1 Eingangshof, 2 Gedeckte Verbindungsgänge, 3 Schulhof, 4 Stichflur, 5 Normalklasse Typ A, 6 Lehrmittel, 7 Normalklasse Typ B, 8 Hauswirtschaftsunterricht, 9 Tonstudio, 10 Rektorat, 11 Lehrerzimmer, 12 Hausmeister, 13 Arzt, 14 Musiksaal, 15 Bibliothek, 16 Halle mit Trinkbrunnen, 17 Nebengebäude mit Toiletten.
3. Eine Freitreppe führt vom Eingangshof zum Innenhof zwischen den Klassentrakten. Über dem Zugang zum oberen Hof das Portal aus Pilzstützen.

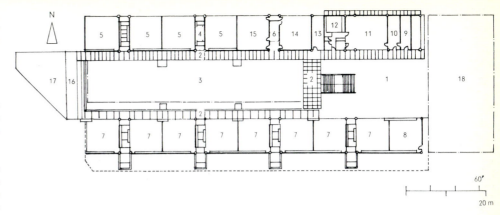

4. Inner courtyard, seen from the annexe. But for narrow ribbons of windows, the classrooms have no windows or doors facing the school yard. Access to the classrooms is from the spur corridors.

5. On the south and west sides of the entrance yard, the slope is supported by retaining walls which also serve as parapets for the upper concourse. The gallery leading to the administration wing (right) is cantilevered.

6. Entrance yard, seen from the open ground floor of the administration wing. The retaining wall is decorated with concrete reliefs.

4. Der Innenhof zwischen den Klassentrakten vom Nebengebäude aus. Die Klassen sind zum Hof bis auf schmale Glasstreifen geschlossen. Ihre Zugänge liegen an den Stichfluren.

5. Stützmauern, die zugleich die Brüstung des oberen Umgangs bilden, fangen den Grund auf der Süd- und Westseite des Eingangshofs ab. Der Zugang zur Verwaltung (rechts) kragt frei aus.

6. Blick von der offenen Stützenhalle unter der Verwaltung auf den Eingangshof. Die Stützmauer ist mit Betonreliefs belebt.

7. With their hyperbolic-paraboloid shell roofs, the ▷ classrooms have top lighting on three sides. The windows towards the spur corridor are non-transparent. In the corner cupboard behind the master's desk are a loudspeaker and teaching implements.

8. Corridor in the annexe with the cupboards containing the teaching implements for the different forms.

9. The wide corridor of the lavatory building at the western end of the courtyard has a 'honeycomb' wall of concrete bricks.

7. Durch die Abdeckung mit HP-Schalen erhalten die Klassenräume von drei Seiten Oberlicht. Die Fenster zum Stichflur sind undurchsichtig verglast. Der Eckschrank hinter dem Lehrertisch enthält Lautsprecher und Lehrmittel.

8. Blick in den Korridor des Nebengebäudes mit den Lehrmittelschränken der einzelnen Klassen.

9. Der breite Korridor des Toilettengebäudes an der westlichen Schmalseite wird durch eine Wabenwand aus Betonformsteinen begrenzt.

Akiro Naito

Secondary School at Yasato-Minami, Ibaraki District, 1962-64
Following the post-war boom in the birth rate, the number of schoolchildren in this village was 667 in 1963 but is expected to drop to 440 in 1972. The new school was therefore required to offer a maximum of flexibility in use. For economic and pedagogic reasons, it was decided to adopt a schooling system where most of the lessons take place in special classrooms, with a small number of standard classrooms serving as 'refuge'. This system has permitted a compact arrangement, with two groups of buildings surrounding a central courtyard. The hexagonal plan of the classrooms enables a number of rooms to be concentrated in a relatively small area, with favourable access conditions. The standard classrooms are concentrated in a three-storey 'tower' with four classrooms on each floor, two staircases and a centrally placed sanitary unit. The classrooms face south and have windows on two sides. The special classrooms are housed in bungalows surrounding the courtyard, with cloakrooms and offices placed in lateral annexes. To reduce walking distances, the layout of the whole group has been kept completely symmetric. Due to the compact arrangement of the classroom wings, traffic area requirements have been reduced to 18 per cent (compared with about 30 per cent. in corridor-type schools). The buildings are erected in reinforced concrete. The special classrooms have hyperbolic-paraboloid shell roofs.

Mittelschule in Yasato-Minami, Bezirk Ibaraki, 1962-64
Infolge des Nachkriegs-Babybooms betrug die Schülerzahl in diesem Dorf 1963 667 Schüler, 1972 werden es nur noch 440 sein. Die neu zu bauende Schule mußte also größtmögliche Flexibilität in der Nutzung bieten. Bei der Planung entschied man sich aus ökonomischen und pädagogischen Gründen für ein Betriebssystem, bei dem der Unterricht im wesentlichen in Spezialklassen abgehalten wird und eine Reihe von Normalklassenzimmern als Ausweichmöglichkeiten zur Verfügung stehen. Dieses System erlaubte eine kompakte Lösung, die aus zwei um einen zentralen Innenhof angeordneten Baugruppen besteht. Der Sechseckgrundriß der Klassen macht es möglich, eine Vielzahl von Räumen auf relativ kleiner Fläche zusammenzufassen und günstig zu erschließen. Je vier Normalklassen pro Geschoß sind in einem dreistöckigen »Turm« mit zwei Treppenhäusern und zentraler Sanitärzelle untergebracht. Sie sind nach Süden orientiert und zweiseitig belichtet. Die Spezialklassen gruppieren sich eingeschossig um den Innenhof. Garderobe und Verwaltung sind als seitliche Flügelbauten an die Spezialklassen angehängt. Um die Verkehrswege kurz zu halten, entstand eine vollkommen symmetrische Anlage. Durch die kompakte Form der Klassentrakte konnte die Verkehrsfläche auf 18 % reduziert werden (bei Korridorschulen rund 30 %). Die Bauten sind in Stahlbeton ausgeführt. Die Dächer der Spezialklassen bestehen aus HP-Schalen.

1. The low buildings are towered over by the three-storey block where the hexagonal plans of the standard classrooms provide a pattern. But, due to the polygonal configuration of their walls and the up-and-down of the hyperbolic-paraboloid shell roofs, even the special-classroom bungalows are of lively appearance.
2. Inner courtyard, seen from the standard classroom tower. The special classrooms are linked by passageways protected by copper roofing.
3. View from north-west. The special classrooms receive most of their daylight from the side of the playing field (in the foreground). In the flat-roofed annexe (background, right) are the children's cloakrooms.
4. Courtyard with arts room, workshop and music room, seen from the administration wing.
5. Plan of ground floor and of a typical floor in the classroom tower.
6. In the natural science classroom, the floor rises in two semi-circular steps. The ceiling, which matches the shape of the hyperbolic-paraboloid roof shells, is lined with acoustic boards.

1. Aus der niedrigen Baugruppe wächst der dreigeschossige Normalklassenturm heraus, der durch die Sechseckgrundrisse der Klassen kräftig gegliedert ist. Aber auch die eingeschossigen Spezialklassen zeigen mit der polygonalen Brechung der Außenwände und dem Auf und Ab der HP-Schalen eine lebhaft bewegte Form.
2. Blick vom Normalklassenturm in den Innenhof. Die Spezialklassen sind durch überdachte Gänge mit Kupfereindeckung verbunden.
3. Ansicht von Nordwesten. Die Spezialklassen werden im wesentlichen vom Schulsportplatz (im Vordergrund) her belichtet. Im Gebäudeteil hinten rechts (mit Flachdach) die Schülergarderobe.
4. Innenhof mit Zeichensaal, Werkraum und Musiksaal, vom Verwaltungsteil her gesehen.
5. Grundriß vom Erdgeschoß und Normalgeschoß des Klassenturms.
6. In der Spezialklasse für naturwissenschaftlichen Unterricht steigt der Boden in zwei halbkreisförmigen Podesten an. Die Decke, die dem Verlauf der HP-Schalen folgt, ist mit Akustikplatten verkleidet.

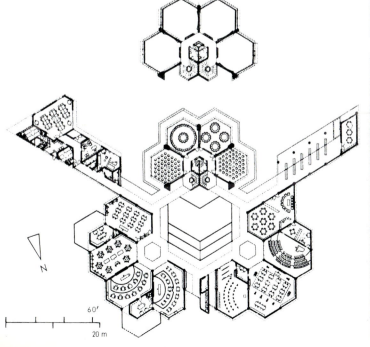

60'
20 m

2. On the sloping ground, the bedroom cells are raised on concrete columns. The floor slabs are projected to form entrance platforms which are protected by slightly vaulted overhanging roof slabs.

2. Im ansteigenden Gelände heben Betonstützen die Wohnzellen vom Boden ab. Die Bodenplatten sind als Eingangsplattformen vorgezogen, darüber kragen die leicht gewölbten Dachplatten aus.

Takamasa Yoshizaka

Students' Centre at Hachioji, near Tokyo

This 'Meeting Place Campus' serves as a venue for symposiums in which 200 students and professors of all faculties take part. They live in 100 cells, each with one, two or three beds which are informally arranged in seven groups, each comprising from nine to seventeen units. The centre of each group is a seminar building which, depending on the size of the 'neighbourhood unit', has accommodation for 10, 20, 30 or 50 people. All the 'neighbourhood units' are, in their turn, grouped around a community centre which also contains sanitary installations and bathrooms. In the hopper-shaped main building, which stands somewhat apart near the access road, are offices, dining hall and kitchen. All buildings are erected in reinforced concrete. The intimately designed 'neighbourhood units' are intended to restore the close personal contact between professors and students which is in danger of getting lost among the 'production line' output of modern universities. Although, because of the modest scale and simple design, construction costs have been relatively low, the campus meets its purpose in an almost ideal manner.

Studentenzentrum in Hachioji bei Tokio

In diesem »Campus der Begegnung« kommen jeweils 200 Studenten und Professoren aller Fakultäten zu Symposien zusammen. Sie wohnen in insgesamt 100 Ein-, Zwei- oder Dreibett-Zellen, die in freier Anordnung sieben Gruppen aus 9 bis 17 Wohneinheiten bilden. Mittelpunkt jeder Wohngruppe ist ein Seminargebäude, das je nach Größe der Nachbarschaft 10, 20, 30 oder 50 Personen Platz bietet. Die Nachbarschaften gruppieren sich ihrerseits um ein Gemeinschaftszentrum mit sanitären Einrichtungen und Bädern. Das Hauptgebäude (siehe Abb. 6 und 7), eine auf der Spitze stehende Pyramide, in der Verwaltung, Speisesaal und Küche untergebracht sind, ist etwas abseits an die Zufahrtsstraße gestellt. Alle Bauten wurden als Stahlbetonkonstruktion ausgeführt. Die eng zusammengeschlossenen Nachbarschaften stellen zwischen Professoren und Studenten den engen persönlichen Kontakt wieder her, der im Massenbetrieb an den Universitäten verlorenzugehen droht. Diese Aufgabe erfüllt der Campus geradezu ideal, obwohl er dank der bescheidenen Konzeption mit geringen Mitteln gebaut werden konnte.

1. Aerial view. The hopper-shaped main building in the foreground is placed in a depression of the ground where the access road widens out into car parks. To the right of the Campus entrance is the pyramid-shaped auditorium for 50 people. The buildings with chimney to the left of it is the community centre with sanitary installations. The seven informally arranged groups of the 100 'cells' enable each resident to preserve a feeling of independence.

1. Luftansicht. Vorn in einer Mulde, wo sich die Zufahrtsstraße zu Parkplätzen erweitert, das trichterförmige Hauptgebäude. Am Dorfeingang rechts die Pyramide des Auditoriums für 50 Personen, links davon das Zentrum mit Bädern und Sanitäreinrichtungen (mit Kamin). Die sieben locker verteilten Gruppen der 100 Wohnzellen geben dem einzelnen Bewohner das Gefühl der Unabhängigkeit und Individualität, gliedern ihn aber eng in die Gemeinschaft ein.

3. The grouping of the bedroom cells is determined by the topography of the ground. The centre of each 'neigbourhood unit' is formed by a piazza with the seminar building.
4, 5. The large auditorium for 200 people and the library are placed somewhat outside the Campus. The large mushroom-type roof shells nearly touch each other; their form is in keeping with the soft lines of the landscape.

3. Die Gruppierung der Hauszellen folgt der Geländebewegung. Im Zentrum jeder Nachbarschaft ist ein Platz gebildet, an dem das Seminargebäude steht.
4, 5. Das große Auditorium für 200 Personen und die Bibliothek sind etwas außerhalb des Campus plaziert. Ihre großflächigen, weit auskragenden Dachschalen berühren sich fast und greifen in ihrer Form die sanfte Modellierung der Landschaft auf.

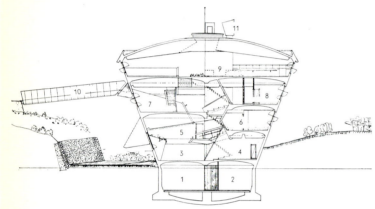

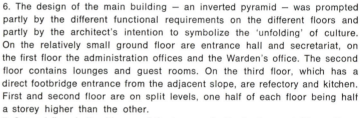

6. The design of the main building — an inverted pyramid — was prompted partly by the different functional requirements on the different floors and partly by the architect's intention to symbolize the 'unfolding' of culture. On the relatively small ground floor are entrance hall and secretariat, on the first floor the administration offices and the Warden's office. The second floor contains lounges and guest rooms. On the third floor, which has a direct footbridge entrance from the adjacent slope, are refectory and kitchen. First and second floor are on split levels, one half of each floor being half a storey higher than the other.

7. Second floor hall, with one of the lounges in the background. The ceilings merely rest on the hopper-shaped outer walls, spanning the rooms without intermediate supports. The pitch of the outer walls is taken up by the inner walls.

8. Section of main building. Key: 1 machinery, 2 electrical plant, 3 entrance hall, 4 secretariat, 5 administrative office, 6 Warden's office, 7 lounge, 8 guest room, 9 refectory, 10 footbridge, 11 air intake turret.

9. The pyramid-shaped roof of the auditorium for 50 people is closely adapted to the ground. An oblique incision in the roof marks the entrance.

6. Die Form des Hauptgebäudes, eine auf der Spitze stehende Pyramide, ergab sich einmal aus den unterschiedlichen funktionalen Erfordernissen auf den verschiedenen Geschoßebenen, zum anderen soll sie nach der Absicht der Architekten das Sichentfalten der Kultur symbolisieren. Im Erdgeschoß mit relativ geringer Grundfläche liegen Eingangshalle und Sekretariat, im 1. Obergeschoß Verwaltung und Direktion. Das 2. Obergeschoß enthält Aufenthaltsräume und Gästezimmer. Im dritten Obergeschoß, das vom benachbarten Hügel über eine Brücke zugänglich ist, sind Speisesaal und Küche untergebracht. Im 1. und 2. Obergeschoß ist die Grundfläche halbiert und um halbe Geschoßhöhe gegeneinander versetzt.

7. Halle im 2. Obergeschoß mit Durchblick in einen Aufenthaltsraum. Die Decken, die nur auf den trichterförmigen Außenwänden aufliegen, überspannen die Innenräume stützenfrei. Durch Schrägstellen auch der Innenwände wird die äußere Bauform wiederholt.

8. Schnitt durch das Hauptgebäude. Legende: 1 Maschinenraum, 2 Elektrozentrale, 3 Eingangshalle, 4 Sekretariat, 5 Verwaltung, 6 Direktion, 7 Aufenthaltsraum, 8 Gästezimmer, 9 Speisesaal, 10 Fußgängerbrücke, 11 Aufbau für Frischluftzufuhr.

9. Das Pyramidendach des Auditoriums für 50 Personen paßt sich dem Gelände an; über dem Eingang ist es schräg ausgeschnitten.

Planning Group/Planungsgruppe Daiichi Kobo

Osaka University of Arts, 1965-67

In 1964, having won the First Prize in the design contest, the Planning Group were entrusted with the realization of the project. Their project is based on a new training scheme for students of arts, design, music and literature which calls for new space concepts and dimensions. The attractive undulating ground favoured a variegated design of the outdoor installations. So far, two stages of the building programme have been realized. The first stage comprised the erection of a group consisting of two four-storey faculty buildings and a workshop wing. The plan of the faculty buildings is windmill-shaped. Each of these staggered blocks is centred on a stairwell with large landings, which serve as a concourse and communication zone. The premises placed on different landing levels serve as specialized lecture rooms for group lectures and individual tasks of advanced students. The workshop wing is a single-storey building, oblong in plan. The buildings erected during the second stage are mainly destined for the basic teaching of first-year students. They include the Auditorium Maximum and two multi-storey faculty buildings with large lecture rooms for 100 to 200 people. The floors of the two buildings are connected with each other by open galleries. The amphitheatrically arranged seats of the auditorium are built into a dell.

Kunstuniversität in Osaka, 1965-67

Die Planungsgruppe erhielt 1964, nachdem sie den 1. Preis im Wettbewerb gewonnen hatte, den Ausführungsauftrag. Ihrem Projekt liegt ein neues Ausbildungsschema für Kunst-, Design-, Musik- und Literaturstudenten zugrunde, das neue Raumkonzeptionen und neue Raumgrößen erfordert. Das bewegte, landschaftlich reizvolle Gelände bot günstige Voraussetzungen für eine abwechslungsreiche Gestaltung der Außenanlagen. Bisher wurden zwei Bauetappen realisiert. Im 1. Bauabschnitt entstand eine Gebäudegruppe aus zwei viergeschossigen Fakultätsbauten und einem Werkstattflügel. Die Fakultätsgebäude sind auf einem windmühlenförmigen Grundriß errichtet. Jeweils im Zentrum dieser versetzt zueinander gestellten Baukörper liegt das Treppenhaus mit großen Podestflächen als Verkehrs- und Kommunikationszone. Die Abteilungsräume, die auf verschiedenen Podesthöhen liegen, dienen den höheren Semestern als Fachunterrichtsräume für Gruppenunterricht und individuelle Aufgaben. Das Werkstattgebäude ist ein eingeschossiger Trakt mit langgezogenem Rechteckgrundriß. Die Gebäudegruppe des 2. Bauabschnitts ist vor allem für die Grundausbildung während der ersten Semester bestimmt. Sie umfaßt das Auditorium Maximum und zwei mehrgeschossige Fakultätsgebaude mit Großräumen für 100 bis 200 Studenten. Die einzelnen Stockwerke der beiden Bauten sind über offene Galerien miteinander verbunden. Das Auditorium mit ansteigendem Gestühl ist in eine Geländemulde hineingebaut.

1. Site plan. First stage: 1 studio building for graphics, photography and interior design, 2 studio building for arts and crafts, industrial design and painting, 3 workshop wing. Second stage: 4 faculty building for basic teaching of architecture, literature and arts, 5 faculty building for general education, 6 auditorium maximum.

1. Lageplan. Erster Bauabschnitt: 1 Ateliergebäude für Graphik, Photographie und Innenarchitektur, 2 Ateliergebäude für Kunsthandwerk, industrielle Formgebung und Malerei, 3 Werkstattgebäude. Zweiter Bauabschnitt: 4 Fakultätsgebäude für die Grundlehre in Architektur, Literatur und Kunst, 5 Fakultätsgebäude für allgemeinen Unterricht, 6 Großer Hörsaal.

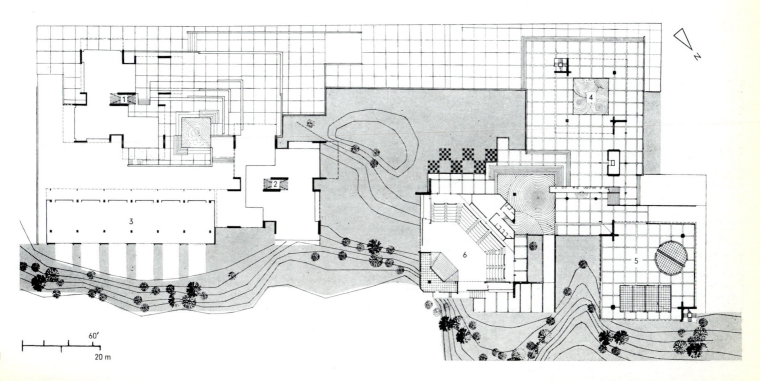

60'

20 m

2. The three buildings erected during the first stage, seen from north-east. It is because of the more even daylight conditions that the workshop wing faces in this direction.
3. View from south-east. The roof of the workshop wing (right) is accessible from the adjacent studio building. The different structural elements such as floors, wall diaphragms and parapets are separated by clearly visible joints.
4. Studio building forming part of the first stage. The premises for junior and senior students are placed on different levels. The stairwell is separated from the lecture rooms by rows of lockers where the students can leave their out-door clothing and implements.

2. Die drei Bauten des 1. Bauabschnitts von Nordosten. Der Werkstattflügel ist wegen des gleichmäßigen Lichtes nach Norden orientiert.
3. Blick von Südosten. Das Dach des Werkstattbaues (rechts) ist vom anschließenden Ateliergebäude aus begehbar. Die Gebäudeelemente wie Decken, seitliche Wandscheiben und Brüstungen sind durch deutlich sichtbare Fugen voneinander getrennt.
4. Ateliergebäude 1. Bauabschnitt. Die Abteilungsräume für die verschiedenen Semester liegen auf unterschiedlichem Niveau. Die Schrankwände, in denen die Studenten Garderobe und Arbeitsgeräte unterbringen, trennen das Treppenhaus von den Unterrichtsräumen.

5. A view across the open gallery connecting the two faculty buildings forming part of the second stage, with the wooded hills in the background. The interplay of man-made and natural contours as an integral part of the overall design concept is convincingly mastered.

5. Durchblick durch die offene Verbindungsgalerie zwischen den beiden Fakultätsgebäuden des 2. Bauabschnitts hindurch auf die bewaldeten Hügelketten der Umgebung. Das Zusammenspiel von gebauter und natürlicher Form als wichtiger Bestandteil der architektonischen Gesamtidee ist überzeugend gemeistert.

6. General view, from the south-east, of the buildings erected during the second stage. The auditorium facing the two faculty buildings is placed in a depression of the ground.

7. The piazza between the buildings is terraced in adaptation to the slope. Its appearance is enlivened by the use of contrasting materials: concrete on the level surfaces and steps; pavement of two different sizes for the adjacent zones and the transitions to the open ground.

6. Gesamtansicht des 2. Bauabschnitts von Südosten. Vor den beiden Fakultätsbauten steht das in eine Geländemulde eingebettete Auditorium.

7. Der Platz zwischen den Gebäuden ist dem Geländeverlauf terrassenartig angepaßt. Er wirkt durch die Verschiedenheit der Materialien sehr lebendig: Beton für die ebenen Flächen, Stufen und Schwellen; Pflasterbelag in zwei Größen für die anschließenden Bereiche und die Übergänge ins freie Gelände.

8. The piazza is further enlivened by the alternation between the brightly lit open spaces and the extensive shaded areas below the column-supported buildings.

9. Faculty building for general education. From the main staircase (left), open galleries run along the different floors. The first and third floor are, on this south-east side, walled up by vertical concrete boards. Behind these walls is a concourse giving access to the different premises.

10. Large training hall, mainly with artificial lighting, for junior students. One of the four main columns of the building, supporting four reinforced concrete edge beams, is visible in the background (right). The ceiling is divided by secondary beams into square bays.

8. Durch die Wechselbeziehung zwischen lichterfüllten Freiflächen und ausgedehnten Schattenzonen unter den auf Stützen stehenden Gebäuden wird eine zusätzliche Gliederung des Platzraumes erreicht.

9. Gebäude für die allgemeine Grundausbildung. Vom zentralen Treppenhaus links führen offene Verbindungsgalerien zu den einzelnen Etagen. Das 1. und 3. Obergeschoß ist nach Südosten durch vertikale Betonfelder geschlossen. Hinter diesen Außenwänden liegt ein Umgang, der die Abteilungsräume erschließt.

10. Großer, überwiegend künstlich beleuchteter Übungsraum für die unteren Semester. Im Hintergrund rechts ist eine der vier Hauptstützen des Gebäudes sichtbar, auf denen vier Randbalken aus Stahlbeton aufliegen. Die Decke ist durch Sekundärträger in quadratische Felder aufgeteilt.

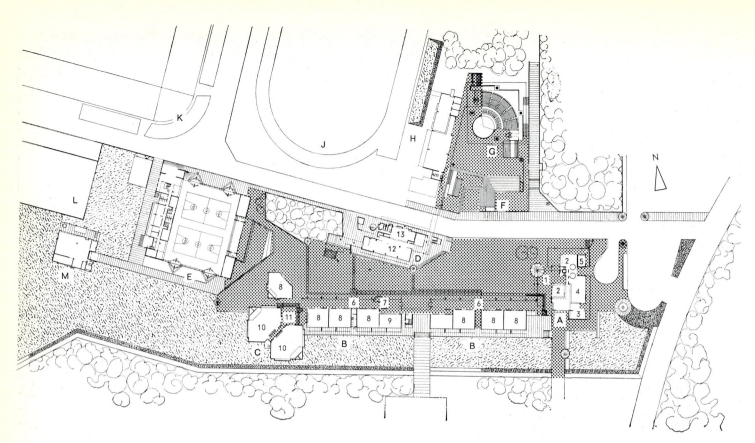

Fumihiko Maki & Associates

Campus of the Rissho University at Kumagaya, 1965-67

Behind the plan for the new campus of Rissho University was the wish to concentrate the entire group as much as possible although the extensive woodlands leave sufficient space even for major extensions. The present group of buildings, representing the first stage of the building programme, will later be supplemented by a large auditorium, another community centre, and dormitories. The present buildings face an oblong pedestrian plaza which runs from west to east with terraces separated by steps and ends up in a wedge-shaped extension at the sports hall at the western end. The woodlands were preserved as much as possible and were allowed to intrude into the plaza so as to form a contrast to the buildings. On the south side, the three-storey administration wing and the likewise three-storey wing with the lecture rooms form a chain of buildings forming a transition to the lower, fan-shaped annexe with the larger lecture rooms. The community centre on the north side of the plaza will later be connected by a bridge across the main access road with the planned future buildings on the north-west side of the campus. The reinforced concrete facades still show the marks of the shuttering.

Campus der Rissho-Universität in Kumagaya, 1965-67

Der neue Campus der Rissho-Universität, dessen erste ausgeführte Bauetappe noch durch ein großes Auditorium, ein weiteres Sozialgebäude und Dormitorien ergänzt werden wird, zeigt das Bemühen, die ganze Anlage möglichst zu verdichten, obwohl in dem ausgedehnten Waldgelände selbst für umfangreiche künftige Erweiterungen genügend Grundstücksfläche zur Verfügung steht. In der jetzigen Ausbaustufe sind die Gebäude an einer plazaähnlichen, in Ost-West-Richtung verlaufenden Fußgängerachse aufgereiht, die mehrfach abgetreppt ist und sich nach Westen vor der abschließenden Sporthalle keilförmig verbreitert. Die ursprüngliche Waldlandschaft wurde soweit wie möglich erhalten und als Kontrast zu den Gebäuden in die Achse mit einbezogen. Im Süden bilden das dreigeschossige Verwaltungsgebäude und der ebenfalls dreigeschossige Hörsaaltrakt eine kettenförmige Formation, die zu dem niedrigeren fächerförmigen Anbau mit den größeren Hörsälen überleitet. Das Sozialgebäude auf der Nordseite der Plaza wird später durch eine Brücke über die Hauptzufahrtstraße mit den Erweiterungsbauten im Nordwesten des Campus verbunden sein. Alle Bauten wurden in schalungsrauh belassenem Stahlbeton ausgeführt.

1. Site plan. Key: A administration wing, B lecture room wing, C annexe with the large lecture rooms, D community centre I, E sports hall, F exhibition building (planned), G auditorium (planned), H community centre II (planned), J athletics sports ground, K baseball pitch, L tennis courts, M heating plant, 1 entrance hall, 2 information desk, 3 interview room, 4 office, 5 control room, 6 connecting corridor, 7 cafeteria, 8 medium-sized lecture rooms, 9 office, 10 large lecture rooms, 11 hall, 12 refectory, 13 kitchen.

1. Lageplan. Legende: A Verwaltungsgebäude, B Hörsaalgebäude, C Anbau mit großen Hörsälen, D Sozialgebäude I, E Sporthalle, F Ausstellung (geplant), G Auditorium (geplant), H Sozialgebäude II (geplant), J Leichtathletikfeld, K Baseballfeld, L Tennisplätze, M Heizzentrale, 1 Eingangshalle, 2 Auskunft, 3 Sprechzimmer, 4 Büro, 5 Kontrollraum, 6 Verbindungsflur, 7 Cafeteria, 8 Mittelgroße Hörsäle, 9 Büro, 10 Große Hörsäle, 11 Halle, 12 Mensa, 13 Küche.

2. The entrance hall of the administration building extends through three storeys. Stairs, landings and galleries create, between the circular columns, the atmosphere of a generously conceived forum.

3. Aerial view from the north. Administration wing (left) and sports hall (right) are separated by the oblong lecture room wing and towards the sports hall, the fan-shaped annexe containing the large lecture rooms. On the near side, the community centre.

2. Die drei Geschosse hohe Eingangshalle des Verwaltungsgebäudes. Treppen, Podeste und Galerien schaffen zwischen den Rundstützen die Atmosphäre eines großzügigen Forums.

3. Luftansicht von Norden. Zwischen Verwaltungsgebäude (links) und Sporthalle (rechts) der langgestreckte Hörsaaltrakt, an den sich zur Sporthalle hin der fächerförmige Anbau mit den großen Hörsälen anschließt. In der Mitte vorn das Sozialgebäude.

4. North-east side of the sports hall, seen from the sports ground. The latticework structure of the roof is supported by a tubular steel framework.
5. A view from the open, raised porch of the administration wing towards the three-storey lecture room (left), the annexe with the large lecture rooms (background, left), and the community centre (right) where the ground floor is occupied by the refectory.
6. Stairs and footbridges lead from the main east-west axis of the campus to the community centre. The backcloth of the plaza is formed by the sports hall.
7. A view from the north towards the administration wing (left) and the lecture room wing further west.
8. The annexe of the faculty building with the large lecture rooms, seen from the north. The wedge-shaped plaza confronting the sports hall on the right is terraced and can serve as a meeting forum.

4. Die Nordostseite der Sporthalle, von den Sportplätzen aus. Eine Stahlrohrkonstruktion trägt das Gitterfachwerk des Daches.
5. Blick aus der offenen, erhöhten Vorhalle des Verwaltungsgebäudes auf den dreigeschossigen Hörsaaltrakt (links), den Anbau mit den großen Hörsälen (hinten links) und das Sozialgebäude (rechts) mit der Mensa im Erdgeschoß.
6. Treppen und Brücken führen von der in Ost-West-Richtung verlaufenden Hauptachse des Campus zum Sozialgebäude. Im Hintergrund als Platzabschluß die Sporthalle.
7. Blick von Norden auf das Verwaltungsgebäude (links) und den nach Westen anschließenden Hörsaaltrakt.
8. Der Anbau des Fakultätsgebäudes mit den großen Hörsälen, von Norden gesehen. Der trichterförmig sich erweiternde Platz vor der Sporthalle rechts ist terrassenförmig abgestuft und kann als Versammlungsforum dienen.

Kunio Mayekawa & Associates

New Buildings of the Gakushuin University at Tokyo, 1959-60
The new Campus consists of four buildings, three of which flank the centrally placed Auditorium Maximum at right angles. On the north side, the piazza is bordered by the oblong four-storey building of the Philosophical Faculty (with the Institutes for Philology, Literature, Economics and Political Sciences). The south side of the piazza is formed by the building — also with four storeys — of the Faculty for Natural Sciences. These two wings are connected by the square two-storey block of the administration building with central hall and sky-lighting, where the ground floor is taken up by two open-plan offices. Two spiral stairs lead to the first floor with the Vice-Chancellor's rooms and conference rooms. The eccentric pyramid of the auditorium, which has direct access from the hall of the administration building, has seats for 700 people. The rhombic units of the reinforced concrete structure of the pyramid, which has a cladding of concrete slabs, remain visible on the inside.

Neubauten der Gakushuin-Universität in Tokio, 1959-60
Der neue Campus setzt sich aus vier Baukörpern zusammen, von denen drei das zentral gelegene Auditorium Maximum im rechten Winkel flankieren. Nach Norden wird der Platz durch das langgestreckte, viergeschossige Gebäude der Philosophischen Fakultät (mit den Instituten für Philologie, Literatur, Volkswirtschaft und Politische Wissenschaften) begrenzt. Den südlichen Querriegel bildet der ebenfalls viergeschossige Bau für die Naturwissenschaften. Bindeglied zwischen diesen beiden Flügeln ist der zweigeschossige, quadratische Verwaltungstrakt mit zentraler Halle und Oberlicht, dessen Erdgeschoß zwei Großraumbüros einnehmen. Zwei Wendeltreppen führen ins erste Obergeschoß, wo Rektorat und Sitzungsräume untergebracht sind. Die verschobene Pyramide des Auditoriums, mit direktem Zugang von der Halle des Verwaltungsgebäudes aus, kann 700 Hörer aufnehmen. Die Tragkonstruktion der außen mit Betonplatten eingedeckten Pyramide besteht aus einem Stahlbetongerippe, dessen rhombische Elemente innen sichtbar sind.

1. Aerial view of the entire group, seen from the east. All the buildings are connected by covered passageways. To the left of the square administration building is that of the Faculty for Natural Sciences, on the right that of the Philosophical Faculty, behind it the pyramid-shaped auditorium. All the flat roofs are accessible. The site in the foreground, right, was later occupied by the library building (cf. page 123).

1. Luftbild der Gesamtanlage von Osten. Alle Bauten sind durch überdachte Gänge miteinander verbunden. Links vom quadratischen Verwaltungsgebäude die Naturwissenschaftliche, rechts die Philosophische Fakultät, dahinter das pyramidenförmige Auditorium. Alle Flachdächer sind begehbar. Rechts im Vordergrund wurde später das Bibliotheksgebäude hinzugefügt (siehe Seite 123).

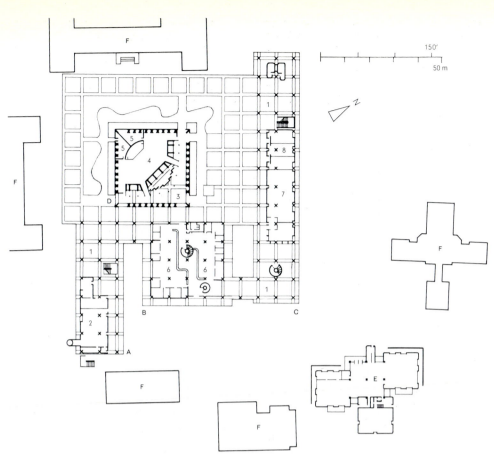

150'

50 m

2. Site plan and floor plans at ground floor level. Key: A Natural Sciences, B Administration, C Philosophy, Political Sciences, Economics, D Auditorium, E Library, F Older buildings, 1 open vestibule with stairs, 2 heating plant and technical installations, 3 auditorium vestibule, 4 auditorium, 5 waiting room, 6 administrative offices, 7 reading room, 8 seminar.

3. View from north-west. In the background the administration building, on the left that of the Philosophical Faculty. Its columns have a square cross-section with deep grooves on all sides so that they are reminiscent of cluster columns and appear to be lighter than they are. The floors and parapets between the columns are projected in loggia fashion in order to provide sun protection for the recessed windows.

2. Lageplan und Grundrisse auf Höhe des Erdgeschosses. Legende: A Naturwissenschaften, B Verwaltung, C Philosophie, Politische Wissenschaften, Volkswirtschaft, D Auditorium, E Bibliothek, F Bestehende Gebäude, 1 Offene Vorhalle mit Treppe, 2 Heizung und technische Räume, 3 Foyer Auditorium, 4 Auditorium, 5 Warteraum, 6 Büros der Verwaltung, 7 Lesesaal, 8 Seminar.

3. Blick von Nordwesten. Im Hintergrund die Verwaltung. Links die Philosophische Fakultät. Ihre im Querschnitt quadratischen Stützen haben an allen Seiten tiefe Einkerbungen, so daß sie an Bündelpfeiler erinnern und optisch leichter wirken. Decken und Brüstungen sind zwischen den Pfeilern loggienartig vorgezogen, um den zurückgesetzten Fenstern Sonnenschutz zu geben.

4. The top of the pyramid is off-centre so as to gain more space for the rising rows of seats. The auditorium is surrounded by grass-covered earth mounds and pools of water.

4. Die Spitze der Pyramide ist aus dem Zentrum nach der Seite verschoben, um für das ansteigende Gestühl mehr Platz zu gewinnen. Das Auditorium wird von bepflanzten Erdwällen und Wasserbecken umzogen.

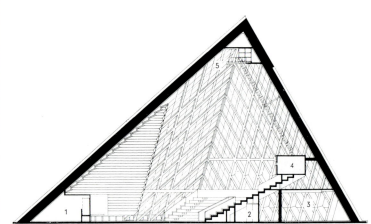

5. Lecture platform of the auditorium, as seen from the rising rows of seats. The aesthetic appearance of the room is governed by acoustic requirements. The rhombic reinforced concrete framework has an infilling of sound-absorbing boards.
6. The outer wall of the otherwise open vestibule of the auditorium is formed by the rhombs of the concrete framework. The rising rows of seats are supported by inclined concrete beams which, in their turn, rest on circular columns.
7. Section of the auditorium. Key: 1 waiting room behind the stage, 2 lavatories, 3 vestibule, 4 projector cabin, 5 lighting control platform.

5. Blick vom aufsteigenden Gestühl des Auditoriums zum Vortragspodest. Die formale Ausbildung des Raumes wird von den Erfordernissen der Akustik bestimmt. Schallschluckplatten fachen das rhombische Stahlbetonskelett aus.
6. Die offene Eingangshalle des Hörsaalgebäudes, die nach außen von den teilweise offenen Rhomben der Skelettkonstruktion begrenzt wird. Das ansteigende Auditorium ruht auf schrägen Betonbalken, die von Rundsäulen getragen werden.
7. Schnitt durch das Auditorium. Legende: 1 Warteraum hinter dem Podium, 2 Toiletten, 3 Foyer, 4 Projektionskabine, 5 Beleuchtungskanzel.

Kunio Mayekawa & Associates

Library of the Gakushuin University at Tokyo, 1962-63
The library building forms part of the new Campus of Gakushuin University (cf. page 120). It stands somewhat apart from the 1959-60 group of buildings on the west side of the large park. The building is composed of three square blocks of identical size which are placed in staggered arrangement around a likewise square central hall. The stairwell forms a self-contained unit in front of the lobby. The much frequented reading rooms are on the ground floor. The east tower, which has a separate staff entrance, serves as book repository; its six storeys are lower than the standard floors of the two other towers which contain catalogue room, lending library, study rooms and reading rooms. The flat roofs serve as outdoor reading rooms. The upper floor premises are visually extended by projecting balconies. The alternation of vertical wall diaphragms and horizontal balcony parapets of recessed windows and projecting terraces has a highly sculptural effect.

Bibliothek der Gakushuin-Universität in Tokio, 1962-63
Die Bibliothek gehört zum neuen Campus der Gakushuin-Universität (siehe Seite 120). Sie steht etwas abseits von den 1959-60 errichteten Gebäuden im Westen des großen Parks. Der Baukörper ist aus drei gleich großen, quadratischen Bauteilen zusammengefügt, die — gegeneinander versetzt — auf drei Seiten eine ebenfalls quadratische Zentralhalle umschließen. Das Treppenhaus ist als selbständiges Element vor die Eingangshalle gestellt. Im Erdgeschoß sind die stark frequentierten Lesesäle untergebracht. Der östliche Turm mit separatem Personaleingang dient als Büchermagazin, dessen 6 Stockwerke niedriger sind als die Normalgeschosse der beiden anderen Türme, die Katalogsaal, Ausleihe, Studien- und Leseräume aufnehmen. Die Flachdächer werden als Lesezimmer im Freien benutzt. In den oberen Geschossen sind die Innenräume durch vorspringende Balkone optisch erweitert. Aus dem Wechsel von vertikalen Wandscheiben und horizontalen Brüstungsbändern an den Balkonen, von zurückgesetzten Fensterflächen und vorgezogenen Terrassen bezieht der Bau seine starke plastische Wirkung.

1. West side with the protruding staircase tower and main entrance. The central part of the building has a reinforced concrete framework, the three towers at the sides are supported by solid wall diaphragms of exposed concrete.

1. Westseite mit vorgezogenem Treppenhaus und Haupteingang. Konstruktion des zentralen Mittelstücks: Stahlbetonskelett, der drei Seitentürme: massive Wandscheiben aus Sichtbeton.

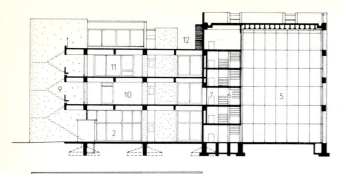

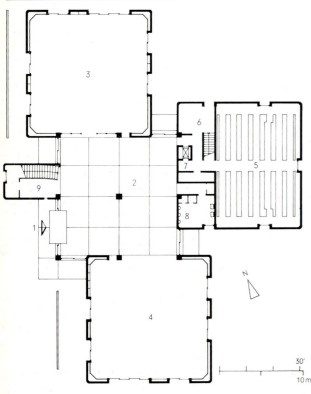

2. Ground floor plan and section. Key: 1 main entrance, 2 vestibule, 3 reading room, 4 periodicals, 5 book repository, 6 staff entrance and secondary stairs, 7 lift, 8 W. C., 9 main stairs, 10 lending library, 11 reading room, 12 roof terrace.
3. From the reading room with newspapers and periodicals, sliding doors (on the left, not visible in the picture) lead to the park-side terrace.
4. The central part of the roof, around the stairwell, is enclosed so as to form a completely glazed lounge. In the background, the top floor of the book repository.

2. Grundriß Erdgeschoß und Schnitt. Legende: 1 Haupteingang, 2 Halle, 3 Lesesaal, 4 Zeitschriftenlesesaal, 5 Büchermagazin, 6 Personaleingang und Nebentreppe, 7 Aufzug, 8 WC, 9 Haupttreppe, 10 Bücherausleihe, 11 Lesezimmer, 12 Dachterrasse.
3. Vom Zeitungs- und Zeitschriftenlesesaal führen Schiebetüren (links, im Bild nicht zu sehen) auf die Parkterrasse.
4. Auf dem Zentralbau steht im Anschluß an das Treppenhaus inmitten der großen Dachterrasse ein ringsum verglaster Aufenthaltsraum. Im Hintergrund das oberste Geschoß des Büchermagazins.

5. Part of the west side. The powerful sculptural treatment results in strong light-and-shade effects which enhance the expressiveness of the building. In the park are small, paved islands with benches.
6. The strong relief effect is also apparent on the windowless walls of exposed concrete which still shows the marks of the shuttering. The rounded corners create harmonious transitions between the facades.
7. The central vestibule with the main entrance faces the park with full-height windows. On the left, the reading room for periodicals.

5. Ausschnitt aus der Westseite. Die mächtige plastische Gliederung ergibt starke Licht- und Schatteneffekte und steigert damit die Ausdruckskraft des Bauwerks. Im Park kleine, durch Platten abgegrenzte Sitzinseln.
6. Auch die geschlossenen Sichtbetonflächen der vertikalen Wandscheiben zeigen ein starkes Relief. Abgerundete Gebäudeecken schaffen harmonische Übergänge von Fassade zu Fassade.
7. Die zentrale Halle mit dem Haupteingang ist zum Park hin durch geschoßhohe Fensterflächen geöffnet. Links der Zeitschriftenlesesaal.

Kimio Yokoyama

Daikyakuden Building in the Daisekiji Temple District, Fujinomoija, 1962-63

The religious centre of the Soka-Gakkai Buddhist sect, which has 15 million members in Japan alone and is spread throughout the world, is located at Fujinomoija in the vicinity of the Fujiyama Mountain in the Shizuoka District. The temple precinct comprises numerous sanctuaries, dwellings and seminaries for priests and novices as well as residential buildings for the many thousand worshippers who take part in a 600-years old ceremony at 1 a. m. every night. The Daikyakuden Building represents, for the time being, the outstanding feature among a group of older buildings. The temple authorities desired that the new building should represent a novel form of sacral architecture without, in principle, abandoning the link with ancient Japanese temple architecture. The building is raised by robust columns above an open ground floor which extends through two storeys. On the first floor are the cloakrooms and lavatories. The sanctuary on the second floor, designed for a congregation of 5,000 worshippers, has a free span of 148 ft. x 115 ft. Vertically, the hall is subdivided by two galleries. The lower one forms an inside balcony which surrounds the entire hall. Yokoyama tried to create a sacral atmosphere by a skilful design of the lighting arrangements and by extending the interior outwards in the form of balconies. The reinforced concrete faces of the columns and balcony undersides are lined with granite. Floors and the two-ply roof are of ribbed reinforced concrete construction.

Daikyakuden-Gebäude im Tempelbezirk Daisekiji in Fujinomoija, 1962-63

Das religiöse Zentrum der buddhistischen Sekte Soka-Gakkai, die allein in Japan 15 Millionen Mitglieder hat und über die ganze Welt verbreitet ist, befindet sich in Fujinomoija in der Nähe des Fujiyama im Bezirk Shizuoka. Der Tempelbezirk besteht aus zahlreichen Kultstätten, Wohnungen und Seminargebäuden für Priester und Aspiranten sowie Wohngebäuden für die vielen tausend Gläubigen, die täglich nachts um 1 Uhr an der über 600 Jahre alten Zeremonie teilnehmen. Das Daikyakuden-Gebäude ist der vorläufige Höhepunkt in einem Ensemble älterer Gebäude. Nach den Wünschen der Auftraggeber sollte der Bau eine neue Form sakraler Architektur darstellen, ohne die prinzipielle Bindung an die historische japanische Tempelarchitektur aufzugeben. Der Baukörper steht auf massigen Stützen über dem freien, zwei Stockwerke hohen Erdgeschoß. Im 1. Obergeschoß sind Sanitätsräume und Garderoben untergebracht. Der Zeremonienraum im 2. Obergeschoß, der 5000 Personen aufnehmen kann, überspannt stützenfrei 45 x 35 m. Seine Höhe ist durch zwei Galeriegeschosse unterteilt, von denen das untere als rings umlaufende Empore in den Saal vorspringt. Yokoyama versuchte durch die Lichtführung und die Erweiterung des Innenraumes über Balkone nach außen eine sakrale Atmosphäre zu schaffen. An den Stützen und Balkonuntersichten ist der Stahlbetonbau mit Granit verkleidet. Das doppelschalige Dach ist eine Stahlbetonrippenkonstruktion.

1. The temple is connected with an administration building by a covered passage. The concave roof forms a counter-point to the overhung main roof.

1. Der Tempel ist durch einen geschlossenen Gang mit einem Verwaltungsgebäude verbunden. Die durchhängende Dachform bildet eine Gegenbewegung zum auskragenden Hauptdach.

2. South side with main stairs. The facade is given a strong horizontal emphasis by the characteristically moulded balcony parapets. The weightiness of the wide roof projection is mitigated by the deeply recessed boxes of the ribbed reinforced concrete construction.

2. Die Südseite mit der Haupttreppe. Durch die vorgezogenen und aufgewölbten Balkonbänder erhält die Fassade eine starke horizontale Gliederung. Die Stahlbetonrippenkonstruktion nimmt mit ihren tiefen Kassetten dem weitauskragenden Dach die Schwere.

3. A view from the altar zone, which is raised by one step, into the sanctuary where the floor is laid out with Tatami mats.

3. Blick von der um eine Stufe erhöhten Altarzone in den Zeremonienraum, dessen Boden mit Tatami-matten ausgelegt ist.

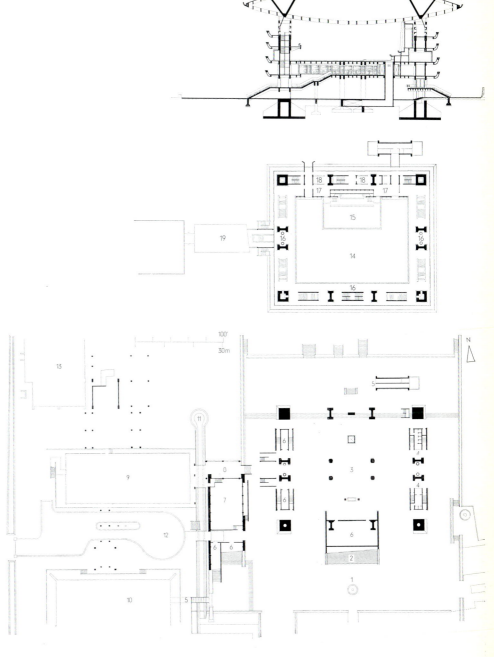

4. North-south section, ground floor plan (bottom) and second floor plan. Key: 1 entrance forum, 2 main stairs, 3 ground floor hall, 4 solid core with ancillary stairs and lavatories, 5 ramp, 6 stores, 7 machinery, 8 passage leading to administration building, 9 administration building, 10 existing building (auditorium), 11 moat, 12 drive, 13 existing building (residential), 14 sanctuary, 15 altar, 16 access gallery, 17 corridor, 18 priests' room, 19 roof of the passage leading to the administration building.

4. Schnitt in Nord-Süd-Richtung, Grundrisse von Erdgeschoß (unten) und 2. Obergeschoß. Legende: 1 Eingangsforum, 2 Haupttreppenaufgang, 3 Erdgeschoßhalle, 4 Festpunkt mit Nebentreppe und Toiletten, 5 Rampe, 6 Lagerraum, 7 Maschinenraum, 8 Passage zum Verwaltungsgebäude, 9 Verwaltungsgebäude, 10 Existierendes Gebäude (Auditorium), 11 Wassergraben, 12 Vorfahrt, 13 Existierendes Gebäude (Wohnheim), 14 Zeremonienraum, 15 Altar, 16 Erschließungsgalerie, 17 Korridor, 18 Priesterraum, 19 Dachaufsicht der Passage.

5. The corner columns are widened out at the base.

6. Square light fittings are mounted in some of the ceiling panels in the sanctuary. At second floor level, the hall is surrounded by glass curtain walls so that the outer balconies appear to be extensions of the interior. In contrast, the walls above the gallery are veiled by latticework and cleft by recesses.

7. The open space at entrance level extends through two storeys and is divided by a system of columns and stairs.

8. A corner of the building, with a view through the open ground floor. The mighty corner columns form the main supports of the building. The design of the wide balconies, which seem to form outwards extensions of the different floor levels, is reminiscent of the horizontal note of traditional Buddhist temples. The underside of the roof corner is designed with great precision.

5. Die Eckpfeiler sind am Stützenfuß strebenartig verbreitert.

6. In der Zeremonienhalle sind in einige Deckenfelder Leuchtwannen eingebaut. Während sich der Raum in Höhe des 2. Obergeschosses durch Glaswände zum Balkon weitet, sind die Wandflächen über der Empore mit einer Gitterstruktur verschleiert und durch Nischen stark gegliedert.

7. Die offene Halle auf Eingangsniveau ist zwei Geschosse hoch und wird durch ein System von Pfeilern und Treppen gegliedert.

8. Blick durch das offene Eingangsgeschoß. Die wuchtigen Eckpfeiler sind die Hauptstützen des Gebäudes. Die vorgezogenen Balkone erweitern die Innenräume der einzelnen Geschosse nach außen und erinnern in ihrer formalen Gestaltung an die horizontale Gliederung traditioneller buddhistischer Tempelbauten. Mit großer formaler Präzision ist die Ecklösung der Dachuntersicht durchgearbeitet.

Sachio Otani + Taneo Oki

Religious Centre of the Tensho Kotai Jingu-Kyo Sect at Tabuse, Yamaguchi District, 1964
The centre of this religious sect, which was founded in Japan shortly after the war, stands in hilly grounds outside the town of Tabuse. The rites of this sect, which is based on Shintoism, consist of sermons interrupted by rhythmic dances which tend to become ecstatic. The group of buildings can be divided into four parts: the sanctuaries proper, the living quarters for Japanese and foreign members of the sect (separated by age, sex and degree of probation), the administration building, and the residence of the founder who is the spiritual head of the more than 300,000 members of the sect. The architects tried to derive, from the rites of the sect, an architectural concept which blends with the landscape and, at the same time, represents a formal interpretation of the religious ceremonies. The result was a rhythmically accentuated group of buildings which, by the staggered arrangement of the different parts, by several penetrations of the structural mass, and by continually changing vistas, attempts to convey something of the character of the 'dancing religion'. The open structure characterized by long, sweeping lines, solid blocks and light 'catwalks' almost conceals the fact that it has a reinforced concrete framework-and-slab construction.

Religiöses Zentrum der Sekte Tensho Kotai Jingu-Kyo in Tabuse, Bezirk Yamaguchi, 1964
Das Zentrum dieser Religionsgemeinschaft, die kurz nach dem Krieg in Japan gegründet wurde, steht im hügeligen Gelände außerhalb der Stadt Tabuse. Die Riten der auf dem Shintoismus basierenden Sekte bestehen aus Predigten, die durch rhythmische, ins Ekstatische gesteigerte Tänze unterbrochen werden. Der Gebäudekomplex umfaßt vier Teile: den eigentlichen Tempelbezirk, die Wohnbereiche für die Mitglieder der Sekte (gegliedert nach Alter, Geschlecht und Grad der Bewährung) und ausländische Gäste, das Verwaltungsgebäude und den Wohnbezirk der Gründerin, die als geistiges Oberhaupt mehr als 300 000 Anhängern vorsteht. Die Architekten waren bemüht, aus den Riten der Religionsgemeinschaft heraus eine Architekturkonzeption zu entwickeln, die sich der Landschaft einordnet und zugleich die Zeremonien der Sekte formal interpretiert. So entstand eine rhythmisch bewegte Gebäudeformation, die durch Staffelung, Durchbrüche und sich ständig verändernde Durchblicke etwas vom Charakter der »tanzenden Religion« sichtbar machen will. Die offene Bauweise mit ihren langen zügigen Linien, massierten Blöcken und leichten, stegförmigen Bauteilen läßt fast vergessen, daß es sich auch hier um eine Stahlbetonkonstruktion handelt, bei der eine Mischung aus Stahlbetonskelett- und Plattenbauweise zur Anwendung kam.

1. On the north side of the Prayer Hall is a large piazza where the members of the sect congregate. Below the smaller prayer hall is an open space of mighty size.
2. East-west section, plan at ground level (left), and plan at second floor level.
3. View from the south. The low building in the foreground, right, is the administration wing. In keeping with its importance, the cubic cluster of the Great Prayer Hall, which is raised one storey above entrance level, is the dominating feature of the whole group. To the right of it rises the concave roof of the smaller prayer hall. An enclosed passageway three storeys above entrance level connects the sanctuaries with the Founder's residence.

1. Auf der Nordseite des Zeremoniengebäudes ist ein großer Platz angelegt, auf dem sich die Gläubigen versammeln. Unter dem kleinen Zeremoniensaal entsteht eine offene Halle von mächtigen Dimensionen.
2. Schnitt in Ost-West-Richtung und Grundrisse des Erdgeschosses (links) und des 2. Obergeschosses.
3. Ansicht von Süden. Im Vordergrund rechts der flache Verwaltungstrakt. Der große Zeremoniensaal, dessen geschlossener, kubischer Baukörper das dominierende Gebäude der Anlage ist, liegt seiner Bedeutung nach ein Geschoß über dem Eingangsniveau. Mit geschwungenem Dach schließt sich der kleine Zeremoniensaal an. Ein geschlossener Gang, drei Geschosse über dem Eingangsniveau, verbindet die Zeremonienräume mit der Wohnung der Gründerin.

Key: 1 piazza, 2 terrace, 3 entrance hall, 4 cloak room, 5 basin, 6 vestibule, 7 pool of water, 8 lavatories, 9 air space above the great prayer hall, 10 small prayer hall, 11 altar, 12 reception.

Legende: 1 Versammlungsplatz, 2 Terrasse, 3 Eingangshalle, 4 Garderobe, 5 Bassin, 6 Vestibül, 7 Wasserbecken, 8 Sanitärräume, 9 Luftraum über dem großen Zeremoniensaal, 10 Kleiner Zeremoniensaal, 11 Altar, 12 Empfang.

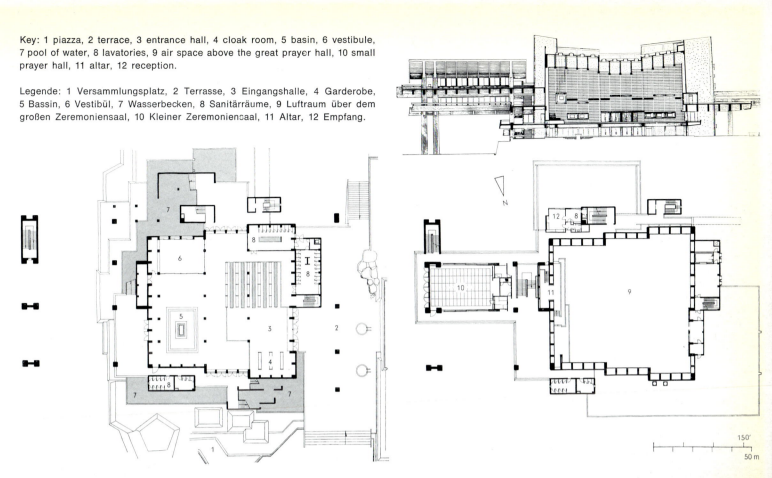

4. The open space facing the entrance hall of the Great Prayer Hall is terraced, the different levels being linked by broad flights of stairs. The smaller prayer hall is placed above the main entrance hall. The solid facades are interrupted by wide terraces which extend the interiors outwards.

5. Altar zone in the Great Prayer Hall. The roof beams, separated by sky lights, are placed on different levels and their underside is irregularly notched. In front of the altar, sound-absorbing boards are suspended from the ceiling for acoustic reasons.

4. Die Plätze vor der Eingangshalle zum großen Zeremonienraum sind terrassiert und durch breite Treppen miteinander verbunden. Der kleine Zeremonienraum liegt über der Haupteingangshalle. Die geschlossenen Fassaden werden durch weit ausladende Terrassen unterbrochen, die die Innenräume nach außen erweitern.

5. Blick auf die Altarzone des großen Zeremoniensaales. Die Deckenunterzüge, zwischen denen Oberlichter angeordnet sind, liegen auf verschiedenen Höhen und sind an der Unterkante unregelmäßig eingekerbt. Vor der Altarzone sind aus akustischen Gründen Schalltafeln von der Decke abgehängt.

1. The historic temple precinct, seen from the priest's room on the first floor.
2. East side with the main entrance and the secondary entrance to the treasury. The inclined outer walls are composed of prefabricated stanchions and concrete grilles. The horizontal emphasis is further enhanced by the lateral overhang of the I-beams of the roof which rest on the box pillars.

Kiyonori Kikutake

Office Building for the Izumo Shrine, 1961-63

Like that other Shinto sanctuary known as Ise Shrine, the Izumo Shrine embodies the tradition of early Japanese architecture. Its prototype dates back to the 6th century; but as its timber is decaying, the building is under continuous reconstruction at cycles of sixty years. Nevertheless, its structure and details continue to appear in their early traditional design without modification. Although the new office building is uncompromisingly modern in making the most of contemporary building techniques, its design is closely related to the historic sanctuary which dominates the temple precinct. The structural framework of the new building consists of two box-shaped pillars of 20 ft. height and 56 ft. circumference which also contain the stairwells, a couple of I-girders of 131 ft. span and 6 ft. 7 in. height, and of floor slabs placed between the girders. The structure also includes a gallery which is supported by columns and girders independent of the outer framework. Among the non-bearing components are the elements of the entrance zone, the grille forming the outer walls, the stairs ramp roofed by hyperbolic-paraboloid shells, and the movable furniture. To the south of the entrance hall, along the east side, is the two-storey treasury whilst the offices, waiting room and guest rooms are placed below the gallery. A ramp on the west side of the building leads to the upper level with the hall of worship in its centre. The structure mostly consists of precast concrete units.

1. Blick aus dem Priesterraum im ersten Obergeschoß auf den historischen Tempelbezirk.
2. Die Ostseite mit dem Haupteingang und dem Nebeneingang zum Schatzraum. Schräge Außenwände aus vorfabrizierten Stützen und Betonlamellen. Die starke Betonung der Horizontalen wird noch gesteigert durch das seitliche Auskragen der I-förmigen Dachträger, die auf den Kastenpfeilern aufliegen.

Verwaltungsgebäude für den Schrein von Izumo, 1961-63

Der Shinto-Schrein von Izumo, dessen Prototyp aus dem 6. Jahrhundert stammt, überliefert, ähnlich wie der Schrein von Ise, die Tradition der frühen japanischen Baukunst. Da das Baumaterial Holz dem Verfall unterworfen ist, wird das Gebäude im Turnus von 60 Jahren neu errichtet. Konstruktion und Detail spiegeln jedoch unverändert die Formenwelt der Frühzeit wider. Das neue Verwaltungsgebäude nützt zwar uneingeschränkt die Möglichkeiten moderner Bautechnik, steht aber hinsichtlich der Form in enger Beziehung zu dem historischen Gebäude, das als Heiligtum den Tempelbezirk beherrscht. Das konstruktive Gerüst des Neubaus besteht aus zwei kastenförmigen Pfeilern von 6 m Höhe und 17 m Umfang, die zugleich die Treppenhäuser enthalten, aus einem Trägerpaar in I-Form von 40 m Spannweite und 2 m Höhe und aus Deckenplatten, die zwischen den Trägern liegen. Ferner gehört zum konstruktiven Aufbau eine Empore, die unabhängig vom äußeren Gerüst auf Stützen und Unterzügen steht. Die Ausstattung setzt sich aus den Elementen der Eingangszone, aus den Lamellen der Außenwände, aus der mit HP-Schalen abgedeckten Treppenrampe und dem beweglichen Mobiliar zusammen. An die Eingangshalle auf der östlichen Längsseite schließt sich nach Süden der zweigeschossige Schatzraum an, während unter der Empore Verwaltung, Warteraum und Gästezimmer zusammengefaßt sind. Eine Rampe, die auf der Westseite vor das Gebäude gesetzt ist, führt auf die Empore, deren Kernstück der Zeremonienraum bildet. Die Konstruktion besteht zum großen Teil aus Betonfertigteilen.

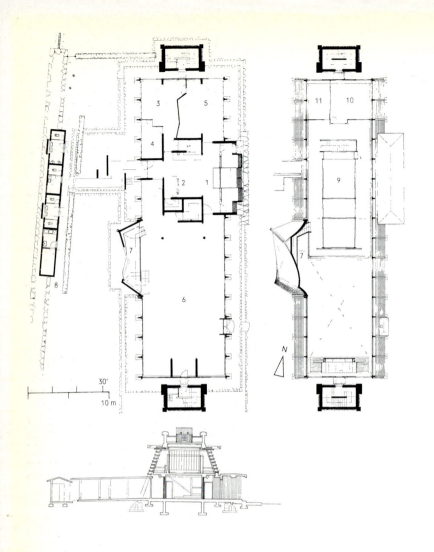

3. Ground floor plan (left), upper floor plan and section. Key: 1 entrance hall, 2 reception, 3 administration, 4 interview room, 5 waiting room, 6 treasury, 7 ramp leading to upper level, 8 annexe with lavatories and washrooms, 9 hall of worship, 10 priest's room, 11 vestry.
4. Treasury. The narrow windows in the inclined outer walls create a diffused lighting effect which is skilfully enhanced by the artificial lighting. On the left the outbuilding with the ramp. Flooring of square wooden blocks.
5. Waiting room. The apertures between the concrete grilles have windows.
6. View from the south, with the box-shaped pillar braced by cross-beams. The architectural kinship to the historic buildings of the temple precinct is emphasized by the diagonal pattern of the wall decorations, by the grilles forming the inclined outer walls, and by the turrets rising above the roof.

3. Grundrisse von Erdgeschoß (links), Obergeschoß und Querschnitt. Legende: 1 Eingangshalle, 2 Empfang, 3 Verwaltung, 4 Sprechzimmer, 5 Warteraum, 6 Schatzraum, 7 Rampe zum Obergeschoß, 8 Nebengebäude mit Toiletten und Waschräumen, 9 Zeremonienraum, 10 Priesterraum, 11 Umkleidezimmer.
4. Der Schatzraum. Die schmalen Fensterstreifen in den schrägen Außenwänden geben eine diffuse Lichtstimmung, die durch die künstliche Beleuchtung geschickt verstärkt wird. Links der Vorbau mit der Rampe. Bodenbelag aus quadratischen Kanthölzern.
5. Der Warteraum. Die Lichtschlitze zwischen den Betonlamellen sind verglast.
6. Ansicht von Süden mit dem kastenförmigen, durch Querbalken ausgesteiften Pfeiler. Die Diagonalornamente der Giebelfelder und die Lamellen der schrägen Außenwände schaffen ebenso formale Beziehungen zu den historischen Bauten des Tempelbezirks wie die aus dem Bauvolumen herausragenden Dachaufbauten.

Kenzo Tange

St Mary's Cathedral at Tokyo, 1964

The cathedral is situated in the Bunkyo district of North Tokyo — a residential area densely built up with low-rise houses. The plan of the church shows two trapezoids in staggered position. The nave is flanked by two low annexes: — a modern interpretation of the aisles of historic churches. It is in these aisles that the main entrances are placed. A third annexe, connected with the cathedral merely by a narrow passageway, contains the sacristy. Above the nave, four dual-curvature hyperbolic-paraboloid shells form a cross which is opened up by skylight ribbons, the shells being braced by cross-beams between these ribbons. At the sides, the skylights merge with the windows which divide the church vertically in a cruciform pattern. The high-altar marks the end of the main axis opposite the processional entrance. In the two aisles are small chapels; one of them also contains the font. The organ is placed above the processional entrance. Below the main altar is a crypt which, with its light-shafts, is reminiscent of early Christian sacral architecture. In this edifice, the non-Christian architect Tange has created a convincing synthesis of structural and symbolic design.

Marienkathedrale in Tokio, 1964

Die Kathedrale steht im Bezirk Bunkyo im Norden von Tokio, in einem relativ dicht, aber niedrig bebauten Wohngebiet. Der Grundriß des Kirchenraumes besteht aus zwei gegeneinander versetzten Trapezen. Zwei niedrige Anbauten begleiten das Hauptschiff: eine moderne Interpretation der Seitenschiffe im historischen Kirchenbau. In diese Seitenschiffe führen auch die Haupteingänge. Ein dritter Anbau, der mit der Kathedrale nur durch einen schmalen Gang verbunden ist, nimmt die Sakristei auf. Über dem Hauptschiff bilden vier doppelt gekrümmte HP-Schalen ein durch Oberlichtbänder geöffnetes Kreuz, wobei Querbalken zwischen den Lichtbändern die Schalen gegeneinander abstützen. Die Oberlichtbänder gehen an den Seiten in Fensterbänder über, die den Raum vertikal teilen und ihn nach den vier Richtungen der Kreuzform öffnen. Der Hochaltar steht am Ende der Hauptachse gegenüber dem Prozessionseingang. In den beiden Nebenschiffen sind kleine Seitenaltäre plaziert, auch der Taufstein ist in einem der Seitenschiffe untergebracht. Die Orgelempore liegt über dem Prozessionseingang. Unter dem Hauptaltar ist eine Kapelle eingebaut, die durch Lichtschächte erhellt wird und in der Stimmung an frühchristliche Sakralarchitektur erinnert. Zusammenfassend läßt sich sagen, daß dem Nichtchristen Tange mit diesem Bauwerk eine überzeugende Synthese aus Konstruktions- und Symbolform gelungen ist.

1. Aerial view. The dominant feature of the design is the cruciform shape. At ground level, the plan is very nearly a convex cross. At the top, this shape recedes into a concave cross of skylight ribbons. The transition is formed by the dual-curvature shells. The general layout of the whole group, including the annexes, was partly governed by the shape of the plot. The 197 ft. high, needle-shaped belfry stands in an isolated position in the piazza close to the processional entrance.
2. Nave with high-altar, seen from one of the low aisles. The end of the low entrance hall is marked by a chapel.
3. Main altar. At the intersection of the skylight ribbons — where a classic basilica has its central cupola linking nave and transept — the four shells are braced by a cruciform system of struts. The high and narrow vertical window behind the altar is the continuation of the skylight ribbon.

1. Luftansicht. Grundidee des Entwurfes ist die Kreuzform. Die Bodenfläche nähert sich im Grundriß einem konvexen Kreuz. Diese Form verjüngt sich nach oben zu einem konkaven, kreuzförmigen Oberlichtband. Zwischen diesen zwei Formen bildet sich die doppelt gekrümmte Schale. Der Gesamtgrundriß des Komplexes, einschließlich der Anbauten, wurde durch den Zuschnitt des Grundstücks mitbestimmt. Der 60 m hohe, nadelförmige Glockenturm steht frei auf dem Platz in der Nähe des Prozessionseingangs.
2. Blick aus dem niedrigen Seitenschiff in den Hauptraum mit dem Hochaltar. Am Ende der niedrigen Eingangshalle steht ein Seitenaltar.
3. Blick auf den Hauptaltar. Im Schnittpunkt der Oberlichtbänder an der Stelle, wo sich in der Vierung der klassischen Basilika Mittelschiff und Querschiff durchdringen, stützt eine kreuzförmige Strebe die vier Schalen gegeneinander ab. Der senkrechte Lichtschlitz hinter dem Altar ist die Fortsetzung des kreuzförmigen Oberlichtes.

4. View from north-west. Above the processional entrance between the two upright hyperbolic-paraboloid roof shells is a broad ribbon of windows. Entrance platform and nave are raised a few steps above the piazza level. The entrances for the congregation are in the aisles.
5. Plan and section. Key: 1 processional entrance, 2 main entrances, 3 waiting room, 4 pump room, 5 aisle, 6 chapel, 7 baptistry, 8 main altar, 9 side entrances, 10 sacristy, 11 light-shafts for the crypt.

4. Ansicht von Nordwesten. Zwischen den beiden aufrechtstehenden HP-Schalen der Dachflächen entsteht über dem Prozessionseingang ein breiter Lichtschlitz. Die Eingangsplattform und das anschließende Hauptschiff sind einige Stufen über das Platzniveau angehoben. Die Eingänge für die Gemeinde liegen in den seitlichen Anbauten.
5. Grundriß und Schnitt. Legende: 1 Prozessionseingang, 2 Haupteingänge, 3 Warteraum, 4 Pumpenraum, 5 Seitenschiff, 6 Seitenaltar, 7 Taufkapelle, 8 Hauptaltar, 9 Nebeneingänge, 10 Sakristei, 11 Oberlichter über den Altären der Unterkirche.

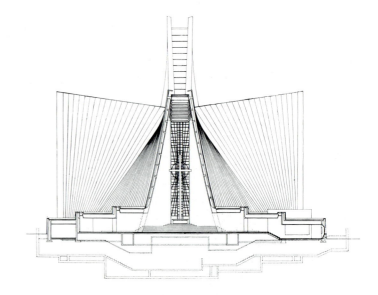

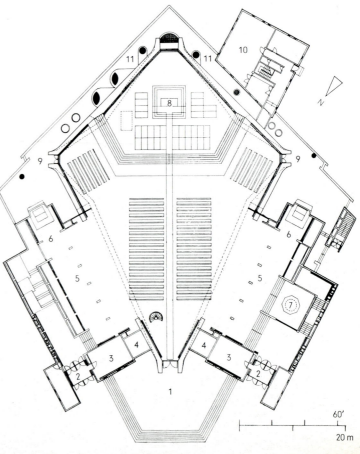

60'

20 m

6. Detail of the cruciform intersection of the skylight ribbons. The hyperbolic-paraboloid shells are braced by cross-struts. The incoming light is filtered through louvres. The exposed concrete of the inner walls still bears the marks of the shuttering.

7. The daylight entering the crypt through the central light-shaft above the altar zone has a plastic effect on the two skew concrete diaphragms flanking the altar.

8. The steeply rising roof marks the choir with the main altar. The roof shells are lined, on the outside, with profiled stainless steel sheeting.

6. Detail des Vierungskreuzes im Schnittpunkt der Oberlichtbänder. Die HP-Schalen werden durch Querrippen gegeneinander abgestützt. Lamellen filtern das einfallende Licht. Die Innenwände aus Sichtbeton sind schalungsrauh belassen.

7. Die kleine Kapelle im Untergeschoß wird durch ein zentrales Oberlicht über der Altarzone erhellt, wobei die Lichtführung zwei schräggestellte Betonscheiben zu Seiten des Altars plastisch heraushebt.

8. Die steil aufsteigende Dachlinie kennzeichnet den Chor mit dem Haupt-altar. Die äußere Verkleidung der Schalen besteht aus profiliertem, rostfreiem Stahlblech.

Kunio Mayekawa & Associates

Museum of Arts at Okayama, 1962-63
The museum ground, accessible from the east and retained by a rubble wall, is about 13 ft. above street level. The museum is a patio-type building of compact appearance with strong horizontal emphasis. It is flanked on the south-east side by a wing containing offices and repositories. A forecourt and a broad flight of stairs leads to the entrance hall which opens up a view of the patio. With the exception of two windows facing the garden in the north and west, the display rooms have artificial lighting only. In contrast, the foyer on the south side has full-height windows facing both the garden and the patio. This foyer is mainly designed for exhibits which should be viewed in daylight. The predominant building materials are brick and untreated concrete. The overall impression of harmony is enhanced by the landscaping of the grounds, with lawns, shrubs, trees and a seemingly random scatter of boulders.

Kunstmuseum in Okayama, 1962-63
Das Grundstück, das von Osten erschlossen und von einer Stützmauer aus Bruchsteinen eingefaßt wird, liegt etwa 4 m über Straßenniveau. Das Museum ist ein kompakt wirkender, in der Horizontalen stark betonter Atriumsbau, an den sich auf der Südostseite ein Büro- und Magazinflügel anschließt. Über einen Vorhof und eine breite Treppe gelangt man zur Eingangshalle, von der aus sich der Blick zum Innenhof öffnet. Die Ausstellungsräume, die nur an zwei Stellen auf der Nord- und Westseite zum Garten hin verglast sind, werden mit Kunstlicht erhellt. Dagegen öffnet sich das Foyer auf der Südseite mit geschoßhohen Glaswänden sowohl zum Garten als auch zum Innenhof hin. Es ist in erster Linie für Objekte vorgesehen, die Tageslicht benötigen. In der Materialwahl dominieren Backstein und schalungsrauher Beton. Die Ausgewogenheit des Gesamteindrucks wird vervollständigt durch die Gestaltung des Außenraumes mit Rasenflächen, Büschen, Bäumen und wie zufällig verteilten Natursteinblöcken.

1. Forecourt, and stairs leading to the main entrance. Owing to the long projection of the rubble wall, the two-storeyed repository building appears to be lower than it is. The different buildings are linked by the broad roof edge of the connecting wing.

1. Vorhof und Treppe zum Haupteingang. Die weit vorgezogene Bruchsteinmauer reduziert optisch die Höhe des zweigeschossigen Magazingebäudes. Das kräftige Dachgesims des Mitteltraktes faßt die einzelnen Gebäudeteile zusammen.

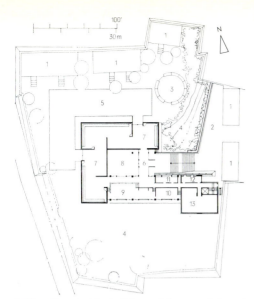

2. Plan. Key: 1 older buildings, 2 fore-court, 3 pool of water, 4 garden, 5 terrace, 6 entrance hall, 7 display room, 8 patio, 9 display room for sculptures, 10 office, 11 cloak room, 12 restoration studio, 13 repository.

2. Grundriß. Legende: 1 Existierende Gebäude, 2 Hof, 3 Wasserbecken, 4 Garten, 5 Terrasse, 6 Eingangshalle, 7 Ausstellungsraum, 8 Innenhof, 9 Ausstellungsraum für Skulpturen, 10 Verwaltung, 11 Toilette, 12 Studien- und Restaurierungsraum, 13 Magazin.

3. One of the display rooms. The rooms are mainly lit by light fittings above the show cases along the walls and by point lamps suspended from the ceiling. The sculpture in the foreground receives daylight through an opening in the wall.

3. Einer der Ausstellungsräume, die im wesentlichen mit Kunstlicht über den längs der Wände aufgereihten Vitrinen und durch Punktleuchten im Raum beleuchtet werden. Die Skulptur vorn erhält durch eine Außenwandöffnung Tageslicht.

4. View from the south. The wing connecting the window-less west wing with the repository is lower than the display rooms and has windows facing the garden. Foyer and garden are linked by two sliding doors. On the right, the office.

4. Ansicht von Süden. Der Verbindungstrakt zwischen dem geschlossenen Westflügel und dem Magazin ist niedriger als die Ausstellungsräume und zum Garten hin verglast. Zwei Schiebetüren führen vom Foyer in den Garten; rechts das Büro.

1. The integral appearance of the group is achieved by applying the same vertical facade structure and using the same materials.
2. A few low windows are the only apertures on the south side.

1. Die vertikale Fassadenstruktur und das gleiche Material geben dem Komplex ein einheitliches Gepräge.
2. Nur wenige, tiefliegende Fenster unterbrechen die Südfassade.

Kunio Mayekawa & Associates

Setagaya District Museum at Tokyo, 1964

As the exhibits in this museum of popular art called for artificial lighting unaffected by daylight fluctuations, a group of largely enclosed buildings was indicated, with but a few shaft-like windows permitting an occasional glimpse of the surrounding park. The group consists of two parts; the cubic two-storey display building and the lower lecture room, connected with the former through a porch. The centre of the display building is formed by a square stairwell which extends through both storeys and receives daylight through domes in the roof. The upper floor is divided into four rooms of equal size which are partially open towards the stairwell and which, because of the window-less outer walls, offer a maximum of wall area for displays. The facades, cast behind climbing steel forms, are rhythmically enlivened by stiffening ribs. In the display building, the floor and roof slabs rest on an inner ring of reinforced concrete columns.

Setagaya-Bezirksmuseum in Tokio, 1964

Da die Ausstellungsobjekte dieses Museums für Volkskunst eine vom wechselnden Tageslicht unabhängige Beleuchtungstechnik verlangten, entstand eine weitgehend geschlossene Baugruppe, deren wenige, schachtartige Fenster nur gelegentlich den Blick in den umgebenden Park freigeben. Die Anlage besteht aus zwei Teilen: dem zweigeschossigen Ausstellungskubus und dem über einen Windfang angeschlossenen, niedrigeren Vortragssaal. Das Zentrum des Ausstellungsgebäudes bildet eine durch beide Geschosse gehende, quadratische Treppenhalle, die durch Oberlichtkuppeln belichtet wird. Das obere Geschoß ist in vier gleich große Säle gegliedert, die sich teilweise zur Zentralhalle öffnen und wegen der geschlossenen Außenmauern viel Wandfläche bieten. Die Fassaden, die mit einer Stahlschalung stufenweise hochbetoniert wurden, sind durch Aussteifungsrippen rhythmisch belebt. Im Ausstellungsbau ruhen die Decken auf einem Innenkranz von Stahlbetonstützen.

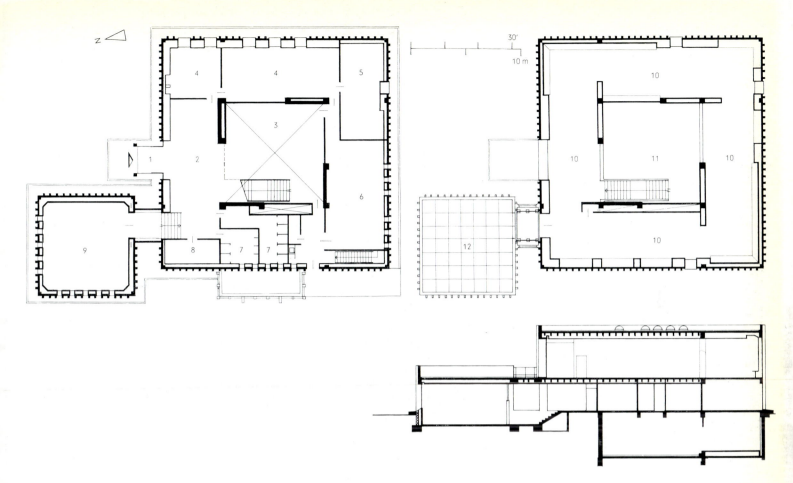

3. Ground floor plan (left), upper floor plan and section. Key: 1 porch, 2 vestibule, 3 central display room, 4 administration, 5 archives, 6 collection, 7 W. C., 8 stores, 9 lecture room, 10 display room, 11 air space above central display room, 12 roof terrace.

4. The showcases are lit from above by fluorescent lamps. All the rooms are effectively illuminated by concealed light fittings in the ceiling. In addition, individual exhibits are picked out by spotlights.

5. Parts of the outer walls of the display rooms are double walls, containing the indirectly lit showcases which, with their broad wooden frames, look almost like paintings.

3. Grundriß von Erdgeschoß (links) und Obergeschoß und Schnitt. Legende: 1 Windfang, 2 Vorhalle, 3 Ausstellungshalle, 4 Verwaltung, 5 Archiv, 6 Sammlung, 7 WC, 8 Lager, 9 Vortragssaal, 10 Ausstellungsraum, 11 Luftraum über der Ausstellungshalle, 12 Dachterrasse.

4. Die Vitrinen werden von oben durch Leuchtstoffröhren beleuchtet. Alle Räume sind durch indirekte, in die Decke eingebaute Lichtquellen gut ausgeleuchtet, Deckenstrahler konzentrieren sich auf Einzelstücke.

5. Die Außenwände der Ausstellungssäle sind teilweise doppelschalig ausgebildet. Sie nehmen die indirekt beleuchteten Vitrinen auf, die mit ihren breiten Holzrahmen fast wie Bilder wirken.

Junzo Sakakura

Museum of Modern Arts at Kamakura, 1951 and 1965
The group of three museum buildings was erected in two stages. Whilst the long and narrow repository wing stands entirely on land, the two exhibition buildings jut out onto a small lake. The older main building, erected in 1951, recalls the ideas of Le Corbusier who was Sakakura's teacher. The centre of the square building is taken up by an atrium where sculptures are exhibited. In the narrower and lower annexe, which is connected with the older part by a small bridge, Japanese architectural notions are blended with Western technology. The curtain walls, consisting of white enamelled steel sheets measuring 2 ft. 7½ in. × 5 ft. 3 in., are interrupted — especially near the corners — by suspended window panes of 18 ft. 5 in. height which seem to integrate the premises with lake and park.

Museum für moderne Kunst in Kamakura, 1951 und 1965
Der Museumskomplex, der sich aus drei getrennten Baukörpern zusammensetzt, wurde in zwei Phasen errichtet. Während das schmale, langgezogene Magazin ganz auf dem Festland steht, wurden die beiden Ausstellungsgebäude in einen kleinen See hinausgebaut. Im Hauptmuseum, 1951 als 1. Bauabschnitt entstanden, sind die Ideen Le Corbusiers spürbar, der Sakakuras Lehrer war. Im Zentrum des quadratischen Baukörpers ist ein Innenhof als Skulpturengarten ausgeschnitten. Beim schmäleren und niedrigeren Erweiterungsbau, der mit dem älteren Bauteil durch eine kleine Brücke verbunden ist, vereinigen sich japanische Architekturvorstellungen mit westlicher Technologie. Die mit 80 x 160 cm großen, weiß emaillierten Stahlblechtafeln geschlossenen Außenflächen werden, vor allem in den Eckbereichen, von 5,60 m hohen, hängenden Glasscheiben unterbrochen, die den See und den Park in die Räume einbeziehen.

1. The two museum buildings, seen from southwest. The facade of the atrium building is lined with asbestos cement boards. Its upper floor has a loggia facing the lake. The lake-side corners of the annexe are deeply recessed and have full-height windows. The framework, based on a column spacing of 22 ft. 2 in. × 39 ft. 8 in., consists of special high-tensile steel which, as a result of oxidation, forms a dark-brown protective film.
2. Through the visual interruption of the walls, the landscape becomes an essential element of interior decoration; on the other hand, the wall area available for display is considerably reduced. On the right is the part of the older building placed over the lake. The ceiling has steel wire netting.

1. Blick von Südwesten auf die beiden Museen. Das Obergeschoß des Atriumbaues, dessen Fassade mit Asbestzementplatten verkleidet ist, öffnet sich über eine Loggia zum See. Die dem Wasser zugewandten Ecken des Erweiterungsbaues sind tief ausgeschnitten und raumhoch verglast. Für die Skelettkonstruktion, der ein Stützenraster von 6,75 x 12,10 m zugrunde liegt, ist ein Spezialstahl hoher Festigkeit verwendet, der bei Korrosion eine dunkelbraune Schutzschicht bildet.
2. Durch die optische Auflösung der Wandflächen wird zwar die Landschaft ein wesentliches Element der Innenraumgestaltung, doch reduziert dieser Effekt beträchtlich die Hängefläche. Rechts der in den See hineingestellte Teil des Altbaues. Deckennetz aus Stahldraht.

144

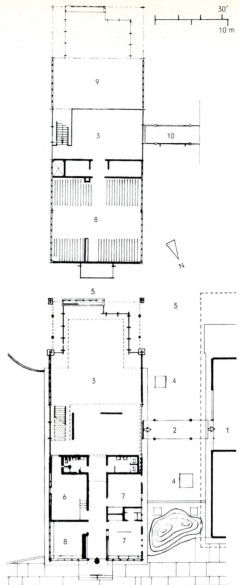

3. At the south-east corner, floor slab and windows are recessed. But the overall shape is restored by the overhung roof.

4. Ground floor and upperfloor plans of the new building. Key: 1 sculptures room, main building, 2 connecting bridge, 3 exhibition room, 4 pedestals for sculptures, 5 pool of water, 6 machinery room, 7 office, 8 stores, 9 space above exhibition room, 10 roof of connecting bridge.

5. Night view from the lake. The facade of the new building is flush with that of the old one.

3. An der Südostecke sind Bodenplatte und Glasflächen zurückgenommen. Das vorstehende Dach faßt jedoch die Gesamtform wieder zusammen.

4. Grundrisse von Erd- und Obergeschoß des Neubaues. Legende: 1 Skulpturensaal des Hauptgebäudes, 2 Verbindungsbrücke, 3 Ausstellungsraum, 4 Sockel für Skulpturen, 5 Wasserfläche, 6 Maschinenraum, 7 Büro, 8 Depot, 9 Luftraum über Ausstellungsraum, 10 Dach der Verbindungsbrücke.

5. Nachtansicht vom See aus. Die Flucht des neuen Baukörpers verläuft bündig mit dem Altbau.

1. Entrance pavilion. The area below the buildings was laid over with boards and also used for display purposes.

1. Der Eingangspavillon. Der Platz unter den Ausstellungstrakten war mit Brettern belegt und als Ausstellungsfläche genutzt.

Yoshinobu Ashihara

Japanese Pavilion at the World Exhibition, Montreal, 1967

The strong horizontal emphasis of the design — interpreting traditional Japanese 'building set' methods in the light of modern building techniques — formed a deliberate contrast to the vertically accentuated skyline of the city. To avoid obstructing the landscape of St Helen's Island, the three vertically and horizontally staggered parts of the pavilion were placed on columns. The vertical stagger was inspired by the idea of water streaming down the terraces. The visitors were taken by an escalator to the top-level exhibition room from which gently inclined ramps led to the two lower levels and finally to the restaurant on the opposite side which was placed in the artificial lake of the Japanese garden. The ends of the up to 113 ft. 2½ in. long prestressed concrete beams, which had been cast in Japan, were covered with aluminium sleeves. The beams and the block shaped spacers were laid out with epoxy cement and vertically tensioned by steel cables. The wall behind the beams consisted of prefabricated light-weight slabs, the ceiling of precast reinforced concrete units. The supporting steel beams of floors and ceilings projected from the facades. Owing to the extensive use of prefabricated components, the pavilion was quickly erected and dismantled (erection within six months).

Japanischer Pavillon auf der Weltausstellung in Montreal, 1967

Der Entwurf, der die traditionelle japanische Blockbauweise mit den Mitteln moderner Bautechnik interpretierte, stellte gegen die vertikal akzentuierte Stadtsilhouette eine stark horizontal betonte Baugruppe. Um die Landschaft der Insel Ste. Hélène nicht abzuriegeln, wurden die drei im Grundriß gegeneinander versetzten und in der Höhe abgestuften Teile des Pavillons auf Stützen gestellt. Die Höhenstufung war durch den Gedanken an Wasser, das über Terrassen herabströmt, inspiriert. Die Besucher wurden mit einer Rolltreppe zum höchstgelegenen Ausstellungsraum hinaufgebracht, von wo sanft geneigte Rampen auf die beiden tieferen Ebenen und schließlich zum gegenüberliegenden Restaurant hinunterführten, das in den künstlichen See des japanischen Gartens hineingebaut war. Die Enden der in Japan hergestellten Spannbetonbalken (größte Länge 34,50 m) waren mit Manschetten aus Aluminium überzogen. Die Balken und die blockförmigen Abstandhalter wurden mit Epoxydzement versetzt und in der Senkrechten mit Stahlkabeln verspannt. Der Wandabschluß hinter den Balken bestand aus vorfabrizierten Leichtbauplatten, die Decke aus Stahlbetonfertigteilen. Als Deckenüberzüge und Fußbodenunterzüge waren Stahlträger verwendet, die über die Fassade vorsprangen. Die überwiegend vorfabrizierten Bauteile ermöglichten kurze Montage- und Demontagezeiten (Aufbau in 6 Monaten).

2. Highest part of the pavilion, with the escalator. The walls behind the beams consist of prefabricated light-weight panels.

2. Der höchste Pavillonteil mit der Rolltreppe. Wandabschluß hinter den Balken aus vorfabrizierten Leichtbauplatten.

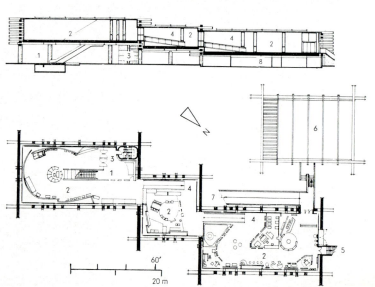

3. A view from the corner of the restaurant building across the Japanese garden towards the staggered main building.
4. Longitudinal section and upper floor plan. Key: 1 escalator, 2 exhibition room, 3 stairs, 4 ramp, 5 fire exit, 6 restaurant, 7 outdoor ramp, 8 administration.

3. Blick von der Ecke des Restaurantgebäudes über den japanischen Garten auf den versetzten, abgetreppten Pavillon.
4. Längsschnitt und Grundriß des Obergeschosses. Legende: 1 Rolltreppe, 2 Ausstellungsraum, 3 Treppe, 4 Rampe, 5 Notausgang, 6 Restaurant, 7 Außenrampe, 8 Verwaltung.

148

5. Model of a modern Japanese living room. Adoption of Western style elements without breaking with Japanese tradition. On the left and in the background were the ramps which connect the different parts of the pavilion.
6. The model living room had an irregularly patterned, suspended box type ceiling.
7. The restaurant building and the Japanese garden.

5. Modellbeispiel eines modernen japanischen Wohnraumes. Übernahme von Stilelementen westlicher Kultur ohne Bruch mit der japanischen Tradition. Links und hinten die Rampen, die die Pavillonteile verbanden.
6. Über dem Musterwohnraum eine abgehängte Kassettendecke in unregelmäßigem Muster.
7. Der Restaurantpavillon mit dem japanischen Garten.

Togo Murano

Nissei Theatre and Nihon'Seimei Administration Building at Tokyo, 1958

This head office building of an insurance company, occupying a corner site in central Tokyo, incorporates a hall for opera, concert and theatre performances and lectures. The severity of the external architecture varies the style elements which, emanating from Japanese tradition, had an influence on the Art Nouveau. The facade, clad with large granite slabs, has storey-high windows which are partitioned by columns and sculptured lintels. The lobby for the seven office floors is entered from the west passage whilst the entrance to the split-level vestibule of the theatre is from the south passage. From the vestibule, stairs and lifts lead to the theatre foyer and balconies. In the theatre hall, which has 1,200 seats, ceiling and walls seem to be organically integrated — a sculptural treatment reminiscent of Antoni Gaudi's designs. This sculptural treatment of walls and ceilings, together with the rich textures of glass mosaic and globular glass castings and the indirect lighting from concealed light fittings, has a mysterious, fantastic effect.

Nissei-Theater und Nihon'Seimei-Verwaltungsgebäude in Tokio, 1958

In dieses Verwaltungsgebäude einer Versicherungsgesellschaft auf einem Eckgrundstück in der Innenstadt Tokios ist ein Saal für Oper, Konzert, Schauspiel und Vorträge eingebaut. Die strenge äußere Form variiert die aus der japanischen Tradition in den Jugendstil eingeflossenen Stilelemente. Die Fensteröffnungen sind geschoßhoch in die mit großen Granitplatten verkleidete Fassade eingeschnitten und durch Säulen und behauene Sturzbalken unterteilt. Die Eingangshalle für die sieben Büroetagen betritt man von der Westpassage aus, die zweigeschossige Halle des Theaters wird von der Südpassage her erschlossen. Aus der Halle führen Treppen und Aufzüge zu den Foyers des Saales und der Ränge. Die plastische Gestaltung des Theaterraums mit 1200 Plätzen, dessen Decke und Wände organisch zusammenwachsen, erinnert an die Architektur von Antoni Gaudí. Die stark bewegte Wand- und Deckenmodellierung ergibt zusammen mit den reichen Texturen aus Glasmosaik und runden Gußglasstücken, unterstützt durch die indirekte Beleuchtung aus versteckten Lichtquellen eine geheimnisvoll-phantastische Wirkung.

1. Detail of the south facade. The different storeys are emphasized by horizontal ribbons of granite slabs. Behind the storey-high windows are loggias, backed by solid walls. The solid granite columns and lintels in the window openings are purely decorative.
2. View from the upper tier on the stage which has a span of 141 ft. and is equipped with vertically and horizontally movable platforms. The curtain design is in keeping with the interior decoration of the room. For theatre performances, the orchestra pit can be hydraulically raised to the level of the stage. Indirect lighting in the cavity between ceiling and wall, additional point lamps in the 'valleys' of the ceiling.

1. Detail der Südfassade. Betonung der Geschosse durch waagerechte Bänder aus Granitplatten. Hinter den geschoßhohen Fenstern liegen Loggien vor geschlossenen Wandscheiben. Säulen und Sturz aus massivem Granit in den Fensteröffnungen erfüllen rein dekorative Absichten.
2. Blick vom oberen Rang auf die Bühne, die mit Hebeplattformen und Schiebeböden ausgestattet ist. Bühnenportal 43 m breit. Vorhang an Raumgestaltung angepaßt. Hydraulischer Hebeboden des Orchestergrabens bei Schauspielen auf das Niveau der Bühne anhebbar. Indirekte Beleuchtung in Hohlkehle zwischen Decke und Wand, zusätzliche Punktleuchten in den Deckenmulden.

3. North-south section. Key: 1 chimney, 2 patio, 3 conference room with top lighting, 4 office, 5 stage, 6 stage curtain, 7 auditorium with tiers, 8 foyer, 9 rigging floor, 10 orchestra pit, 11 theatre entrance hall, 12 open porch, 13 basement garage, 14 control centre, 15 stores, 16 machinery, 17 electrical plant.
4. Plans of ground floor (left) and first floor. Key: 1 open porch, 2 lobby for office floors, 3 entrance hall to theatre, 4 machinery room below orchestra pit, 5 rigging floor, 6 ramp leading to rigging floor, 7 office and porter's lodge at stage entrance, 8 entrance and exit of basement garage, 9 theatre foyer, 10 auditorium, 11 orchestra pit, 12 stage with horizontally and vertically movable platforms, 13 cloakrooms and technical plant, 14 air space above open plan office.

3. Schnitt in Nord-Süd-Richtung. Legende: 1 Schornstein, 2 Lichthof, 3 Konferenzsaal mit Oberlicht, 4 Büroraum, 5 Bühnenhaus, 6 Bühnenvorhang, 7 Zuschauerraum mit Rängen, 8 Foyer, 9 Unterbühne, 10 Orchestergraben, 11 Eingangshalle des Theaters, 12 Offene Vorhalle, 13 Tiefgarage, 14 Kontrollzentrum, 15 Lager, 16 Maschinenraum, 17 Elektrozentrale.
4. Grundrisse von Erdgeschoß (links) und 1. Obergeschoß. Legende: 1 Offene Vorhalle, 2 Eingangshalle des Büroteils, 3 Eingangshalle des Theaters, 4 Maschinenraum unter Orchestergraben, 5 Unterbühne, 6 Zufahrt zur Unterbühne, 7 Büro und Pförtnerloge am Bühneneingang, 8 Einfahrt und Ausfahrt der Tiefgarage, 9 Theaterfoyer, 10 Zuschauerraum, 11 Orchestergraben, 12 Bühnenhaus mit Schiebe- und Hebebühnen, 13 Garderoben und technische Räume, 14 Luftraum über Großraumbüro.

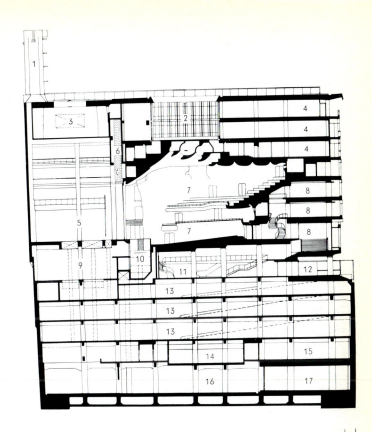

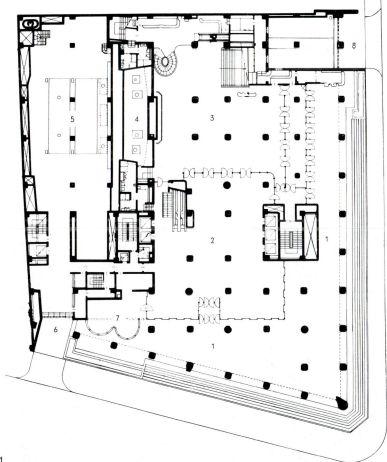

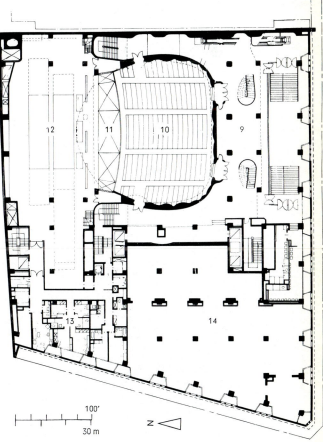

100'
30 m
N

5. Detail of wall and ceiling. For acoustic reasons, wall and ceiling have been given a highly irregular and curvilinear shape (the effect was previously tested on 1 in 50 and 1 in 10 models). Ceiling texture composed of circular glass castings embedded in the concrete, interrupted by visible air outlet tubes and, in the 'valleys', point lamps.

6. Wall facing of glass mosaic pieces of different sizes. The fresh-air inlet ducts protrude from the wall.

5. Wand- und Deckendetail. Raumhülle aus akustischen Gründen sehr unregelmäßig und kurvenreich (Wirkung an Modellen im Maßstab 1 : 50 und 1 : 10 erprobt). Deckentextur aus runden, in den Beton eingegossenen Gußglasstücken, dazwischen sichtbare Entlüftungsröhren. In den Mulden Punktstrahler.

6. Wandverkleidung aus Glasmosaiksteinen verschiedener Größe. Frischluftkanäle wulstartig aus der Wand vorgezogen.

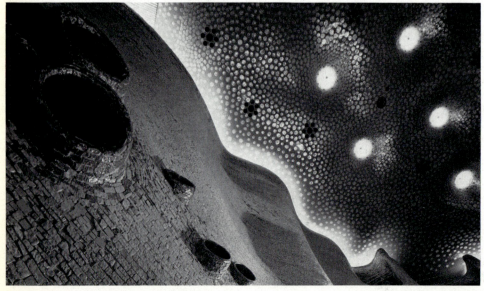

7. From the theatre entrance hall, a broad flight of stairs and an escalator lead to the mezzanine above the colonnade. Black-patterned marble flooring. There is a deliberate contrast between the refined profile treatment of the aluminium ceiling and the heavy, granite-clad columns.
8. The different foyer levels are linked by two freely suspended flights of curved stairs.

7. In der Eingangshalle des Theaters führen eine breite Treppe und eine Rolltreppe auf das Galeriegeschoß über dem Säulengang. Hallenboden: schwarzgeflammter Marmor. Materialgegensatz zwischen fein profilierter Aluminiumdecke und den schweren, granitverkleideten Pfeilern.
8. Saal und Foyers der Ränge sind durch zwei frei geschwungene Treppen verbunden.

Kunio Mayekawa & Associates

Municipal Festival Hall at Tokyo, 1958-61

The Festival Hall, erected for the quincentenary celebrations of the city, covers an area of some 80,730 sq. ft. and contains premises for many different purposes. On the ground floor is the large auditorium for 2,327 people which extends through three storeys, the foyer, the exhibition rooms and the administrative offices. On the first floor, extending through two storeys, is a conference room with garden terrace and restaurant. On the second floor are further conference rooms, meeting rooms as well as a music library for books and records with the necessary studios. In the basement are the stage, an orchestra pit that can be lowered, rehearsal rooms, artists' dressing rooms, ancillary premises and technical installations. The large auditorium (floor area 16,469 sq. ft.; stage measuring 59 ft. × 72 ft.) is designed for orchestral concerts, opera, theatre and ballet performances whilst the first floor hall is used for minor musical events and for conferences. The multi-purpose character of this centre is also apparent from the roof landscape which is, however, held together by a platform that surrounds all of it except the top part of the stage of the large auditorium on the south side. From this all-embracing horizontal element, the various top structures emerge like sculptures, conveying an impression of plasticity which is also characteristic for the facades. The structural framework consists of steel and reinforced concrete. Inside and outside, the dominating feature is the wall cladding of concrete slabs in which pieces of white marble are embedded.

Städtische Festhalle in Tokio, 1958-61

Die Festhalle, die zur 500-Jahrfeier der Stadt auf einer Grundfläche von rund 7 500 m² errichtet wurde, birgt in sich ein sehr umfangreiches Raumprogramm. Im Erdgeschoß liegen der große Saal, der durch drei Stockwerke geht und 2 327 Personen faßt, das Foyer, Ausstellungsräume und die Büros der Verwaltung. Das 1. Obergeschoß wird von einem zweigeschossigen Konferenzsaal mit Gartenterrasse und Restaurant eingenommen. Im 2. Obergeschoß befinden sich weitere Konferenzräume, Sitzungszimmer sowie eine Musikbibliothek für Bücher und Schallplatten mit den dazugehörigen Aufnahmeräumen, Studios usw. Das Untergeschoß gliedert sich in Bühne, versenkbaren Orchesterraum, Probenräume, Künstlergarderoben, ergänzt durch Nebenräume und technische Einrichtungen. Der große Saal (1 530 m², Bühne 18 x 22 m) ist für Orchesterkonzerte, Opern-, Theater- und Ballettaufführungen bestimmt, während im Saal des 1. Obergeschosses musikalische Darbietungen in kleinerem Rahmen und Konferenzen stattfinden. Die sich in der Dachlandschaft ausprägende Vielzahl von Funktionen, für die dieses Zentrum geplant ist, wird durch eine Plattform optisch zusammengefaßt, aus der nur der Bühnenturm des großen Saales nach Süden ausbricht. Aus diesem horizontalen, den ganzen Bau konzentrierenden Element ragen die verschiedenen Aufbauten wie Skulpturen heraus, eine Plastizität, die übrigens auch die Fassaden charakterisiert. Das konstruktive Gerüst besteht aus Stahl und Stahlbeton. Innen und außen dominiert die Wandverkleidung mit Betonelementen, in die weiße Marmorbrocken eingegossen sind.

1. This aerial photograph from the east shows the overall situation in Ueno Park. In the centre the Festival Hall, to the right the Museum of Western Art, designed by Le Corbusier. The railway installations just visible in the foreground had a highly detrimental influence on the overall plan.
2. Main entrance on the east side. On the left, the facade of the exhibition room, accentuated by vertical concrete posts. Next to it, the full-height glass frontage of the two-storey foyer. The moulded roof rests on the heavy concrete columns of the framework structure, based on a grid of 32 ft. 10 in.

1. Die Luftaufnahme von Osten zeigt die Gesamtsituation im Ueno-Park. Im Zentrum die Festhalle, rechts das Museum für westliche Kunst von Le Corbusier. Durch die im Vordergrund gerade noch erkennbare Bahnanlage wurde die Planung des Baukomplexes stark beeinträchtigt.
2. Der Haupteingang auf der Ostseite. Links die durch vertikale Betonstreben akzentuierte Fassade des Ausstellungsraumes, an die sich die vom Boden bis zur Decke verglasten Wandflächen des zwei Geschosse hohen Foyers anschließen. Das aufgewölbte Dach des Gebäudes ruht auf den schweren Betonstützen der Skelettkonstruktion, der ein Raster von 10 m zugrunde liegt.

154

3. View from the terrace of the Museum of Western Art on the north side and roof landscape of the Festival Hall. Unfortunately, the fencing of the museum zone, not envisaged by Le Corbusier, spoils the spatial and architectural inter-relation of the different buildings.

4. The sculpture garden, designed by Masayuki Nagare, is placed on a gentle south slope and reached from the upper foyer of the conference room. On the left the 69 ft. high stage tower, next to it the large concert and theatre hall. On the right, the roof platform is overtowered by the peculiarly shaped roof of the smaller auditorium.

5. The foyer of the large concert hall at ground floor level (with the western main entrance in the background) is connected with the upper foyer by a ramp. The floor is patterned by stone strips and multi-coloured triangular tiles so that carpet-like bays are formed. The irregularly arranged point lamps on the ceiling form a 'milky way' diagonally across the room.

3. Blick von der Terrasse des Museums für westliche Kunst auf Nordfassade und Dachlandschaft der Festhalle. Die von Le Corbusier nicht vorgesehene Einzäunung des Museumsbereiches unterbricht leider die räumliche und bauliche Beziehung der Gebäude zueinander.

4. Vom oberen Foyer vor dem Konferenzsaal aus erreicht man den von Masayuki Nagare gestalteten Skulpturengarten, der nach Süden leicht abfällt. Links der 21 m hohe Bühnenturm, anschließend der große Saal. Aus der Plattform steigt rechts das Schanzendach des kleinen Auditoriums auf.

5. Das Foyer des großen Saales im Erdgeschoß (im Hintergrund der westliche Haupteingang), das mit dem oberen Foyer durch eine Rampe verbunden ist. Der Fußboden ist durch eingelassene Steinstreifen und verschiedenfarbige Dreieckplättchen so gegliedert, daß teppichartige Felder entstehen. Die unregelmäßig verteilten Punktstrahler zeichnen eine diagonal durch den Raum führende »Milchstraße« an die Decke.

6. First floor plan. Key: 1 ramp leading to conference room, 2 upper foyer of conference room, 3 conference room, 4 lowerable orchestra pit, 5 gallery restaurant, 6 office, 7 gallery, 8 projection, 9 floodlights, 10 air space above the large hall, 11 air space above the stage, 12 sculpture garden (forming a terrace in front of the conference room foyer), 13 air space above the foyer of the large hall, 14 air space above entrance hall, 15 cloak room of the conference hall.

7. Ground floor plan. Key: 1 entrance hall, 2 display room, 3 lowerable stage of conference hall, 4 stage entrance, 5 office, 6 management reception room, 7 foyer of the large hall, 8 terrace facing the large foyer, 9 cloak room, 10 large hall, 11 floodlights, 12 lighting control, 13 stage tower, 14 side stage, 15 rehearsal room.

8. The smaller auditorium is mainly used for conferences. The translators' cabins are placed inside the concrete walls designed by Masayuki Nagare and are provided with narrow peep-holes towards the hall. The folded acoustic screen in the rear of the stage, consisting of matt-finished metal plates, looks like a modern sculpture.

9. Interior of the large theatre and concert hall. In keeping with acoustic requirements, the suspended ceiling units can be adjusted. The seat covers, uni-coloured in the centre of the hall, are held in brighter shades on the seats nearer the walls. The walls on either side are, up to the fourth tier, covered with sculptured wooden decorations, created by Ryokichi Mukai.

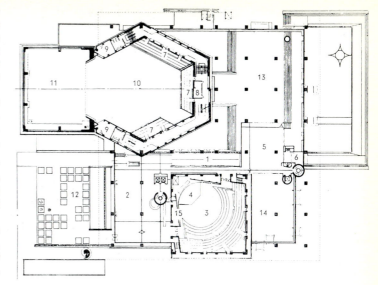

6. Grundriß des 1. Obergeschosses. Legende: 1 Rampe zum Konferenzsaal, 2 Oberes Foyer vor dem Konferenzsaal, 3 Konferenzsaal, 4 Versenkbares Orchesterpodium, 5 Galerierestaurant, 6 Büro, 7 Galerie, 8 Projektion, 9 Scheinwerfer, 10 Luftraum über dem großen Saal, 11 Luftraum über der Bühne, 12 Skulpturengarten (Terrasse vor dem Foyer des Konferenzsaales), 13 Luftraum über dem Foyer vor dem großen Saal, 14 Luftraum über der Eingangshalle, 15 Garderobe des Konferenzsaals.

7. Grundriß des Erdgeschosses. Legende: 1 Eingangshalle, 2 Ausstellungsraum, 3 Versenkbühne des Konferenzsaals, 4 Künstlereingang, 5 Büro, 6 Empfangsraum der Direktion, 7 Foyer des großen Saals, 8 Terrasse vor dem großen Foyer, 9 Garderobe, 10 Großer Saal, 11 Scheinwerfer, 12 Beleuchter, 13 Bühnenhaus, 14 Seitenbühne, 15 Proberaum.

8. Im kleineren Auditorium werden hauptsächlich Konferenzen abgehalten. Die Übersetzerkabinen sind in die von Masayuki Nagare gestalteten Betonwände eingelassen und haben schmale Sehschlitze zum Saal hin. Wie eine moderne Skulptur mutet der gefaltete Akustikschirm auf der Rückseite des Podiums an, der aus mattierten Metalltafeln besteht.

9. Blick in den großen Theater- und Konzertsaal. Den Erfordernissen der Akustik entsprechend können die abgehängten Deckenelemente verstellt werden. Die im Mittelfeld überwiegend einfarbig gehaltene Bestuhlung wird in den seitlichen Zonen durch hellere Bezüge unterbrochen. Über beide Seitenwände ziehen sich bis zum 4. Rang plastische Holzornamente, die aus der Werkstatt von Ryokichi Mukai stammen.

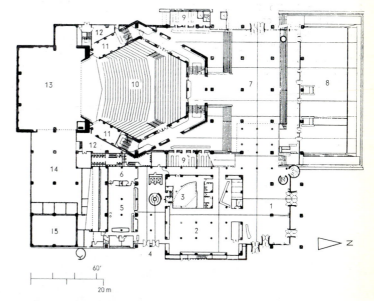

Saicho Otani

Municipal Children's Centre at Shibuya, Tokyo, 1961-63

In large cities, the opportunities for children to play and occupy themselves are constricted more and more by new buildings and traffic installations. The City of Tokyo therefore decided to create a Children's Centre which was designed, for the first time, to comply with an ambitious educational programme, requiring plenty of space. As the site in a residential zone available for this purpose was restricted, the building had to be developed in height. Functionally, the premises can be classified in five groups: (1) entrance hall, foyer and theatre, (2) exhibition rooms, (3) assembly rooms and classrooms for music and arts lessons, (4) laboratory and workshops, (5) administration.

These premises are spread over five upper floors and two basements and, being used for different purposes, have separate entrances. Adjacent to the entrance hall on the ground floor is the central staircase which can also be used as an extension of the theatre foyer. There is a separate entrance for the theatre hall which has 800 seats. The administrative offices are placed in a projecting south wing which likewise has its own entrance from the open porch. Another part of the building, placed on columns across forecourt and entrance hall, contains a large exhibition room, opening up towards a terrace on the south side. A good part of the third floor consists of a roof terrace so that the area above the theatre hall can be used as an open-air stage. Adjacent to the central staircase is a cafeteria. In the wing projecting above the entrance hall are library, classrooms and conference rooms. The top floors, which have a much reduced floor area, are taken up by further display rooms in conjunction with a studio and a music and records library. The building has a reinforced concrete framework with a column spacing of 25 ft. Because of the individual treatment accorded to the different parts of the building as regards orientation, lighting and proportions, the centre has become a highly differentiated ensemble. But its aesthetic integrity has been preserved by the leitmotif of the roof troughs whose sides are formed by vertically profiled concrete elements.

1. Entrance to the theatre hall. For acoustic reasons, walls and ceilings are divided into irregular panels.
2. With its portico extending through three storeys, the main entrance on the south side has a monumental effect. On the different levels, the individual wall-flanked troughs of varying width are conspicuous.

1. Blick auf den Eingang des Theatersaals. Wände und Decke sind aus akustischen Gründen in unregelmäßige Flächen gegliedert.
2. Der Haupteingang auf der Südseite bekommt durch das drei Stockwerke hohe Freigeschoß eine monumentale Wirkung. Auf den verschiedenen Ebenen sind die unterschiedlich breiten, seitlich geschlossenen Wannen gut zu erkennen.

3. Aerial view. It is from the staggered arrangement
of the different storeys that the building derives
its characteristic variegation. The roof terraces are
accessible and inter-connected by stairs.
4. Section and ground floor plan. Key: 1 open portico, 2 administration, 3 entrance hall, 4 theatre
foyer, 5 theatre hall, 6 stage, 7 passage.

3. Luftansicht. Durch Versetzen der einzelnen Geschosse erhält der Baukörper seine starke Gliederung. Die begehbaren Dachterrassen sind durch
Treppen miteinander verbunden.
4. Schnitt und Grundriß des Erdgeschosses. Legende: 1 Offene Vorhalle, 2 Verwaltung, 3 Eingangshalle, 4 Foyer des Theatersaals, 5 Theatersaal, 6 Bühne, 7 Passage.

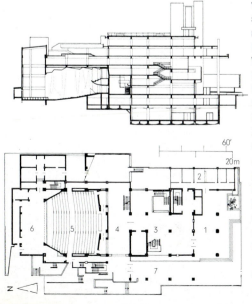

Städtisches Kinderzentrum in Shibuya, Tokio, 1961-63

Neubauten und ständig wachsende Verkehrsanlagen beschneiden den Aktions- und Spielraum
der Kinder in der Großstadt immer stärker. Die Stadt Tokio plante deshalb ein Kinderzentrum,
bei dem erstmalig ein pädagogisch und räumlich gleich umfassendes Programm verwirklicht
werden sollte. Da nur ein relativ beschränkter Bauplatz in einem Wohngebiet zur Verfügung
stand, mußte das Gebäude vertikal entwickelt werden. Die Räume lassen sich ihrer Bestimmung nach in fünf Gruppen zusammenfassen: 1. Eingangshalle, Foyer und Theater, 2. Ausstellungsräume, 3. Versammlungs- und Unterrichtsräume für Musik und Zeichnen, 4. Labor und
Werkstätten, 5. Verwaltung. Diese Gruppen verteilen sich auf fünf Obergeschosse und zwei
Untergeschosse und haben wegen ihrer unabhängigen Nutzung jeweils separate Eingänge.
Im Erdgeschoß liegt im Anschluß an die Eingangshalle das zentrale Treppenhaus, das auch als
Erweiterung des Theaterfoyers benutzt werden kann. Der Theatersaal mit separatem Eingang
hat 800 Sitzplätze. In einem nach Süden herausgezogenen Vorbau, ebenfalls mit eigenem
Zugang von der offenen Vorhalle aus, ist die Verwaltung untergebracht. Ein Gebäudeteil, der
auf Stützen quer über dem Vorplatz und über der Eingangshalle steht, enthält einen großen
Ausstellungsraum, der sich auf eine Terrasse auf der Südseite öffnet. Das 3. Obergeschoß
ist zum guten Teil Dachterrasse; so wird die Fläche über dem Theatersaal als Freilichtbühne
benutzt. Eine Cafeteria liegt im Anschluß an die zentrale Treppe. In dem Teil, der über die
Eingangshalle vorkragt, sind Bibliothek, Unterrichts- und Konferenzräume untergebracht. Auf
die obersten Geschosse, deren Fläche stark reduziert ist, verteilen sich weitere Ausstellungsräume in Verbindung mit einem Atelier sowie ein Musik- und Schallplattenraum. Die Konstruktion besteht aus einem Stahlbetonskelett mit einem Achsmaß von 7,50 m. Aus der individuellen
Behandlung der einzelnen Raumeinheiten in bezug auf Lage, Belichtung und Proportion entstand ein stark differenzierter Baukörper, den jedoch das Leitmotiv der seitlich mit vertikal
profilierten Betonelementen geschlossenen Wannen formal zusammenfaßt.

Kunio Mayekawa & Associates

Kanagawa Youth Centre at Yokohama, 1961-62
Together with the concert hall and library built in 1954, the youth house forms a municipal centre which is accessible from a common entrance forum on the east side of the site. The Youth Centre is composed of a western part with the large diagonally placed multi-purpose auditorium and of a square eastern part which contains the smaller meeting and common rooms. A portico leads to the foyer of the hall which can accommodate 1,000 people and, being equipped with revolving stage, backstage wings and lowerable orchestra pit, is perfectly suited for theatrical performances. Outdoor stairs and a terrace lead to the entrance hall of the second part of the building, a large exhibition centre with a high ceiling which raises the upper floors to a level above the auditorium. On the second and third floors are meeting and lecture rooms, offices and a planetarium; on the roof terrace are an observatory and a restaurant. The building materials differ with the different functions:— Auditorium and stage are tiled with clinkers whilst the block-shaped, enclosed meeting room building, where the deeply recessed loggias provide the only architectural feature, has a reinforced concrete structure with outer walls of untreated concrete.

Kanagawa-Jugendzentrum in Yokohama, 1961-62
Zusammen mit der 1954 gebauten Konzerthalle und Bibliothek bildet das Jugendhaus ein städtisches Zentrum, das über ein gemeinsames Zugangsforum auf der Ostseite des Grundstücks erschlossen wird. Das Jugendzentrum gliedert sich in den Westteil mit dem großen, übereck gestellten Mehrzwecksaal und den quadratischen Ostteil mit den kleineren Versammlungs- und Gemeinschaftsräumen. Ein überbauter Säulengang führt zum Foyer des Saales, der 1000 Zuschauer faßt und mit Drehbühne, Seitenbühnen und versenkbarem Orchestergraben perfekte Theateraufführungen erlaubt. Über Freitreppen und eine Außenterrasse erreicht man die Eingangshalle des zweiten Bauteils, einen großen, überhöhten Ausstellungsraum, der die Obergeschosse über den Theaterkomplex hochhebt. Das 2. und 3. Obergeschoß enthält Versammlungs- und Vortragsräume, Büros und ein Planetarium; auf der Dachterrasse stehen ein Observatorium und ein Restaurant. Entsprechend den unterschiedlichen Funktionen sind auch verschiedene Materialien verwendet: Saalbau und Bühnenturm wurden außen mit Klinkern verkleidet, während das blockhaft geschlossene Versammlungsgebäude, das nur durch tief eingekerbte Loggien gegliedert wird, als Stahlbetonbau nach außen schalungsrauh belassene Sichtbetonflächen zeigt.

1. General view from the east. In the background, left, the clinker-tiled auditorium. The ribbons of loggias in the four-storey block of the youth house (foreground) have the appearance of being milled into the concrete.

1. Gesamtansicht von Osten. Links hinten der mit Klinkern verkleidete Theaterbau. Am viergeschossigen Block des Jugendhauses (vorn) wirken die Bänder der Loggien wie eingefräst.

2. Pedestrians reach the Centre through the underpass below the drive which leads to the car park on the right.

3. Section, ground floor plan (bottom) and second floor plan. Key: 1 portico, 2 foyer, 3 cloak rooms, 4 side entrance with porter's lodge, 5 auditorium, 6 stage, 7 backstage wing, 8 restaurant, 9 flies, 10 hall, 11 youth welfare office, 12 library, 13 office, 14 hobby room, 15 preparation rooms and laboratories for working groups, 16 observatory, 17 restaurant, 18 exhibition room.

4. For acoustic reasons, the walls of the hexagonal multi-purpose auditorium are sub-divided into sharp-cornered strips and lined with sound-absorbing material.

2. Fußgänger erreichen das Zentrum durch die Unterführung, über die die Zufahrt zum Parkplatz rechts eine Brücke bildet.

3. Schnitt und Grundrisse des Erdgeschosses (unten) und des 2. Obergeschosses. Legende: 1 Überbauter Säulengang, 2 Foyer, 3 Garderobe, 4 Nebeneingang mit Pförtnerloge, 5 Zuschauerraum, 6 Bühne, 7 Seitenbühne, 8 Restaurant, 9 Bühnenturm, 10 Halle, 11 Jugendamt, 12 Bibliothek, 13 Büro, 14 Bastelraum, 15 Vorbereitungsräume und Labors für Arbeitsgruppen, 16 Observatorium, 17 Restaurant, 18 Ausstellungsraum.

4. Die Wände des im Grundriß sechseckigen Mehrzwecksaals sind aus akustischen Gründen in winklig gebrochene Streifen unterteilt und mit Schallschluckplatten verkleidet.

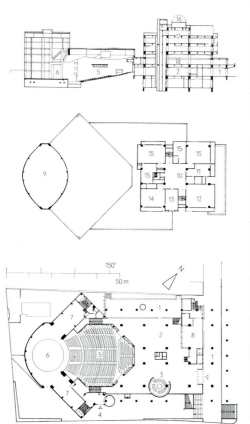

Masato Otaka & Associates

Cultural Centre of the Chiba District, 1964-67
This cultural centre of the Chiba District is being erected in the central area of the town on a site of some 123,800 sq. ft. Ultimately, the centre will comprise four parts: a 'Hall of Culture' (floor area 78,931 sq. ft.), a small building used mainly for wedding ceremonies (6,698 sq. ft.), a central library (21,291 sq. ft.) and a museum. The 'Hall of Culture' and the ceremonial building are already standing. The hall occupies the centre of the entire group and will serve as a link between ceremonial building and library by which it is flanked on either side across terraced plazas. Otaka's notion of 'group design' in architecture is here clearly evident. Instead of adopting the conventional distinction between interior decoration and facade design, he endeavours to design the human environment as an integrated whole. In this case, he tried to find a group design capable of expressing the activities of highly concentrated cultural life in a town. The entrance hall extends through the main building in the transverse direction and creates a link with both sides. Its central part is raised, thus adding a vertical extension. The foyers are placed on different levels and are likewise extended

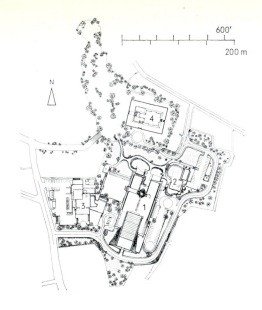

into the third dimension by open galleries leading to the balconies and loggias. The plan of the hall has a trapezoidal shape widening out towards the stage, which creates a highly dynamic impression. There is room for 1,800 people. On the other side of the entrance hall, opposite the foyer, are an exhibition room and a smaller lecture room for 250 people. Administrative offices and backstage rooms are spread over entrance floor and basement. On the first floor is a restaurant, connected with the foyer by a gallery. The concrete structure of the building is left exposed; the outer walls of the large hall consist of hyperbolic-paraboloid shells.

Bezirkskulturzentrum in Chiba, 1964-67

Dieses Zentrum, kultureller Mittelpunkt des Bezirks Chiba, steht in der Innenstadt auf einem rund 11 500 m² großen Grundstück. Im Endausbau wird es vier Teile umfassen: die Kulturhalle (überbaute Grundfläche 6 865 m²), das Gemeinschaftsgebäude, das vorwiegend für Hochzeitszeremonien verwendet wird (622 m²), die projektierte Zentralbibliothek (1 977 m²) und ein geplantes Museum. Im ersten Bauabschnitt wurden Kulturhalle und Gemeinschaftshaus gebaut. Die Halle liegt im Zentrum der Gesamtanlage und ist zugleich Bindeglied zwischen Gemeinschaftshaus und Bibliothek, die auf den beiden Längsseiten durch terrassierte Plätze an das Hauptgebäude angeschlossen werden. Otakas Idee von der »Gruppenform« in der Architektur wird hier sehr deutlich. Statt die klassische Unterscheidung zwischen Innenarchitektur und Fassadengestaltung zu machen, versucht er, die Umwelt des Menschen als Einheit zu gestalten. In diesem Fall war er bemüht, eine Gruppenform zu finden, die die Aktivität konzentrierten, kulturellen städtischen Lebens auszudrücken vermag. Die Eingangshalle durchdringt das Hauptgebäude in der Querrichtung und schafft eine Verbindung nach zwei Seiten. Durch ihr überhöhtes Mittelstück ist sie auch nach oben geöffnet. Das Foyer ist auf verschiedene Ebenen verteilt und wird durch offene, galerieartige Verbindungsgänge zu den Balkonen und Loggien ebenfalls in die dritte Dimension erweitert. Der Saal mit seiner im Grundriß trapezförmigen, im Raumeindruck sehr dynamisch wirkenden Form verbreitert sich zur Bühnenöffnung hin. Er bietet Platz für 1 800 Personen. Auf der anderen Seite der Eingangshalle, dem Foyer gegenüber, schließt sich ein Ausstellungsraum und ein kleiner Vortragssaal für 250 Personen mit Bühne an. Die Verwaltung und die Nebenräume der Bühnen sind über das Eingangsgeschoß und über das Untergeschoß verteilt. Das erste Obergeschoß nimmt ein Restaurant auf, das über eine Galerie mit dem Foyer verbunden ist. Die Bauten sind in Sichtbeton ausgeführt; die Außenwände des großen Saales bestehen aus HP-Schalen.

1. View from the north. Even the roof landscape illustrates Otaka's notion of an interrelated group design. The pyramid in the foreground forms the roof of the transverse entrance hall. The trapezoidal roof in the background is that of the large auditorium.
2. The cultural centre stands on a raised platform which, along the entrance drive to the car park from the south side, is supported by retaining walls. In the otherwise solid south wall of the auditorium is the stage entrance.
3. Site plan. Key: 1 hall of culture, 2 ceremonial building, 3 central library (planned), 4 museum (planned).
4. West entrance of the auditorium. The hyperbolic-paraboloid shells forming the walls of the auditorium have an external cladding of profiled concrete panels.

1. Ansicht von Norden. Auch die Dachlandschaft macht Otakas Idee von der sich durchdringenden Gruppenform deutlich. Im Vordergrund die Pyramide über der quer verlaufenden Eingangshalle, dahinter das trapezförmig ansteigende Dach des großen Saals.
2. Das erhöhte Plateau, auf dem das Kulturzentrum steht, wird nach Süden entlang der Zufahrtsstraße zu den Parkplätzen durch Stützmauern abgefangen. In der geschlossenen Südwand des Saalbaues der Bühneneingang.
3. Lageplan. Legende: 1 Kulturhalle, 2 Gemeinschaftsgebäude, 3 Geplante Zentralbibliothek, 4 Geplantes Museum.
4. Der Eingang zum großen Saal auf der Westseite. Die Wände des Saales aus HP-Schalen sind außen mit profilierten Betonplatten verkleidet.

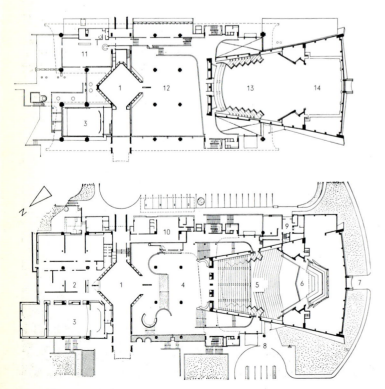

5. Split-level foyer of the auditorium. The skylight ribbon along the centre line meets the transverse axis of the entrance hall above the pyramid-shaped central concourse.
6. Ground floor plan (bottom) and first floor plan of the Hall of Culture. Key: 1 entrance hall with pyramid-shaped central concourse, 2 exhibition rooms, 3 small lecture room, 4 foyer, 5 main auditorium, 6 stage, 7 stage entrance, 8 drive and entrance of auditorium, 9 secondary entrance, artists' dressing rooms, and technical plant, 10 administration, 11 restaurant, 12 air space above foyer, 13 air space above auditorium, 14 flies.

5. Das auf zwei Ebenen verteilte Foyer vor dem großen Saal. Das Oberlichtband in der Längsachse führt auf die Querachse der Eingangshalle mit dem pyramidenförmigen Zentralraum.
6. Grundrisse von Erdgeschoß (unten) und 1. Obergeschoß der Kulturhalle. Legende: 1 Eingangshalle mit pyramidenförmiger Erweiterung, 2 Ausstellungsräume, 3 Kleiner Vortragssaal, 4 Foyer, 5 Zuschauerraum des großen Saals, 6 Bühne, 7 Bühneneingang, 8 Vorfahrt und Eingang zum großen Saal, 9 Nebeneingang, Künstlergarderoben und technische Räume, 10 Verwaltung, 11 Restaurant, 12 Luftraum über Foyer, 13 Luftraum über Zuschauerraum, 14 Bühnenhaus.

7. Entrance plaza on the west side.
8. Longitudinal section. Key: 1 pyramid-shaped concourse in the centre of the entrance hall, 2 exhibition room, 3 foyer, 4 large auditorium, 5 stage, 6 stage entrance, 7 machinery, 8 electrical plant.
9. Above the rising stalls of the auditorium are two rows of eight-seat boxes which extend over the entire width of the hall, growing organically out of the wall.
10. The projecting, almost window-less upper floor of the ceremonial building contains the rooms for the wedding rites. In contrast, the lower floor has full-height windows and is therefore, but for the high and narrow diaphragms supporting the upper floor, kept largely transparent.

7. Die Plaza vor dem Haupteingang auf der Westseite.
8. Längsschnitt. Legende: 1 Pyramidenförmige Erweiterung der Eingangshalle, 2 Ausstellungsraum, 3 Foyer, 4 Großer Saal, 5 Bühne, 6 Bühneneingang, 7 Maschinenraum, 8 Elektrozentrale.
9. Im großen Saal folgen zwei Ränge dem ansteigenden Gestühl des Parketts. Die Rangbalkone, die über die ganze Breite des Saales gehen, sind zu Einheiten mit je 8 Plätzen zusammengefaßt und wachsen organisch aus der Wandscheibe in den Saal hinein.
10. Im auskragenden, nahezu fensterlosen Obergeschoß des Gemeinschaftsgebäudes liegen der Zeremonienraum und Nebenräume für die Hochzeitszeremonie. Das Unterteil zwischen den schmalen, hohen Stützscheiben ist verglast und weitgehend transparent gehalten.

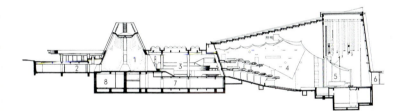

Sachio Otani

International Conference Centre near Kyoto, 1963-66
Asia's largest conference centre, designed for international congresses of all kinds, is situated in a magnificent, virgin landscape to the north of Kyoto. Using a carefully planned classification of the premises, the architect developed a basic element consisting of three zones. Each of these elements is a functionally self-contained unit consisting of a conference hall, with ancillary rooms along the side, and offices above. An optional number of these units can be arranged in longitudinal or transverse juxtaposition. This gave rise to a geometrical system of upright and inverse trapezoids and triangles on a rectangular plan. The basic units — vestibule, large conference room, small conference room — are of different size, though otherwise identical, and are combined in a 'cluster'. The large hall in the centre of the entrance floor extends through three storeys, with numerous galleries. The adjacent large conference hall for 2,000 people is yet another storey higher and can be reached from all four levels. On the first floor level are three smaller conference rooms for 550, 170 and 100 people, respectively; they, too, extend through three storeys. On the fourth floor are the administrative offices, on the fifth floor the offices of the delegates. Linked to the entrance hall at basement level is a large banqueting hall. The load-bearing structure of this extremely variegated and strongly textured building consists of a steel framework clad with strong pre-cast reinforced concrete units.

1. South-west elevation. The group of buildings is staggered vertically and horizontally and faces a large artificial lake.
2. View from south-east. In the foreground, right, the solid gable wall of the large conference hall; on the left, the glass-curtained single-storey building with the rooms of the delegations.

1. Südwestansicht der sich in der Höhe und Tiefe staffelnden Bauanlage, vor der sich ein großer künstlicher See ausbreitet.
2. Ansicht von Südosten. Vorn rechts der geschlossene Giebel des großen Konferenzsaales, links der verglaste, eingeschossige Gebäudeteil mit den Delegationsräumen.

Internationales Konferenzzentrum bei Kyoto, 1963-66
Das größte Konferenzzentrum Asiens, in dem internationale Kongresse aller Art abgehalten werden, liegt nördlich von Kyoto in einer nahezu unberührten, großartigen Landschaft. Der Architekt entwickelte mit Hilfe einer sorgfältigen Klassifizierung der Räume ein dreizoniges Grundelement. Dieses bildet eine jeweils funktionell selbständige Raumgruppe, die aus Konferenzsaal, seitlichen Bedienungszellen und darüberliegenden Büros besteht und in der Länge wie in der Breite beliebig oft addiert werden kann. Auf diese Weise entstand ein geometrisches System aus stehenden und liegenden Trapezen und Dreiecken mit rechtwinkligem Grundriß. Die gleichartigen, aber verschieden großen Grundeinheiten — Vorhalle, großes Konferenzelement, kleines Konferenzelement — sind zu einem »Cluster« zusammengefaßt. Die große zentrale Halle im Mittelpunkt des Eingangsgeschosses entwickelt sich mit zahlreichen eingeschobenen Galerien über drei Stockwerke. Der sich ihr anschließende große Konferenzsaal für 2 000 Personen ist noch ein Geschoß höher und kann von allen vier Geschossen aus erreicht werden. Auf dem Niveau des 1. Obergeschosses liegen drei kleinere Konferenzsäle mit 550, 170 und 100 Plätzen; auch sie reichen durch drei Geschosse. Im 4. Obergeschoß sind die Räume für die Verwaltung, im 5. Obergeschoß die Büros der Delegierten untergebracht. Im Untergeschoß liegt im Zusammenhang mit der Eingangshalle ein großer Bankettsaal. Das tragende Gerippe des außerordentlich reich gegliederten und kräftig strukturierten Bauwerks besteht aus einer Stahlkonstruktion, die mit starken Stahlbeton-Fertigteilen ummantelt wurde.

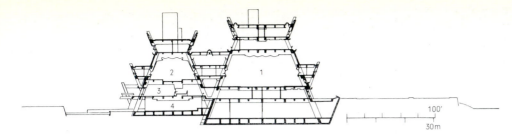

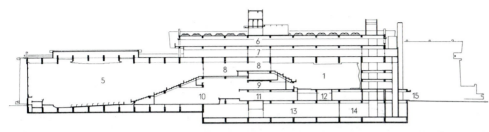

3. Cross-section and longitudinal section. Key: 1 conference room for 550 people, 2 conference room for 170 people, 3 conference room for 50 people, 4 banqueting hall, 5 large conference room for 2 000 people, 6 delegates' offices, 7 administration, 8 public lounge, 9 delegates' lounge, 10 central hall, 11 lobby, 12 kitchen, 13 air-conditioning, 14 heating, 15 staff entrance.
4. A view of the main wing which projects towards south-east.

3. Quer- und Längsschnitt. Legende: 1 Konferenzsaal für 550 Personen, 2 Konferenzsaal für 170 Personen, 3 Sitzungssaal für 50 Personen, 4 Bankettsaal, 5 Großer Konferenzsaal für 2000 Personen, 6 Büros der Delegierten, 7 Verwaltung, 8 Öffentlich zugängliche Lounge, 9 Lounge für Delegierte, 10 Zentrale Halle, 11 Lobby, 12 Küche, 13 Klimaanlage, 14 Heizung, 15 Eingang für das Personal.
4. Blick auf den nach Südosten vorspringenden Haupttrakt.

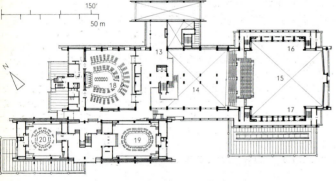

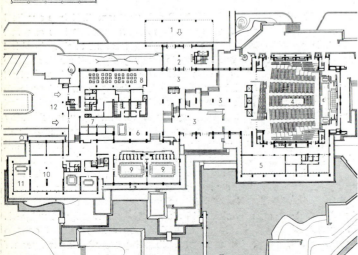

5. The strictly symmetric large conference room, conspicuously sub-divided by the trapezoidal structural frames, extends through four storeys. Along the walls on either side are the press rooms and translators' cabins.

6. Conference room for 550 people. Its walls and ceiling show a variety of design elements. Direct and indirect lighting is provided by fluorescent lamps, glass spheres and spotlights.

7. Ground floor plan (bottom) and first floor plan. Key: 1 entrance for delegations, 2 vestibule, 3 central hall, 4 large conference room for 2,000 people, 5 delegates' offices, 6 exhibition zone, 7 information, 8 cafeteria, 9 conference room, 10 administration, 11 management, 12 auxiliary entrance to the smaller conference rooms, 13 access gallery, 14 air space above the central hall, 15 air space above the large conference room, 16 press room, 17 translators' cabin, 18 conference room for 550 people, 19 conference room for 170 people, 20 conference room for 100 people.

8. Foyer of the large conference room, facing the lake. The different levels are reached by ramps and stairs. On the left, the gallery at first floor level.

5. Der streng axial angelegte, große Konferenzsaal, den die trapezförmigen Rahmenträger deutlich gliedern, zieht sich durch vier Geschosse. Rechts und links an den Außenwänden die Kabinen für Presse und Simultanübersetzer.
6. Der Konferenzsaal für 550 Personen, der im Wand- und Deckenbereich eine Vielfalt von Gestaltungselementen zeigt und durch Leuchtröhren, Kugelleuchten und Punktstrahler direkt und indirekt beleuchtet wird.
7. Grundriß von Erdgeschoß (unten) und 1. Obergeschoß. Legende: 1 Eingang für Delegationen, 2 Vorhalle, 3 Zentrale Halle, 4 Großer Konferenzsaal für 2000 Personen, 5 Räume für Delegierte, 6 Ausstellungsbereich, 7 Information, 8 Cafeteria, 9 Sitzungszimmer, 10 Verwaltung, 11 Direktion, 12 Nebeneingang zu den kleineren Konferenzsälen, 13 Erschließungsgalerie, 14 Luftraum über der zentralen Halle, 15 Luftraum über dem großen Konferenzsaal, 16 Pressekabinen, 17 Übersetzerkabinen, 18 Konferenzsaal für 550 Personen, 19 Konferenzsaal für 170 Personen, 20 Konferenzsaal für 100 Personen.
8. Blick in das nach der Seeseite orientierte Foyer vor dem großen Konferenzsaal, dessen verschiedene Niveaus durch Rampen und Treppen erschlossen werden; links die Galerie im 1. Obergeschoß.

Takeo Satow & Associates

Town Hall and Cultural Centre of the Kotow District, Tokyo, 1965
Town hall and community centre form an L-shaped group of buildings at the edge of a park.
The two zones are linked by the open entrance hall which extends through the full height of
the building and also serves as a passage from the town hall square to the park at the back.
Both buildings stand on a platform which is one storey above ground level. Broad flights
of stairs lead up to the entrance hall level on either side. The foyer of the administration
wing is slightly retracted, leaving a passage between the entrance hall and the terrace on the
narrow north side of the building. From this platform, the municipal offices of the first and
second floor are reached by an open flight of stairs. The multi-purpose room, extending
through the full height and width of the south wing, has accommodation for 1,200 persons.
Through the entrance portico, one enters the foyer which likewise extends through the full
height of the building and is linked by stairs with the different tiers. The faces of the
reinforced concrete framework still show the marks of the shuttering. Some of the walls
have a brick in-filling. Despite its considerable size, the entire group conveys an elegant and
light impression which is enhanced by the isolated pilotis in the ground floor, by the conspicuous
gap created by the entrance portico and by the transparency of the sun louvres which form
a fine-meshed concrete grille in front of the curtain walls on the west side.

Rathaus und Kulturzentrum des Stadtteils Kotow in Tokio, 1965
Rathaus und Gemeindezentrum bilden eine L-förmige Baugruppe am Rande eines Parks. Die
beiden Bereiche sind durch die offene, gebäudehohe Eingangshalle miteinander verbunden; sie
dient auch als Durchgang vom Rathausplatz zu dem auf der Rückseite des Zentrums gelegenen
Park. Der plattformartige Sockel für beide Bauten ist gegenüber dem umliegenden Gelände um
Stockwerkshöhe angehoben. Breite Treppen führen auf beiden Seiten zum Niveau der Eingangshalle hinauf. Das Foyer des Verwaltungstrakts wurde etwas zurückgenommen; so entsteht ein
Verbindungsgang zwischen der Eingangshalle und der Terrasse auf der nördlichen Schmalseite
des Baues. Von diesem Podest aus erreicht man über eine frei stehende Treppe die städtischen
Ämter im 1. und 2. Obergeschoß. Der Mehrzwecksaal, der die volle Höhe und Breite des Süd-
flügels ausfüllt, faßt 1 200 Personen. Durch den Eingangsportikus betritt man das ebenfalls
gebäudehohe Foyer, von dem aus Treppen zu den verschiedenen Rängen führen. Die Sichtflächen der Stahlbeton-Skelettkonstruktion wurden schalungsrauh belassen. Die Wände sind zum
Teil mit Ziegelmauerwerk ausgefacht. Trotz seiner beträchtlichen Dimensionen wirkt der ganze
Komplex feingliedrig und leicht, ein Eindruck, zu dem die frei stehenden Pilotis im Erdgeschoß
ebenso beitragen wie das Aufreißen des Baukörpers durch den Eingangsportikus und die
Transparenz der Sonnengrills, die als feinmaschige Betongitter vor die Glaswände der Westseite
gesetzt sind.

1. West side, seen from the park. The sun protection louvres are interrupted for the roof terrace
above the administration wing. The horizontality
of the building is further emphasized by the slender campanile.
2. A view of the monumental open portico. A restaurant, accessible from two gangways, is placed
like a box between the two wings. The spiral
stairs on the left lead to the first floor.

1. Westansicht von der Seite des Parks aus. Die
Sonnenschutzlamellen sind im Bereich der Dachterrasse über dem Verwaltungstrakt unterbrochen.
Der schlanke Uhrturm, der wie ein Campanile abseits steht, läßt den Betrachter die Horizontalität
des Zentrums noch deutlicher wahrnehmen.
2. Blick in die monumentale, offene Eingangshalle.
Über zwei Verbindungsstege ist ein Restaurant
kastenartig zwischen die beiden Baukörper eingefügt. Die Wendeltreppe links führt zum 1. Obergeschoß.

3. Entrance portico, seen from the east. The pavement consists of concrete-embedded gravel. On the left, the entrance to the foyer of the hall; on top, the strong supporting structure of the restaurant suspended at first floor level.

3. Die Eingangshalle von Osten. Der Bodenbelag besteht aus in Beton eingegossenen Naturkieseln. Links der Eingang zum Foyer des Saales, am oberen Bildrand die kräftige Unterkonstruktion des im 1. Geschoß eingehängten Restaurants.

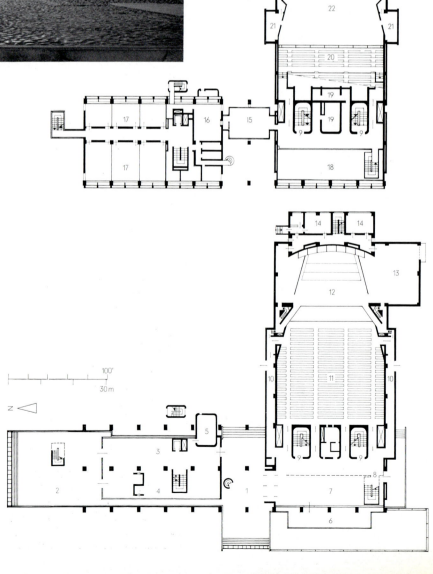

4. Ground floor plan (bottom) and first floor plan. Key: 1 entrance portico and passage, 2 north terrace, 3 lobby of administration wing, 4 cafeteria, 5 office, 6 terrace, 7 foyer, 8 stairs leading to lower tier, 9 stairs leading to upper tier, 10 side passage to stalls and proscenium, 11 stalls, 12 stage, 13 backstage wing, 14 rigging rooms, 15 restaurant, 16 kitchen, 17 conference rooms, 18 air space above foyer, 19 W. C., 20 lower tier, 21 lighting and sound control cabin, 22 air space above stalls, 23 air space above stage, 24 air space above backstage wing, 25 artists' dressing rooms and stores.

4. Grundrisse von Erdgeschoß (unten) und 1. Obergeschoß. Legende: 1 Eingangsportikus und Passage, 2 Nordterrasse, 3 Eingangshalle des Verwaltungsflügels, 4 Cafeteria, 5 Büro, 6 Terrasse, 7 Foyer, 8 Treppe zum ersten Rang, 9 Treppen zum zweiten Rang, 10 Seitengang zum Parkett und Bühnenhaus, 11 Parkett, 12 Bühne, 13 Seitenbühne, 14 Vorbereitungsräume, 15 Restaurant, 16 Küche, 17 Versammlungsräume, 18 Luftraum über Foyer, 19 WC, 20 Erster Rang, 21 Beleuchter- und Tonkabine, 22 Luftraum über dem Parterre-Zuschauerraum, 23 Luftraum über der Bühne, 24 Luftraum über der Seitenbühne, 25 Künstlergarderoben und Lager.

5. The comparatively narrow foyer of the multi-purpose hall is visually extended by the full-height glass curtain wall. The isolated stairs at the rear end lead to the balcony facing the lower tier. The upper tier is reached via the enclosed stairwell on the left. Access to the lighting control cabins is from the third floor balcony.

6. Interior of the auditorium. The curved faces of the suspended acoustic ceiling, together with the underview of the lower tiers, form a predominant design feature which contrasts with the block-shaped, strongly chiselled concrete walls. The indirect lighting is derived from light fittings built into the sides. The relief effect of the walls is further enhanced by the alternation of light and shade.

5. Das verhältnismäßig schmale Foyer vor dem Mehrzwecksaal wird durch die raumhohe Außenverglasung optisch erweitert. Die frei stehende Treppe an der hinteren Schmalseite führt zum Balkon vor dem 1. Rang. Der Zugang zum 2. Rang liegt in den geschlossenen Treppenkernen links. Vom Balkon im 3. Obergeschoß aus sind die Beleuchterkabinen zugänglich.

6. Teilansicht des Saales. Die geschwungenen Flächen der abgehängten Akustikdecke bilden zusammen mit der Untersicht des 1. Ranges ein bestimmendes gestalterisches Moment, das im Gegensatz steht zu den blockhaft gegliederten Wänden aus Beton, der mit dem Meißel stark genarbt wurde. Der Saal wird durch seitlich eingebaute Lichtquellen indirekt beleuchtet; die reliefhafte Wirkung der Wände wird durch die Licht- und Schattenmodulation noch gesteigert.

Kunio Mayekawa & Associates

Setagaya Community Centre and Town Hall at Tokyo, 1958-60

The Setagaya Centre, built in two stages, is an important example for the relatively frequent type of building where the town hall of an administrative district is combined with the local cultural and community centre — a dual function which is generally also expressed in the design of the building. The Setagaya Centre is situated in a densely populated district and has a trapezoidal plan which is bordered by streets on all four sides. In sheer size, the multi-purpose auditorium with 1,326 seats is the largest part of the group. Adjoining it southwards and northwards is a T-shaped two-storey wing containing a small assembly hall, library, restaurant and offices. The second stage of the programme comprised the erection of the town hall proper which stands on the narrow northern side of the plot. In the centre of this square five-storey building is a large patio from which an open flight of stairs leads to the first floor gallery. The Council Chamber is on the fourth floor. A joint entrance forum is formed by a large piazza, half-a-storey above street level, which is surrounded by the buildings of the centre on three sides. Exposed reinforced concrete has been consistently used both inside and outside the buildings.

2. Town hall, seen from the auditorium. At the edge of the depressed courtyard, a ramp leads to the low-level car parks. The piazza is decorated with a pavement pattern of stone setts and concrete flags, forming stripes and squares.

2. Blick vom Saalbau auf das Rathaus. Am Rand des vertieften Hofes führt eine Rampe zu den Parkplätzen im Untergeschoß. Der Platz ist mit Natursteinen und Betonplatten in Streifen und Quadrate unterteilt.

Setagaya-Gemeinschaftszentrum und Rathaus in Tokio, 1958-60

Das Setagaya-Zentrum, in zwei Bauphasen entstanden, ist ein wichtiges Beispiel für den verhältnismäßig häufigen Bautyp, bei dem das Rathaus eines Verwaltungsbezirks mit einem lokalen Kultur- und Gemeinschaftszentrum kombiniert wird — eine Doppelfunktion, die sich meist auch in der Gebäudeform ausdrückt. Das Setagaya-Zentrum liegt in einem dicht bevölkerten Stadtteil auf trapezförmigem Grundstück, das auf allen vier Seiten von Straßen begrenzt wird. Der Baukörper des Mehrzwecksaales mit 1326 Sitzplätzen ist von der Baumasse her das größte Gebäude der Anlage. Ihm schließt sich nach Süden und Norden ein zweigeschossiger, T-förmiger Querbau an, in dem ein kleiner Versammlungssaal, Bibliothek, Restaurant und Büroräume untergebracht sind. Als zweiter Bauabschnitt wurde das Rathaus an der nördlichen Schmalseite des Grundstücks errichtet. Im Mittelpunkt dieses fünfgeschossigen Gebäudes, das einen quadratischen Grundriß hat, liegt ein großer Lichthof; von hier aus führt eine Freitreppe zur Galerie des 1. Obergeschosses. Im 4. Obergeschoß befindet sich der Sitzungssaal. Eine ausgedehnte Platzanlage, die auf drei Seiten von den Gebäuden des Zentrums umschlossen wird, bildet das gemeinsame, gegenüber Straßenniveau um ein halbes Geschoß erhöht liegende Eingangsforum. Die Gebäude wurden einheitlich innen und außen aus sichtbar belassenem Stahlbeton ausgeführt. 174

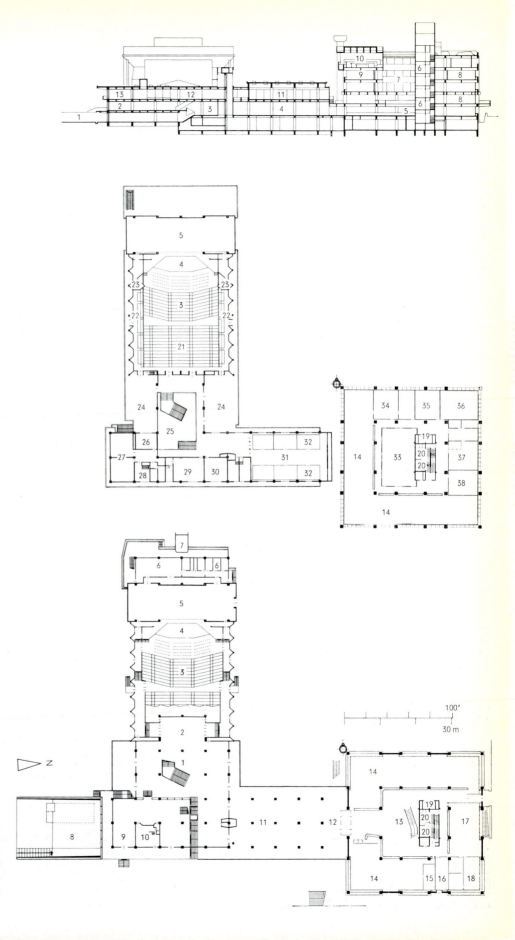

1. General view. Auditorium (left) and town hall are of the same height, but differ greatly in their architectural design. The solid outer walls of the auditorium are accentuated by vertical ribs whilst the town hall facade is sub-divided by horizontal window ribbons. The integrating element is the connecting wing which has a horizontal emphasis.

1. Gesamtansicht. Das Saalgebäude (links) und das Rathaus haben dieselbe Höhe. Die architektonische Gestaltung beider Bauten unterscheidet sich stark. Die geschlossenen Außenwände des Saales sind durch die Auffaltung der Wand senkrecht gegliedert, die Fassaden des Rathauses werden durch waagerechte Fensterbänder unterteilt. Der betont horizontale Verbindungsbau bewirkt den städtebaulichen Zusammenschluß.

3. North-south section. Key: 1 garden, 2 restaurant, 3 foyer, 4 open connecting passage, 5 town hall concourse, 6 W. C., 7 patio, 8 office, 9 assembly hall, 10 council chamber, 11 exhibition room, 12 administration, 13 banqueting hall.
4. Ground floor plan (bottom), first floor plan of auditorium (centre, left), and third floor plan of town hall (centre, right). Key: 1 foyer, 2 cloak room, 3 front stalls, 4 orchestra pit, 5 stage, 6 artists' dressing rooms, 7 ventilation shaft, 8 garden, 9 restaurant, 10 kitchen, 11 covered passageway, 12 porch, 13 public concourse, 14 municipal offices, 15 archives, 16 waiting room, 17 cashier, 18 accountancy department, 19 lift, 20 W. C., 21 rear stalls, 22 gallery, 23 lighting control cabin, 24 terrace, 25 air space of auditorium, 26 room for wedding ceremonies, 27 banqueting hall, (Japanese and European), 28 kitchen, 29 administration, 30 discussion room, 31 exhibition room, 32 assembly hall, 33 patio, 34 executive, 35 film room, 36 conference room, 37 telephone switchboard, 38 post room.

3. Schnitt in Nord-Süd-Richtung. Legende: 1 Garten, 2 Restaurant, 3 Foyer, 4 Offener Verbindungsgang, 5 Rathaushalle, 6 WC, 7 Lichthof, 8 Büro, 9 Versammlungsraum, 10 Ratssaal, 11 Ausstellungsraum, 12 Verwaltung, 13 Festraum.
4. Grundrisse von Erdgeschoß (unten), 1. Obergeschoß des Saalbaues (Mitte links) und 3. Obergeschoß des Rathauses (Mitte rechts). Legende: 1 Foyer, 2 Garderobe, 3 Vorderer Sperrsitz, 4 Orchestergraben, 5 Bühne, 6 Schauspielergarderoben, 7 Ventilationsschacht, 8 Garten, 9 Restaurant, 10 Küche, 11 Überdeckter Verbindungsgang, 12 Windfang, 13 Rathaushalle, Publikumsbereich, 14 Bürozone, 15 Archiv, 16 Warteraum, 17 Kasse, 18 Buchhaltung, 19 Aufzug, 20 WC, 21 Hinterer Sperrsitz, 22 Galerie, 23 Beleuchterkabine, 24 Terrasse, 25 Luftraum Halle, 26 Hochzeitsraum, 27 Festraum (japanisch und europäisch), 28 Küche, 29 Verwaltung, 30 Diskussionsraum, 31 Ausstellungsraum, 32 Versammlungsraum, 33 Lichthof, 34 Abteilungsleiter, 35 Filmraum, 36 Konferenzraum, 37 Telefonzentrale, 38 Postraum.

5. The main stairs in the town hall patio lead to the first floor gallery. The piazza pavement extends into the vestibule.

6. A view from the forum towards the 65 ft. high town hall and the two-storey connecting wing to the south of it. The council chamber projecting from the fourth floor is supported by five main girders and covered by a heavy roof slab. The chimney at the south-west corner of the building provides a strong sculptural accent.

7. One of the open-plan offices. The only separation between the office space and the public concourse is formed by counters which follow the alignment of the inner columns.

5. Die Haupttreppe im Lichthof des Rathauses führt zur Galerie im 1. Obergeschoß. Der Bodenbelag des Platzes ist bis in die Eingangshalle hineingezogen.

6. Ansicht vom Forumsplatz auf das 20 m hohe Rathaus und den nach Süden anschließenden, zweigeschossigen Verbindungsbau. Im 4. Obergeschoß kragt der auf fünf Tragbalken auflagernde und mit einer schweren Dachplatte gedeckte Sitzungssaal aus. Der Kamin an der Südwestecke des Gebäudes bildet einen starken plastischen Akzent.

7. Blick in ein Großraumbüro. Die Räume sind nur durch die Theken, die in der Flucht der Innenstützen stehen, vom Publikumsbereich getrennt.

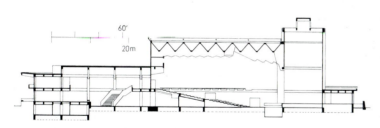

8. Due to the ribs, it was possible to construct the outer walls of the auditorium as relatively thin concrete structures without columns or girders. In order to improve the acoustics, the suspended ceiling is divided into separate stripes.
9. Longitudinal section of foyer and auditorium.
10. North side of the multi-purpose auditorium. The pavement of the forum between the three buildings is an alternation of large concrete flags and small stone sett paving. With this decorative pattern, the monumental concrete facade of the auditorium is greatly enlivened.

8. Durch die Auffaltung konnten die Außenwände des Saalgebäudes in relativ dünner Betonkonstruktion ohne Stützen und Unterzüge ausgeführt werden. Um die Akustik zu verbessern, ist die abgehängte Decke in Streifenelemente unterteilt.
9. Längsschnitt durch Foyer und Theatersaal.
10. Nordansicht des Mehrzwecksaales. Der Forumsplatz zwischen den drei Baukörpern ist abwechselnd mit großformatigen Betonplatten und Kleinpflaster belegt. Diese ornamentale Gliederung wirkt sehr lebendig vor der monumentalen Betonfassade des Saales.

Community Centre of the Saitama District, Urawa, 1963-66

The Community Centre is the cultural as well as administrative centre of the Saitama District. It comprises three buildings, arranged in accordance with their importance and size. The group is dominated by the nine-storey office tower, placed at the lowest point of the site. The large auditorium with 1,500 seats and a stage suitable for all kinds of events stands on the highest point. As it was not possible to combine the two auditoriums in one group, the smaller one for 500 people which is mainly used for lectures and meetings was placed between the pre-existing library and the office tower. The whole group is visually integrated by terraced piazzas on two levels. The first terrace is placed one storey above main road level and forms an entrance forum for the foyers of the auditoriums. The second terrace above the foyers is a large yet intimate piazza, flanked by buildings but open towards south and east. Two of the three sub-surface floors contain rehearsal rooms for the auditoriums as well as exhibition and store rooms whilst the lowest basement serves as a garage. The office tower houses the district administration. It also contains, on the third to sixth floors, meeting rooms which are available to clubs and associations. The structure is one of steel and reinforced concrete, the outer walls have a clinker cladding. The clinker pavement of the piazzas form various decorative patterns.

Gemeinschaftszentrum des Bezirks Saitama in Urawa, 1963-66

Das Gemeinschaftszentrum ist der kulturelle Mittelpunkt des Bezirks Saitama und Sitz der Verwaltung. Es umfaßt drei Gebäude, die ihrer Bedeutung und Größe entsprechend angeordnet wurden. Der Büroturm mit neun Geschossen steht dominierend an der tiefsten Stelle des Geländes. Das große Auditorium, mit 1 500 Plätzen und einer für Veranstaltungen aller Art geeigneten Bühneneinrichtung, wurde auf der höchsten Stelle plaziert. Da man beide Saalbauten nicht zusammenlegen konnte, wurde das kleine Auditorium mit 500 Plätzen, das besonders für Vorträge und Versammlungen benutzt wird, zwischen der bereits bestehenden Bibliothek und dem Büroturm angeordnet. Um alle Gebäude zusammenzufassen, legte der Architekt auf zwei Ebenen platzartige Terrassen an. Die erste Terrasse liegt ein Geschoß über dem Niveau der Hauptstraße und bildet das Eingangsforum vor den Foyers der Auditorien. Die zweite Terrasse über den Foyers ist ein großer, durch die Gebäude abgeschlossener, intimer Platz, der sich nach Süden und Osten öffnet. Die beiden oberen der drei unterirdischen Geschosse enthalten Übungsräume für die Auditorien sowie Ausstellungs- und Lagerräume, das dritte Untergeschoß dient als Tiefgarage. Im Büroturm ist die Bezirksverwaltung untergebracht. Außerdem enthält das 3. bis 6. Geschoß Versammlungsräume, die auch von Klubs und Vereinen benutzt werden. Die Konstruktion ist in Stahl und Stahlbeton ausgeführt, wobei die Außenwände mit Klinkern verblendet wurden. Die Plätze sind mit Klinkerplatten in verschiedenen Ornamenten belegt.

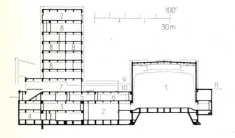

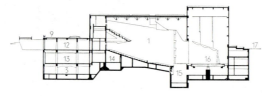

1. East-west section through office tower and large auditorium (left), and longitudinal section of the large auditorium. Key: 1 large auditorium, 2 machinery, 3 garage, 4 kitchen, 5 hall, 6 library, 7 foyer, small auditorium, 8 office and meeting rooms, 9 upper piazza, 10 lower piazza, 11 side street, 12 foyer, large auditorium, 13 exhibition room, 14 W. C., 15 orchestra pit, 16 stage, 17 main road.

1. Schnitt in Ost-West-Richtung durch Büroturm und großes Auditorium (links) und Längsschnitt durch den großen Saal. Legende: 1 Großes Auditorium, 2 Maschinenraum, 3 Garage, 4 Küche, 5 Halle, 6 Bibliothek, 7 Foyer kleines Auditorium, 8 Büro- und Versammlungsräume, 9 Oberer Terrassenplatz, 10 Unterer Terrassenplatz, 11 Seitenstraße, 12 Foyer großes Auditorium, 13 Ausstellungsraum, 14 WC, 15 Orchestergraben, 16 Bühne, 17 Hauptstraße.

2. View from the north. The nine-storey office tower provides a conspicuous landmark. A broad flight of stairs leads from the side street to upper piazza.
3. On the south side, the scene is dominated by the office tower and the solid cube of the stage tower. The balconies are formed by curved extensions of the floor slabs.
4. A view from the library across the terraced piazza on the town. Flanked by buildings, the piazzas seem to form intimate courtyards, an impression which is further enhanced by the islands of greenery with their stools.

2. Ansicht von Norden. Der neungeschossige Büroturm ist als Wahrzeichen des Zentrums weithin sichtbar. Eine breite Treppe führt von der Seitenstraße zur oberen Terrasse.
3. Auf der Südseite wird das Straßenbild bestimmt durch den Büroturm und den geschlossenen Kubus des Bühnenhauses. Die Kragplatten der Balkone entwickeln sich bogenförmig aus den Geschoßdecken.
4. Blick vom Bibliotheksgebäude über die Terrassen auf die Stadt. Durch den seitlichen Abschluß wirken die Terrassen wie intime Höfe, ein Eindruck, den die Grüninseln mit ihren Sitzplätzen noch steigern.

7. The foyer of the large auditorium is placed one storey below upper piazza level. Because of the heavy concentrated loads, the columns are reinforced by consoles.

8. Small auditorium. Behind the isolated side wall is the stage entrance. The rear wall is lined with acoustic boards with irregular, decoratively arranged recesses. The wall is illuminated by floodlights mounted in the ceiling which provide a strong relief effect.

9,10. Large auditorium. The continuity of walls and ceiling, which are lined with plastically moulded plywood, strikes a note of grandeur. The prismatic ridges of the wall lining not only serve to improve the acoustics but also to guide the light from the wall-mounted fittings upwards along the ceiling so as to emphasize the continuity of space. The front stalls can be removed so as to make way for a sunken orchestra pit which ends flush with the stage extensions on either side.

7. Das Foyer des großen Auditoriums im Geschoß unter der oberen Terrasse. Wegen der großen Deckenlasten sind die Stützen durch Konsolen verstärkt.

8. Das kleine Auditorium. Hinter der frei stehenden Seitenwand liegt der Zugang zur Bühne. Die Rückwand ist mit Akustikplatten verkleidet, aus denen in unregelmäßiger, dekorativer Gliederung Nischen ausgespart wurden. Die Wand wird von eingebauten Deckenleuchten angestrahlt und erhält dadurch ein starkes Relief.

9, 10. Das große Auditorium. Der Saal ist mit plastisch verformten Sperrholzplatten ausgekleidet. Die kontinuierliche plastische Durchformung von Wand und Decke schafft einen großzügigen Raumeindruck. Die prismatischen Stege der Wandverkleidung verbessern nicht nur die Akustik, sie leiten auch das Licht der Wandleuchten nach oben bis in die Decke hinein und unterstreichen so das Raumkontinuum. Die ersten Sitzreihen des Parketts können entfernt werden, so daß ein versenkter Orchestergraben entsteht, der bündig mit den seitlichen Vorderbühnen abschließt.

5. Night view of the upper piazza, seen from the north. The light from the fittings placed in wall-mounted concrete boxes radiates both upwards and downwards. In the green islands and flower troughs are mushroom-shaped lamps.

6. Entrance floor plan (left) and standard floor plan of the office tower, with layout plan (right). Key: 1 large auditorium, 2 stage, 3 backstage wing, 4 stores, 5 artists' dressing rooms, 6 lighting control cabin, 7 restaurant, 8 lift landing of office tower, 9 boiler room, 10 foyer, 11 entrance hall, 12 small auditorium, 13 podium, 14 projector cabin, 15 pool of water, 16 lower piazza, 17 standard floor of office tower, 18 upper piazza, 19 roof of small auditorium, 20 existing library.

5. Nachtaufnahme des oberen Terrassenplatzes von Norden. Die in Betonkästen eingebauten Beleuchtungskörper an den Mauern strahlen gleichzeitig nach unten und oben. Auf den Grüninseln und den Blumenkästen sind Pilzleuchten plaziert.

6. Grundrisse von Eingangsgeschoß (links) und Normalgeschoß, Büroturm mit Situationsplan (rechts). Legende: 1 Großes Auditorium, 2 Bühne, 3 Kulissen, 4 Lager, 5 Künstlergarderobe, 6 Beleuchter, 7 Restaurant, 8 Büroturm Aufzugshalle, 9 Heizung, 10 Foyer, 11 Eingangshalle, 12 Kleines Auditorium, 13 Podium, 14 Projektion, 15 Wasserbecken, 16 Unterer Terrassenplatz, 17 Büroturm Normalgeschoß, 18 Obere Terrasse, 19 Dachaufsicht kleines Auditorium, 20 Existierende Bibliothek.

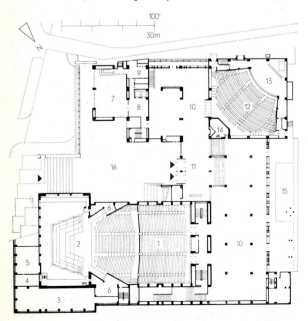

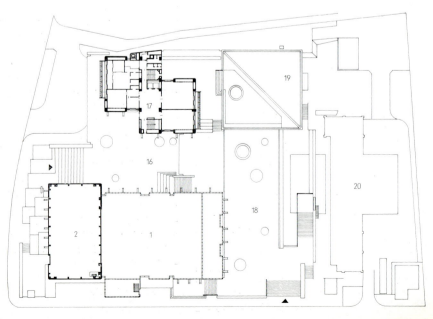

Kenzo Tange

Administration building of the Kagawa District at Takamatsu, 1959

The group of buildings, occupying a comparatively narrow site hemmed in by low-rise housing, consists of two parts with clearly distinct functions. The low community centre with the assembly and congress hall extends over the whole length of the site; but as it is placed on columns of two storeys height, an amply dimensioned pedestrian passage remains open at ground level. Adjoining the open ground floor is a garden in traditional Japanese style which forms a link between the low wing and the square nine-storey office tower. The ground floor of the latter, forming an open plan, contains lobby, a display room and public concourses. The office floors occupying the first to the seventh floor are largely standardized. They have a solid core with stairs and lavatories, surrounded by open-plan offices with movable partitions. The outer walls of the office floors are formed by full-height glass sliding doors which give on to continuous all-round balconies. In this way, the interiors are extended outwards, and sun protection is provided for the floor below. The eighth floor is designed as a roof terrace; its central part is overtowered by an open-topped superstructure with viewing platform an tea-room. Both buildings are of the reinforced concrete framework type.

Verwaltungsgebäude des Bezirkes Kagawa in Takamatsu, 1959

Der Gesamtkomplex, der auf einem relativ beengten Arreal mit niedriger Nachbarbebauung errichtet wurde, besteht aus zwei ihrer Funktion nach klar unterschiedenen Baukörpern. Der flache Gemeinschaftstrakt mit dem Versammlungs- und Kongreßsaal erstreckt sich über die ganze Länge des Grundstücks. Da er auf zwei Geschosse hohen Stützen steht, ergibt sich auf der Ebene des Erdgeschosses eine großzügig bemessene Fußgängerpassage. An das offene Stützengeschoß schließt sich ein im traditionellen japanischen Stil gehaltener Garten an, der vom Flachbau zu dem neungeschossigen Bürogebäude mit quadratischem Grundriß überleitet. Dessen Erdgeschoß, eine große Raumeinheit, enthält Eingangshalle, Ausstellungsraum und Aufenthaltszonen für das Publikum. Die Büroetagen vom 1. bis zum 7. Obergeschoß sind weitgehend standardisiert. Sie haben einen festen Kern mit Treppen und Sanitärräumen, um den sich die Büroflächen erstrecken, deren Trennwände beliebig versetzt werden können. Die Außenwände der Büroetagen sind als geschoßhohe Glasschiebetüren ausgebildet, die sich auf allseitig umlaufende Balkone öffnen. Diese erweitern den Innenraum nach außen und geben zugleich den tieferliegenden Geschossen Sonnenschutz. Das 8. Obergeschoß wurde als begehbare Terrasse ausgebaut. Auf dieser Terrasse steht über dem Verkehrskern ein im oberen Teil offener Aufbau mit Aussichtsplattform und Teeraum. Beide Bauteile sind als Stahlbetonskelettbauten ausgeführt.

1. The road space is enlarged by the open ground floor of the low wing, which extends through two storeys. The module of the column spacing creates a scale relationship with the closely adjoining private houses, mostly consisting of small timber houses. The dominating part is the square administration building, overtowered by the superstructure above the central core.

1. Durch das zweigeschossige, offene Stützengeschoß unter dem Querbau wird der Freiraum der Straße vergrößert. Die Stützenteilung schafft eine maßstäbliche Beziehung zu der eng anschließenden Nachbarbebauung, die überwiegend aus kleinen Holzhäusern besteht. Dominierender Bauteil ist der quadratische Verwaltungsbau mit dem hochgezogenen Gebäudekern.

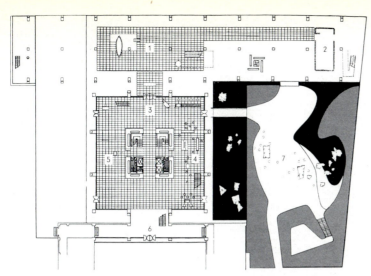
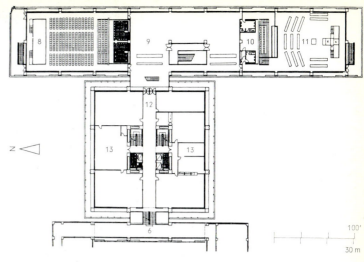

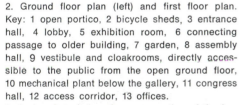

2. Ground floor plan (left) and first floor plan. Key: 1 open portico, 2 bicycle sheds, 3 entrance hall, 4 lobby, 5 exhibition room, 6 connecting passage to older building, 7 garden, 8 assembly hall, 9 vestibule and cloakrooms, directly accessible to the public from the open ground floor, 10 mechanical plant below the gallery, 11 congress hall, 12 access corridor, 13 offices.

3. A view from below the open portico of the low wing across the rock garden onto the south side of the office tower with its glass-curtained, two-storey entrance hall. The appearance of the double-curtained facade is governed by the rhythm of the high and narrow cantilever beams and the long horizontal lines of the balcony slabs and parapets.

2. Grundrisse von Erdgeschoß (links) und 1. Obergeschoß. Legende: 1 Offene Stützenhalle, 2 Abstellraum für Fahrräder, 3 Eingangshalle, 4 Lobby, 5 Ausstellungsraum, 6 Verbindungsgang zum bestehenden Gebäude, 7 Garten, 8 Versammlungssaal, 9 Vorhalle mit Garderoben, für das Publikum vom Stützengeschoß im Parterre aus direkt zugänglich, 10 Mechanische Anlagen unter der Galerie, 11 Kongreßsaal, 12 Erschließungsflur, 13 Büros.

3. Blick aus dem offenen Stützengeschoß des Querriegels über den Steingarten hinweg auf die Südfront des Bürogebäudes, dessen zweigeschossige Eingangshalle verglast ist. Das Bild der zweischichtigen Fassade wird bestimmt durch den Rhythmus der schmalen, hohen Kragbalken und die langen Horizontallinien der Balkonplatten und -brüstungen.

4. The open space below the low wing is linked by sett pavings with the garden and by concrete slabs with the road. The stairs in the foreground lead to the vestibule of the assembly hall.
5. Detail of the south facade of the office block. The main girders at the columns are, outside the facade, split into two beams, more compatible with the high and narrow profiles of the secondary beams projecting from the cross girders. The full-height glass windows forming the curtain wall are set back behind the main girders.
6. View from the south.

4. Die Freifläche unter dem Quertrakt ist im Anschluß an den Garten mit Kieseln, im Anschluß an die Straße mit Betonplatten belegt. Die Treppe im Vordergrund führt zur Vorhalle des Versammlungsraumes.
5. Detail der Südfassade des Bürogebäudes. Die Hauptträger an den Stützen sind vor der Fassade in zwei Teile gespalten. Ihre Form paßt sich damit den schmalen, hohen Profilen der Sekundärträger vor den Hauptunterzügen an. Die vom Boden bis zur Decke verglasten Außenwände sind hinter die Hauptträger zurückgesetzt.
6. Ansicht von Süden mit dem Balkon vor dem Kongreßsaal.

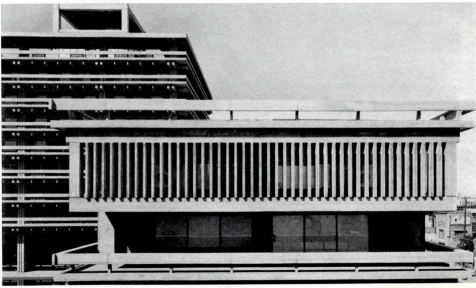

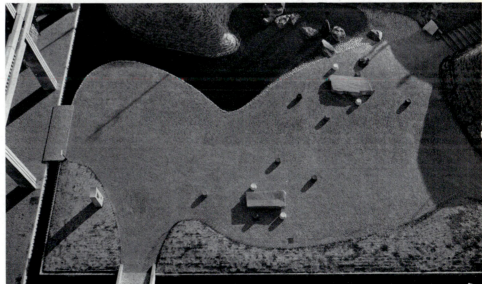

7. The entrance hall of the administration building is also used as an exhibition room. On the side facing the garden are benches for visitors. Behind the isolated, tiled wall are the stairs leading to the office floors.
8. The open-air space of the garden linking the buildings enlarges the entrance hall of the administration block and the open portico of the low wing. It is designed in the traditional Japanese style with pool, terrace, and rocks.

7. Die Eingangshalle des Verwaltungsgebäudes wird auch als Ausstellungsraum verwendet. Auf der Gartenseite stehen Sitzbänke als Wartezone für die Besucher. Hinter der Wandscheibe mit Keramikverkleidung liegt die Treppe zu den Büroetagen.
8. Der Garten zwischen den Gebäuden erweitert als Außenraum die Eingangshalle des Bürogebäudes und die offene Stützenhalle des Auditoriumtraktes. Er ist mit Wasserbecken, Steinterrasse und Felsen im Stil historischer japanischer Gärten gestaltet.

Kenzo Tange

Kurashiki Town Hall, 1960

Already in the Edo period (1615—1868), the harbour town of Kurashiki used to be an important commercial centre. Moreover, it has a centuries-old reputation as a centre of ceramic art. The industrial boom at present experienced by the city through the processing of steel and wool has overwhelmed the historic city centre. That is why a new city centre is to be built in a number of stages, with Kenzo Tange's new Town Hall setting the scale. The block-like building stands across the end of a piazza which will later be faced by a City Hall on the opposite side. The open space on either side of the Town Hall is, as it were, made part of the building by the centrally placed entrance hall which is open towards each of the long sides. This hall extends through two storeys and is flanked by two load-bearing cores, containing stairs and lavatories. The large Council Chamber is placed on the second floor, above the entrance hall, and is likewise two storeys high, overtowering the roof terrace. The central zone, consisting of entrance hall, Council Chamber and stairwells, is surrounded by the traffic zone. In the open-plan offices of the first floor, which are those most frequented by the public, the corridors are separated from the offices proper merely by waist-high counters. On the second floor are the more secluded municipal offices for one or more persons, reached by a double-H system of corridors. The compact shape of the building is textured by a lattice pattern of apertures and sculptural features which is unrelated to the different storeys so that these are, to some extent, almost camouflaged. Concrete has been used almost exclusively.

Rathaus in Kurashiki, 1960

Die Hafenstadt Kurashiki war bereits in der Edozeit (1615—1868) ein bedeutender Handelsplatz. Als Zentrum der Keramikkunst hat sie sich ihren Ruf über Jahrhunderte bewahrt. Dem industriellen Aufschwung, den die Stadt gegenwärtig durch die Verarbeitung von Stahl und Wolle erlebt, ist das historische Zentrum nicht mehr gewachsen. Deshalb soll nach einem Stufenplan ein neues Stadtzentrum gebaut werden, für das Kenzo Tanges neues Rathaus als erstes ausgeführtes Gebäude den Maßstab setzt. Der blockhafte Baukörper steht quer am Ende eines Platzes, auf dessen gegenüberliegender Seite die Stadthalle entstehen wird. Der Freiraum vor und hinter dem Rathaus ist durch die Eingangshalle, die in der Mittelachse liegt und sich nach beiden Längsseiten öffnet, in den Bau einbezogen. Die zweigeschossige Halle wird durch zwei tragende Kerne, die Treppen und Sanitärräume umschließen, seitlich begrenzt. Im zweiten Obergeschoß ist über der Eingangshalle der große Ratssaal plaziert, der zweigeschossig die begehbare Dachterrasse überragt. Die Kernzone aus Halle, beziehungsweise Ratssaal und Treppenblöcken, wird von der Verkehrszone umschlossen. In den Großraumbüros des ersten Obergeschosses, wo die Ämter mit dem stärksten Publikumsverkehr untergebracht sind, werden die Korridore von der eigentlichen Bürofläche nur durch brüstungshohe Theken abgetrennt. Im zweiten Obergeschoß erschließt ein Flursystem in Form eines doppelten H die Einzel- und Mehrpersonenbüros der Stadtverwaltung. Die kompakte Blockform des Gebäudes wird durch gitterartige Durchbrechungen texturiert und plastisch gegliedert. Diese Gliederung ist unabhängig von den Geschoßhöhen, die stellenweise geradezu verschleiert werden. Als Material ist fast durchweg Beton verwendet.

2. The town hall dominates the urban scene which ▷ has still largely preserved its historic appearance.

2. Das Rathaus als Dominante im Stadtbild, das in seiner historischen Form weitgehend erhalten ist.

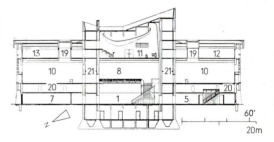

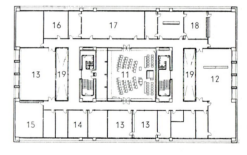

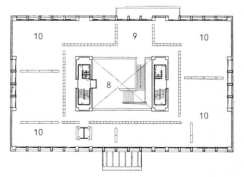

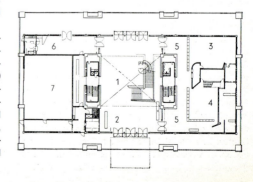

1. Longitudinal section (top) and plans (bottom to top) of ground floor, first floor and second floor. Key to plans: 1 entrance hall, 2 information desk, 3 cashier, 4 citizens' advice bureau, 5 waiting room, 6 restaurant, 7 garage for municipal vehicles, 8 air space above entrance hall, 9 corridor leading to balcony, 10 municipal offices (Welfare Department, City Treasurer, Health Department, Public Works Department, etc.) 11 council chamber, 12 library, 13 conference room, 14 office, 15 rest room and lounge, 16 press office, 17 staff office, 18 Lord Mayor's parlour, 19 light well, 20 mezzanine floor, with records office and archives, 21 traffic core with stairs and W. C.

1. Längsschnitt (oben) und Grundrisse (von unten nach oben) von Erdgeschoß, 1. Obergeschoß und 2. Obergeschoß.
Legende zu den Plänen: 1 Eingangshalle, 2 Information, 3 Kasse, 4 Beratung, 5 Warteraum, 6 Restaurant, 7 Garage für städtische Fahrzeuge, 8 Luftraum über der Halle, 9 Korridor zum Balkon, 10 Städtische Ämter (Sozialamt, Steueramt, Gesundheitsamt, Tiefbauamt usw.), 11 Ratssaal, 12 Bibliothek, 13 Konferenzraum, 14 Büro, 15 Ruhe- und Aufenthaltsraum, 16 Presseamt, 17 Personalamt, 18 Amtsräume des Oberbürgermeisters, 19 Lichtschacht, 20 Mezzaningeschoß mit Registratur und Archiv, 21 Verkehrskern mit Treppe und WC.

3. The design of the corner, composed of prefabricated concrete units of different sizes, is derived from traditional timber constructions methods.

4. Behind the lattice pattern of the outer wall, the windows are recessed so as to form deeply shaded loggias. Even in the facade, the stairwells are recognizable from the stronger columns and the projecting roof beams.

3. Die Ecklösung der Fassade, die aus vorfabrizierten Betonelementen verschiedener Größen gestaltet wurde, ist von der traditionellen Holzbauweise abgeleitet.

4. Hinter der Gitterstruktur der Außenwand sind die Fensterflächen so weit zurückgesetzt, daß tief verschattete Loggien entstehen. Die Treppenkerne zeichnen sich auch in der Fassade durch verstärkte Stützen und auskragende Dachbalken ab.

5. The first floor corridors are open towards the entrance hall. The internal stairs are placed within the structural cores. The main stairs form an open flight through the entrance hall. The dominating material is concrete which has even been used for the banisters.

6. Council Chamber. The suspended ceiling matches the shape of the roof which overtowers the roof terrace. The visitors' gallery, separated from the Chamber by a parapet, has its own entrance.

7. The completely enclosed Council Chamber is illuminated by top lighting at the front wall. The councillors' seats are radially orientated towards the chairman's dais.

5. Die Korridore des 1. Obergeschosses sind zur Eingangshalle hin offen. In den konstruktiven Kernen sind die internen Verbindungstreppen untergebracht. Die Haupttreppe führt frei durch die Halle. Als Material herrscht Beton vor, in dem auch die Treppengeländer ausgeführt sind.

6. Blick in den Ratssaal. Die abgehängte Decke folgt der Dachform des über die Dachterrasse emporgezogenen Ratssaales. Der Besucherrang ist durch eine Brüstung vom Saal getrennt und hat einen separaten Eingang.

7. Der rundum geschlossene Saal wird durch Oberlicht über der Stirnwand beleuchtet. Die Sitzreihen der Gemeinderäte sind radial auf das Präsidentenpodest ausgerichtet.

Kiyonori Kikutake

Tatebayashi Town Hall, 1962-63

The new Town Hall was meant to set the scale for the future development of this town with a population of 70,000 which consists mainly of two-storey timber houses of conventional type. The seven-storey building stands on a hillock and has two entrances. The vestibule with its main entrance on the west side projects as a porch. Because of the sloping ground, the ground floor is reached via a ramp and the first floor via stairs. The municipal departments open to the public are placed in open-plan offices on the ground floor and first floor. The second floor, forming a low mezzanine, contains records and technical plant. From the third floor upwards, the rectangular plan is replaced by a cruciform layout as the premises are extended on all four sides beyond the concrete cores at the corners which contain the stairs and installation shafts. On the fifth floor are the Council Chamber, which extends through two storeys, as well as conference rooms. The bearing structure of the building is formed by the four concrete towers in conjunction with an internal system of stanchions. The structural floors of the projecting storeys as well as all the other floor slabs are of reinforced concrete. The external appearance of the Town Hall is governed by the massive robustness of the corner towers projecting above the roof, which is further accentuated by the lightness of the glass curtain walls by which the cantilevered office floors are surrounded on all sides.

Rathaus in Tatebayashi, 1962-63

Mit dem Neubau des Rathauses sollte in der 70 000 Einwohner zählenden Stadt, die überwiegend aus traditionellen zweigeschossigen Holzhäusern besteht, ein Maßstab für die Zukunft gesetzt werden. Das siebengeschossige Gebäude steht auf einem Hügel; es wird von zwei Eingängen erschlossen. Die Halle mit dem Haupteingang auf der Westseite ist vor das Gebäude gezogen. Bedingt durch das Gefälle des Geländes erreicht man das Erdgeschoß über eine Rampe, während eine Treppe ins erste Obergeschoß führt. Die städtischen Ämter mit Publikumsverkehr sind im Erdgeschoß und im 1. Obergeschoß in Großräumen untergebracht. Das 2. Obergeschoß, ein niedrigeres Zwischengeschoß, enthält Registratur- und Maschinenräume. Vom 3. Obergeschoß an ändert sich die rechteckige Grundrißform in eine kreuzförmige, da die Räume nach allen vier Seiten über die in den Gebäudeecken stehenden Betonblöcke mit den Treppen und Installationsschächten auskragen. Im 5. Obergeschoß liegt der zwei Geschosse hohe Ratssaal sowie die Konferenzräume. Die Tragkonstruktion des Gebäudes wird von den vier Betontürmen in Verbindung mit einem innen liegenden Stützensystem gebildet. Die Decken der auskragenden Geschosse bestehen wie alle übrigen Geschoßdecken aus Stahlbeton. Der äußere Eindruck des Rathauses wird bestimmt durch die geschlossenen, über das Dach emporgezogenen Ecktürme und die auskragenden, nach allen Seiten geöffneten Büroetagen, deren leichte, gläserne Vorhangwände die Massigkeit der Eckpfeiler noch unterstreichen.

1. The 90° stagger of the oblong corner towers provides an interesting variant to the symmetric design of the building.
2. A view from the roof terrace of the Town Hall of drive and main entrance. In contrast to the symmetric architectural design, the landscaping is informal.
3. At night, the contrast between the transparent curtain walls and the massive corner towers is particularly evident. On the left, the west-side projection of the entrance hall.

1. Die im Grundriß rechteckigen Türme sind von Ecke zu Ecke um 90° gedreht, wodurch der symmetrische Aufbau des Baus spannungsvoll variiert wird.
2. Blick von der Dachterrasse des Rathauses auf die Zufahrtsstraße und den Haupteingang. Die Außenanlagen sind im Gegensatz zur symmetrischen Gebäudearchitektur frei gestaltet.
3. Bei Nacht tritt der Kontrast zwischen den transparenten Vorhangwänden und den massigen Eckpfeilern besonders deutlich hervor. Links die auf der Westseite vorgezogene Haupteingangshalle.

4. In accordance with their structural function, the corner towers are massive and mainly enclosed whilst the office floors project from the core of the building and are open on all sides.

5. The Council Chamber on the fifth floor receives daylight from all sides through the high-level windows which give on to the roof terrace. The ceiling is formed by a curved roof shell reinforced by diagonal beams.

6. The main entrance is placed far in front of the building on a mezzanine level which is connected with the ground floor by a ramp and with the first floor by a flight of stairs.

4. Die Ecktürme als statisch bedingte Gebäudeteile sind ihrer Funktion nach massiv und weitgehend geschlossen, während die Bürogeschosse aus dem Gebäudekern vorkragen und nach allen Seiten geöffnet sind.

5. Der Ratssaal im 5. Obergeschoß wird von der Dachterrasse her durch hochliegende Fensterbänder auf allen Seiten belichtet. Eine durch Diagonalbalken verstärkte, gekrümmte Dachschale bildet die Decke.

6. Der Haupteingang ist weit vor das Gebäude vorgezogen. Er liegt auf einem Zwischengeschoß und ist mit dem Erdgeschoß durch eine Rampe verbunden, während eine Treppe ins 1. Obergeschoß hinaufführt.

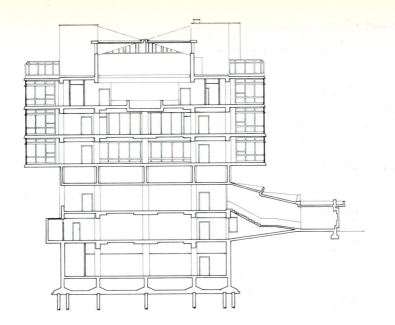

7. East-west section and plans of ground floor (bottom, left), first floor (bottom, right), third floor (centre, left) and fifth floor (centre, right). Key: 1 ramp, 2 open-plan office, 3 access corridor, 4 interview room, 5 reception room, 6 caretaker, 7 entrance hall, 8 office for several persons, 9 ante-room, 10 Lord Mayor's parlour, 11 Town Clerk, 12 Council Chamber, 13 councillors' seats, 14 spectators' gallery, 15 library, 16 rest room, 17 conference room, 18 cloak room, 19 office of the Chairman of the Council, 20 administration, 21 committee rooms.

7. Schnitt in Ost-West-Richtung und Grundrisse von Erdgeschoß (unten links), 1. Obergeschoß (unten rechts), 3. Obergeschoß (Mitte links) und 5. Obergeschoß (Mitte rechts). Legende: 1 Rampe, 2 Bürogroßraum, 3 Erschließungskorridor, 4 Besprechungsraum, 5 Empfangsraum, 6 Hausmeister, 7 Eingangshalle, 8 Mehrpersonenbüro, 9 Vorzimmer, 10 Amtszimmer des Bürgermeisters, 11 Amtsleiter, 12 Ratssaal, 13 Sitze der Stadträte, 14 Zuschauer, 15 Bibliothek, 16 Ruheraum, 17 Konferenzraum, 18 Garderobe, 19 Parlamentspräsident, 20 Büro der Verwaltung, 21 Arbeitsraum für Ausschüsse.

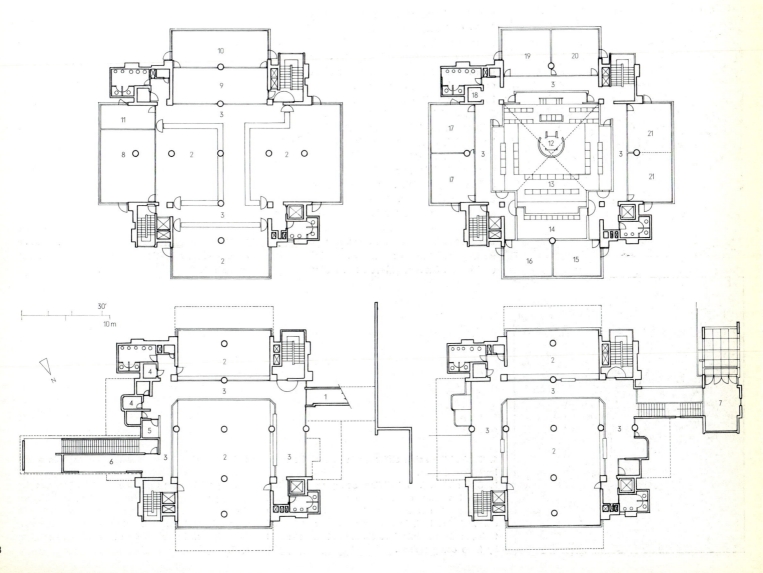

Kenzo Tange

Radio and Press Centre at Kofu, 1964-66

The radio and press centre at Kofu, which apart from numerous studios and editorial premises also contains printing works and warehouses, was designed during the years 1962–64, i. e. at the same time as the buildings for the Olympic Games. In accordance with the 'Manifesto of the Metabolists' of 1960, Kenzo Tange here tried for the first time to realize his idea of the multi-functional user of a building. His idea was based on the notion that a building consists of two types of space units, namely those of a permanent character and flexible zones depending on future developments. The permanent units comprise stairs, lifts, lavatories, power mains, etc. The flexible zones are mainly designed for human occupation, i. e. for work or recreation. The permanent units can easily be combined within the structural elements of a 'superstructure' which, in this case, consist of sixteen cylindric towers. The flexible zones are independent of the structure so that they permit a high degree of freedom in utilization and permutation, and can be extended outwards. The structural framework of the building is provided by the reinforced concrete cylinders which serve as load-bearing elements. These cylinders are fitted with brackets designed to support the floor slabs. The structure can be extended both horizontally and vertically. The outer walls consist of prefabricated units which may be either windows or solid wall panels. The inner partitions are formed by movable reinforced concrete units. With such systems, individual parts of the building may be designed by different architects, and the principle may be applied to entire urban structures.

Rundfunk- und Pressezentrum in Kofu, 1964-66

Gleichzeitig mit den Olympiabauten entstand in den Jahren 1962–64 der Entwurf für das Rundfunk- und Pressezentrum in Kofu, das neben den verschiedensten Studio- und Redaktionsräumen auch Druckerei- und Lagerräume enthält. Gemäß dem Manifest der Metabolisten von 1960 versuchte Kenzo Tange hier zum erstenmal, seine Idee von der multifunktionalen Benutzbarkeit eines Bauwerks zu realisieren. Er ging davon aus, daß ein Gebäude aus zwei Raumgruppen besteht, den fixen Raumeinheiten und den von der Entwicklung abhängigen, flexiblen Raumzonen. Die festgelegten Einheiten sind Raumgruppen wie Treppen, Aufzüge, sanitäre Zellen und Energieversorgungsschächte. Die flexiblen Räume sind vorwiegend »menschliche« Räume, also Arbeits- und Erholungsbereiche. Die fixen Räume lassen sich leicht in den konstruktiven Elementen einer »Superstruktur« zusammenfassen. Bei diesem Bauwerk wurden sie in den 16 zylindrischen Türmen untergebracht. Die flexiblen Räume sind unabhängig von der Konstruktion, so daß eine innere Flexibilität und Austauschbarkeit und ein Wachstum nach außen möglich ist. Das konstruktive Gerüst des Gebäudes bilden die Stahlbetonzylinder als tragende Elemente. An diesen Zylindern sind Auflagekonsolen für die Deckenelemente vorgesehen. Die Struktur ist horizontal und vertikal erweiterbar. Die Außenwände bestehen aus vorgefertigten Teilen, entweder aus Fensterelementen oder aus geschlossenen Wandscheiben. Die Innenwände werden aus versetzbaren Stahlbetonelementen gebildet. Mit solchen Systemen ist es möglich, daß mehrere Architekten einzelne Gebäudeabschnitte unterschiedlich gestalten und ganze Stadtstrukturen nach diesem Prinzip entstehen.

1. 'Eye' of the spiral staircase in one of the load-bearing cylinders.
2. South side. The building occupies a central site in the town, opposite the railway station. It overtowers the surrounding buildings and clearly demonstrates that, in coping with new structural tasks, modern architecture should not be detracted by false compromises.

1. Blick in das Auge einer Wendeltreppe in einem der tragenden Zylinder.
2. Südansicht. Das Gebäude steht im Zentrum der Stadt, gegenüber dem Hauptbahnhof. Es überragt die umliegende Bebauung und macht deutlich, daß die moderne Architektur bei der Bewältigung neuer Bauaufgaben keine falschen Kompromisse machen muß.

3. North-south section (top, right) and plans of basement (bottom, left), ground floor (bottom, right), second floor (centre, left), third floor (centre, right) and sixth floor (top, left). Key: 1 lettable space, 2 air-conditioning plant, 3 paper stores, 4 machinery, 5 electrical plant, 6 entrance hall, 7 air-conditioning shafts, 8 goods elevators, 9 store room, 10 W. C., 11 oil stores, 12 lift and stairwell shaft, 13 dining room, 14 kitchen, 15 drug store, 16 newspaper printing works, 17 machinery, sales, 18 packing room, 19 television camera van, 20 setting and printing plant, 21 editorial offices, 22 reproduction, 23 book binding, 24 photographic section, 25 production planning, 26 roof garden, 27 management, 28 electronic data processing, 29 cashier, 30 office, 31 conference room, 32 library, 33 small TV studio, 34 preparation for TV transmissions, 35 large TV studio (extending through two storeys), 36 store room, 37 radio editing, 38 film editing.

3. Schnitt in Nord-Süd-Richtung (oben rechts) und Grundrisse von Untergeschoß (unten links), Erdgeschoß (unten rechts), 2. Obergeschoß (Mitte links), 3. Obergeschoß (Mitte rechts) und 6. Obergeschoß (oben links). Legende: 1 Vermieteter Raum, 2 Klimaanlage, 3 Papierlager, 4 Maschinenraum, 5 Elektrozentrale, 6 Eingangshalle, 7 Klimakanäle, 8 Lastenaufzüge, 9 Abstellraum, 10 WC, 11 Öllager, 12 Fahrstuhl- und Treppenschacht, 13 Speisesaal, 14 Küche, 15 Drugstore, 16 Zeitungsdruckerei, 17 Maschinen, Verkauf, 18 Verpackungsraum, 19 Fernseh-Übertragungswagen, 20 Setzerei und Druckerei, 21 Redaktion, 22 Reproduktion, 23 Buchbinderei, 24 Photoabteilung, 25 Produktionsplanung, 26 Dachgarten, 27 Direktion, 28 Elektronische Datenverarbeitung, 29 Kasse, 30 Büro, 31 Konferenzraum, 32 Bibliothek, 33 Kleines TV-Studio, 34 Vorbereitung für TV-Aufnahmen, 35 Großes TV-Studio (zwei Geschosse), 36 Abstellraum, 37 Rundfunkredaktion, 38 Filmredaktion.

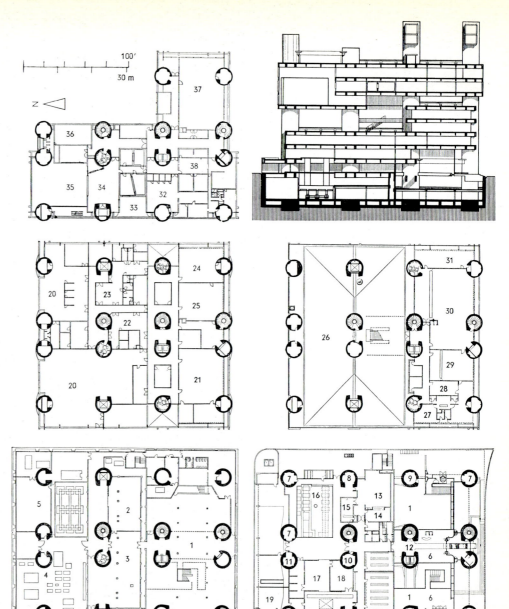

4. West elevation. On the ground floor are service entrances and the loading bays of the printing works; in the foreground, a public car park.
5. The dominating element of the structure is provided by the load-bearing cylinders from which the different floors are suspended. The irregular composition clearly demonstrates the many ways in which the system can be varied.

4. Ansicht von Westen. Im Erdgeschoß Serviceeingänge und Laderampe der Druckerei, im Vordergrund der öffentliche Parkplatz.
5. Dominierendes Element der Gebäudestruktur sind die tragenden Zylinder. Zwischen ihnen werden die einzelnen Geschosse eingehängt. Die starke Gliederung des Baukörpers läßt die große Variationsmöglichkeit des Systems klar erkennen.

6. The lobbies at basement, ground floor and first floor level form part of a single, large hall where the stairs are freely placed in the centre and are connected with the different levels merely by footbridges.
7. Main entrance hall with the reception desk on the left and the entrance in the background.

6. Eine Treppe verbindet die Eingangshallen des Untergeschosses, des Erdgeschosses und des 1. Obergeschosses miteinander. Sie steht als freie Form in einem großen Raum und ist nur über Podeste mit den einzelnen Geschossen verbunden.
7. Blick von der Haupteingangshalle auf den Eingang. Links die Pförtnerloge.

8. South passage with main entrance. The entrance floor is raised a few steps above street level. The main entrance is placed in the centre line between two cylinders of the 'multisystem' and projects beyond the facade so that it is accessible from three sides.

9. Roof terrace at third floor level. The brackets at the cylinders are designed to support additional floors which might be added in future. In the open space shown here, there would be room for two further floor slabs.

8. Blick durch die Südpassage auf den Haupteingang. Das Eingangsgeschoß ist einige Stufen über das Straßenniveau angehoben. Der Haupteingang liegt in der Achse des »Multisystems« zwischen zwei Zylindern und ist vor die Gebäudefassade gezogen, so daß er von drei Seiten zugänglich ist.

9. Blick über die Dachterrasse des 3. Obergeschosses. Die Auflagekonsolen an den Zylindern sind für künftige Erweiterungen vorgesehen. In den freien Raum können bei Bedarf noch zwei Geschosse eingehängt werden.

Togo Murano + Mori

Head office of the Chiyoda Seimei Life Insurance Company at Tokyo, 1966
The head office of this great Japanese insurance company is situated in a dormitory suburb of Tokyo which mainly consists of low-rise houses. A central piazza is surrounded by a U-shaped group of three buildings, viz. a very deep six-storey block with two rows of central columns, a slender eleven-storey office block, and a three-storey entrance building. In the six-storey main block, the part between the central columns, containing the traffic core, lavatories and archives, has a superstructure with partitioned offices, rising three storeys above the roof terrace covering the outer parts of the lower floors which are taken up by open-plan offices. The entrance building has three storeys; its ground floor is occupied by the staff canteen, the first floor by a large and a small conference room. Both floors are flanked by arcades or terraces facing an L-shaped pool of water immediately adjoining the building and main block. Because of the sloping ground, the entrance hall is on the same level as the second floor of the main block. All the buildings have a concrete-clad steel framework structure. The floor slabs are extended beyond the facades, forming loggia-type galleries. The ¼ in. thick facade panels, consisting of four parts, are of aluminium cast in sand moulds.

Verwaltungsgebäude der Lebensversicherungs-Gesellschaft Chiyoda Seimei in Tokio, 1966
Die Hauptverwaltung einer großen japanischen Versicherungsgesellschaft liegt in einem Randgebiet von Tokio mit vorwiegend zweigeschossiger Wohnbebauung. Der U-förmige Komplex besteht aus drei um einen zentralen Platz gruppierten Baukörpern: einem sehr tiefen Hauptgebäude mit 6 Stockwerken, einem elfgeschossigen, scheibenförmigen Bürohochhaus und einem dreistöckigen Eingangsgebäude. In dem dreibündigen Hauptgebäude liegen an den beiden Außenseiten Großraumbüros, im mittleren Bund sind Verkehrskerne, Sanitär- und Registraturräume zusammengefaßt. Dieser Mitteltrakt ist drei Geschosse über die begehbare Dachterrasse hochgezogen; der Aufbau nimmt kleinere Büroräume auf. Das Eingangsgebäude ist ein dreigeschossiger Baukörper, auf dessen unterster Ebene der Angestellten-Speisesaal liegt. Der große und kleine Sitzungssaal sind im mittleren Geschoß untergebracht. Sowohl der Speisesaal als auch die Sitzungssäle öffnen sich über Arkadengänge oder Terrassen auf einen künstlichen See, der L-förmig vor Eingangs- und Hauptgebäude angelegt ist. Die Eingangshalle liegt wegen des ansteigenden Geländes auf gleicher Höhe wie das 2. Obergeschoß des Hauptgebäudes. Die Konstruktion der Bauten besteht aus Stahl mit Betonummantelung. Die Geschoßdecken sind so weit vor die Fensterwände gezogen, daß hinter den vorgesetzten Fassadenelementen begehbare loggienartige Umgänge entstehen. Die in einer Sandform gegossenen Aluminium-Fassadenelemente werden aus vier Teilen zusammengesetzt und haben eine Wandstärke von 5,5 mm.

1. General view from south-east. On the left the three-storey entrance building, in the background the six-storey main block with its three-storey superstructure, on the right the eleven-storey office building. Below the central piazza are a deep-level garage and club rooms.

1. Gesamtansicht von Südosten. Links der dreigeschossige Eingangsbau, im Hintergrund das sechsgeschossige Hauptgebäude mit seinem dreigeschossigen Aufbau, rechts das elfgeschossige Scheibenhochhaus. Unter dem zentralen Platz liegen die Tiefgarage und Clubräume.

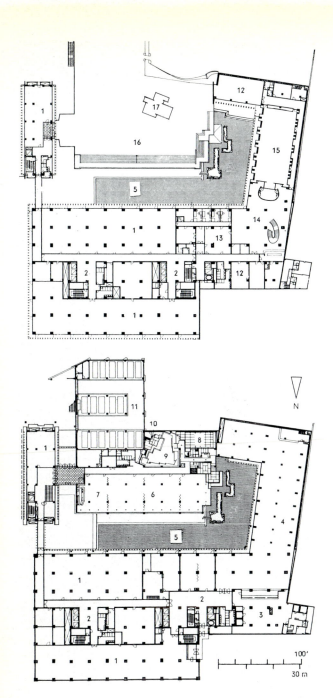

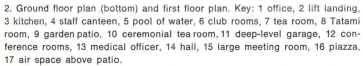

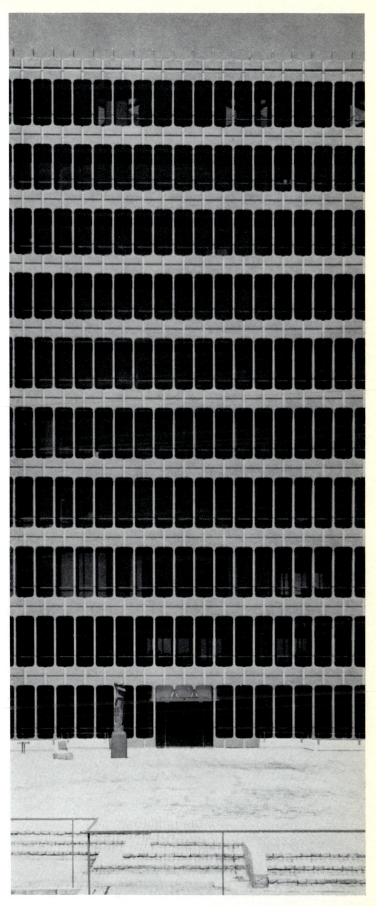

2. Ground floor plan (bottom) and first floor plan. Key: 1 office, 2 lift landing, 3 kitchen, 4 staff canteen, 5 pool of water, 6 club rooms, 7 tea room, 8 Tatami room, 9 garden patio, 10 ceremonial tea room, 11 deep-level garage, 12 conference rooms, 13 medical officer, 14 hall, 15 large meeting room, 16 piazza, 17 air space above patio.
3. Part of the facade of the multi-storey office building on the east side of the central piazza.

2. Grundrisse von Erdgeschoß (unten) und 1. Obergeschoß. Legende: 1 Büro, 2 Aufzugvorhalle, 3 Küche, 4 Angestelltenspeisesaal, 5 See, 6 Clubräume, 7 Teeraum, 8 Tatamiraum, 9 Atriumgarten, 10 Teezeremonienraum, 11 Tiefgarage, 12 Konferenzräume, 13 Arzt, 14 Halle, 15 Großer Sitzungssaal, 16 Platz, 17 Luftraum über dem Atriumgarten.
3. Ausschnitt aus der Fassade des scheibenförmigen Bürohochhauses auf der Ostseite der zentralen Platzanlage.

4,5. The pool of water is accentuated by fountains and small rock islands designed in the tradition of the Japanese garden. Although the windows are set back behind the deeply shaded galleries, the precise and strict rhythm of the aluminium units gives the facades an almost classic appearance.
6. Garden patio, seen from the main block. On the left the multi-storey building with the passage connecting it to the main block.

4, 5. Der künstlich angelegte See erhält seine Akzente durch Fontänen und inselartige Steinkompositionen, die aus der Tradition des japanischen Gartens heraus gestaltet sind. Trotz der tiefen Schattenzonen in den Umgängen vor den zurückgesetzten Fensterwänden wirken die Fassaden durch die Präzision und den strengen Rhythmus der Aluminiumelemente fast klassisch.
6. Blick vom Hauptgebäude in den Innengarten. Links die Hochhausscheibe mit dem Verbindungsgang zum Hauptbau.

7,8. Detail and general view of lobby and main entrance. The cruciform light fittings are placed in front of the side windows. The room is optically enlarged by the mirror effects of the flooring.

7, 8. Detail und Ansicht von Eingangshalle und Haupteingang. Die kreuzförmigen Beleuchtungskörper sind vor den Fenstern der seitlichen Außenwand plaziert. Der Raum wird durch die Spiegeleffekte des Fußbodens optisch erweitert.

Nikken Sekkey Komu Co.
Shoji Hayashi (Planning Director/Planungsleiter)

Palaceside Building at Tokyo, completed in 1966

The Palaceside Building in the vicinity of the Imperial Palace forms the end and climax of a whole chain of head office buildings of large Japanese companies located in this Chiyoda District of Tokyo. It provides a choice example for the way in which the problems arising from the multi-functional utilization of such a building can be tackled. In addition to storeys with lettable offices, there is a storey with conference rooms, two shopping parades, a newspaper printing works, store rooms, deep-level garages and an underground railway station. With such a great mixture of functions, flexibility in room utilization is of particular importance, calling for consistent separation of load-bearing structure, access facilities and installations. The problem of optimising the traffic flows and the shape of the site, which is surrounded by streets on all sides, led to the adoption of a design where the total floor area of nearly 1,292.300 sq. ft. is spread over ten storeys above ground and six storeys below ground. In the plan, the group is seen to consist of two oblong blocks, placed parallel to each other in staggered arrangement and separated by a service road which provides access to the vertical traffic centres. These are self-contained cylindrical towers placed at the ends in the angle between the two blocks. Apart from stairs and lifts, they also contain lavatories and cloakrooms. In this way, it was possible to utilize 82 per cent. of the total floor area of the standard floors. The vertical installation shafts for the supply and drainage mains of the different floors are placed in fully enclosed twin towers at the far ends, rectangular in plan and separated by a fire escape stairwell. Ground floor and first basement are mainly used for shopping parades, linked by stairs and light wells. In the second basement are the concourse of an underground railway station and the printing works of a daily paper which also occupy the third and fourth basement. In the second, third and fourth basement, interconnected by escalators and ramps, are deep-level garages. The fifth and sixth basement contain machinery such as air-conditioning plants and an electric sub-station as well as store rooms, a restaurant and public baths. Above the upper shopping parade are seven office floors, above them one floor with conference rooms and a floor with technical plant. The roof, designed as a roof garden, is accessible to the public. The office floors are subdivided into area units of 84 ft. width and 77 ft., 5 in. depth which can be let in sections. The tenants are free to use their sections for open-plan offices or to sub-divide them into cubicles by means of demountable partitions. The building has a concrete-clad steel framework structure with a column spacing of 21 ft. and a span of 75 ft. There is a basic module of 16 in. The floor slabs consist of solid reinforced concrete. The two main facades have glass curtain walls. On the south side, special aluminium louvres provide sun protection. The two cylindrical traffic towers are clad with concave concrete units, the installation towers at the ends are clad with clinkers.

Palaceside-Bürogebäude in Tokio, fertiggestellt 1966

Das Palaceside Building in der Nachbarschaft des Kaiserpalastes bildet den Abschluß und Höhepunkt einer ganzen Kette von Verwaltungsgebäuden großer japanischer Firmen, die in diesem Stadtgebiet, dem Bezirk Chiyoda, ihren Standort haben. Es ist ein Musterbeispiel für die Bewältigung der Probleme, die sich aus der multifunktionalen Nutzung eines solchen Bauwerks ergeben. Außer Geschossen mit vermietbaren Büros enthält es eine Etage mit Konferenzräumen, zwei Ladenstraßen, eine Zeitungsdruckerei, Lagerräume, Tiefgaragen und eine U-Bahnstation. Bei einer so starken Funktionsmischung kommt der Variabilität in der Raumaufteilung besondere Bedeutung zu; sie bedingt eine konsequente Trennung von Tragkonstruktion, Erschließung und Installation. Das Problem der optimalen Verkehrsführung und der Zuschnitt des allseitig von Straßen umfahrenen Grundstücks legten eine Bauform nahe, bei der die knapp 120 000 m² große Nutzfläche auf 10 Geschosse über der Erde und auf 6 Untergeschosse verteilt ist. Als Grundriß wählte man eine zweibündige Anlage aus zwei langgestreckten Baukörpern, die gegeneinander versetzt sind und durch eine zentrale Innenstraße in der Längsachse erschlossen werden. Sie verbindet die vertikalen Verkehrselemente untereinander, die als separate, zylindrische Baukörper vor die Stirnseiten in die Winkel zwischen den beiden Trakten gesetzt wurden. Neben Treppen und Aufzügen enthalten sie auch die sanitären Einrichtungen. Auf diese Weise konnte bei den Normalgeschossen eine Nutzfläche von 82 % der gesamten Geschoßfläche erreicht werden. Die vertikalen Installationsschächte zur Ver- und Entsorgung der einzelnen Etagen sind in rechteckigen, geschlossenen Zwillingstürmen mit dazwischenliegender Nottreppe vor die Giebelfronten gesetzt. Das Erdgeschoß und das 1. Untergeschoß dienen vorwiegend als Einkaufsetagen mit Ladenstraßen, die durch Treppen und

1. On the north side, the site is flanked by multi-level expressways. On the south side, the drives and main entrances face the moat of the Imperial Palace.

1. Das Grundstück wird auf der Nordseite von Schnellstraßen auf verschiedenen Ebenen tangiert. Die Vorfahrten und Haupteingänge sind nach Süden zum Wassergraben des Kaiserpalastes orientiert.

Deckenöffnungen miteinander verbunden sind. Im 2. Untergeschoß liegen die Verteilerhalle einer U-Bahnstation und die Druckereiräume einer Tageszeitung, die sich auch auf das 3. und 4. Untergeschoß verteilen. Wageneinstellplätze sind im 2., 3. und 4. Untergeschoß untergebracht. Diese Geschosse sind durch Rolltreppen und Rampen miteinander verbunden. Das 5. und 6. Untergeschoß enthält Maschinenräume wie Klimaanlage und Transformatorenstation sowie Lagerräume, Restaurant- und Baderäume. Über dem oberen Ladengeschoß liegen 7 Büroetagen, darüber ein Geschoß mit Konferenzräumen und ein technisches Geschoß. Die als Dachgarten gestaltete Dachfläche ist für die Öffentlichkeit zugänglich. Die Büroetagen sind in Flächeneinheiten von 25,60 m Breite und 23,60 m Tiefe unterteilt, die abschnittsweise vermietet werden. Je nach Bedarf können die Mieter ihre Abschnitte als Bürogroßraum nutzen oder mit demontablen Trennwänden in Einzelräume unterteilen. Das Gebäude wurde als Stahlskelettkonstruktion mit Betonummantelung in einem Stützenabstand von 6,40 m und einer Stützweite von 16,80 m errichtet. Der Modul beträgt 0,40 m. Die Decken bestehen aus massiven Stahlbetonplatten. Die Außenwände der zwei Längsfassaden sind ganz in Glas aufgelöst. Auf der Südseite dienen vorgesetzte Blenden aus Aluminiumlamellen als Sonnenschutz. Die beiden Zylinder für den Vertikalverkehr wurden mit konkaven Betonelementen verkleidet, die Installationstürme vor den Giebelwänden haben eine Verkleidung aus Klinkern.

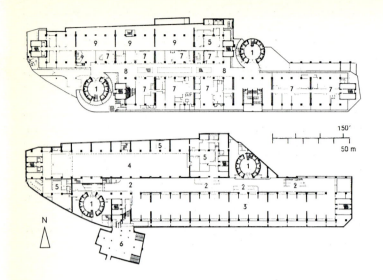

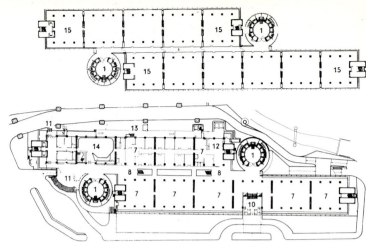

2. Plans of second basement (bottom, left), first basement (top, left), ground floor (bottom, right) and standard floor (top, right). Key: 1 traffic and installation towers, 2 passage and ramps to the parking floors, 3 parking area, 4 air space above printing works, 5 offices, stores and recreation rooms of the printing works, 6 concourse of underground station, 7 shops, 8 service road, 9 printing shop, 10 main entrance, 11 secondary entrance, 12 post office, 13 loading bay, 14 entrance hall, 15 open-plan offices.
3. View from the Hirakawa Gate, one of the entrances to the Imperial Palace, on the south-east side of the building. At this angle, only one of the two oblong blocks can be recognized so that the building appears to be less massive.

2. Grundrisse von 2. Untergeschoß (links unten), 1. Untergeschoß (links oben), Erdgeschoß (rechts unten) und Normalgeschoß (rechts oben). Legende: 1 Verkehrs- und Installationstürme, 2 Durchfahrt und Rampen zu den Parkgeschossen, 3 Parkfläche, 4 Luftraum über der Druckerei, 5 Büro-, Lager- und Sozialräume der Druckerei, 6 Verteilerhalle der U-Bahnstation, 7 Läden, 8 Innere Straße, 9 Arbeitsräume der Druckerei, 10 Haupteingang, 11 Nebeneingang, 12 Postamt, 13 Laderampe, 14 Empfangshalle, 15 Bürofläche.
3. In der Schrägansicht von Südosten, hier vom Hirakawa-Tor, einem Zugang zum Kaiserpalast, aus, ist nur einer der versetzten Trakte zu erkennen, wodurch der Baukörper weniger massiv wirkt.

4. In the front of the all-glass facade on the south side is a filigree lattice-work of horizontal sun louvres and freely mounted rain-water pipes. Additional sun protection is provided by external slat blinds.

5. Eastern traffic tower and south-wing roof terrace, seen from the western tower. Roof terraces and traffic towers are linked by footbridges. The way in which the concrete elements of the outer walls are fastened to the steel structure of the traffic towers is apparent in the foreground.

6. A view of the 33 ft. wide central shopping parade at ground floor level. On the right, the entrance to the lift landing in one of the cylindrical traffic towers.

4. Vor die Ganzglasfassade der Südseite ist ein filigranes Gitter aus horizontalen Sonnenschutzlamellen und frei vor die Fenster montierten Regenrohren gesetzt; zusätzlicher Sonnenschutz durch außenliegende Lamellenjalousien.

5. Blick vom westlichen Verkehrsturm auf das östliche Gegenstück und die Dachterrasse des Südtraktes. Die Dachterrassen und die Verkehrstürme sind untereinander durch Brücken verbunden. Im Vordergrund ist zu erkennen, wie die Außenwandelemente aus Beton an der Stahlkonstruktion der Verkehrstürme befestigt sind.

6. Blick in die 10 m breite, zentrale Ladenstraße des Erdgeschosses. Rechts der Eingang zu der Aufzugshalle im Vertikalverkehrszylinder.

7. The canopy above the main entrance is a steel structure suspended from steel columns. The aluminium louvres protecting the facade are sub-divided into units of 21 ft. 4 in. Between them run the freely mounted rain-water pipes which are sub-divided into lengths of one storey's height and, with their inlet hoppers, form an important element of the facade design.

8. A view from the main lobby through the fully glazed porch onto the drive. Floors and walls are of travertine.

9. Lift landing in one of the traffic towers. Above the bench in the centre is a likewise centrally placed light fitting suspended from the ceiling. In the gap between the lifts is an emergency staircase.

7. Das Vordach über dem Haupteingang ist eine Stahl-Hängekonstruktion auf Stahlstützen. Die Aluminium-Lamellenblenden vor der Fassade sind in Einheiten von 6,50 m unterteilt. Dazwischen laufen die frei vor den Fenstern montierten Regenabflußrohre, die in Längen von jeweils Geschoßhöhe unterteilt sind und mit ihren Einlauftrichtern ein wichtiges Element der Fassadengestaltung bilden.

8. Blick aus der Haupteingangshalle durch den Ganzglaswindfang auf die Vorfahrt. Boden und Wände aus Travertin.

9. Aufzugshalle in einem Vertikalverkehrszylinder. Über der Sitzbank im Zentrum eine ebenfalls zentrale Leuchte in der abgehängten Decke. Zwischen den Fahrstühlen eine Nottreppe.

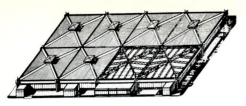

Noriaki Kurokawa & Associates

Canning plant of the Nitto-Sukushin Company at Sagae, Yamagata District, 1964

As fruit canning is confined to the fruit picking season from June to October while, at other times, the plant is used for the manufacture of corned beef, the design called for maximum flexibility, permitting a rapid change of machinery at the seasonal change-over times as well as future extensions of the building in any direction. In its initial phase, the hall has a floor area of 25,750 sq. ft. and consists of eight structural units measuring 56 ft. $\times$ 56 ft. each, a module determined by the size and arrangement of the equipment. All service areas such as toilets, stores and tanks are contained in removable boxes attached to the perimeter of the building. At the corners of the square module are column clusters consisting of four steel pipes, tied together with welded gusset plates. The main girders, consisting of a latticework of tubular steel, are placed diagonally across the bays. Above these main girders are shed-type skylights which intersect at ventilation shafts in the centre. As the building had to be erected very quickly, all the structural parts and infillings were pre-fabricated.

1. Isometric drawing of the roof structure.
2. Site plan of present arrangement (left) and proposed future layout (right). Key: 1. administration, 2 recreational building, 3 research institute, 4 meat canning plant, 5 boiler room, 6 electric substation, 7 stores for empty cans, 8 conveyor belt, 9 fruit canning plant, 10 stores for finished products, 11 store rooms, 12 oil tank.

1. Isometrie der Dachkonstruktion.
2. Situationsplan des jetzigen Zustands (links) und der vorgesehenen Sanierung (rechts). Legende: 1 Verwaltung, 2 Sozialgebäude, 3 Forschungsinstitut, 4 Fabrikationshalle für Fleischwaren, 5 Boiler, 6 Elektrozentrale, 7 Lager für leere Dosen, 8 Förderband, 9 Fabrikationshalle für Obstkonserven, 10 Lager für Fertigwaren, 11 Lagerhallen, 12 Öltank.

Konservenfabrik der Nitto-Sukushin-Company in Sagae, Bezirk Yamagata, 1964

Da sich die Herstellung von Obstkonserven auf die Erntesaison von Juni bis Oktober konzentriert und in der übrigen Zeit Cornedbeef produziert wird, mußte die Fabrik mit größter Flexibilität gebaut werden. Es sollte möglich sein, die Maschinen bei der saisonalen Produktionsumstellung in kürzester Zeit auszutauschen; ferner waren die Voraussetzungen für ein beliebiges Erweitern der Fabrikationshalle nach allen Seiten zu schaffen. In der jetzigen Ausbaustufe hat die Halle eine Grundfläche von 2392 m². Sie setzt sich aus 8 Konstruktionseinheiten von 17 x 17 m zusammen, ein Modulmaß, das sich aus den Abmessungen der Maschinen und ihrer Aufstellung ergab. Alle Nebenräume wie Toiletten, Lager und Tanks sind als austauschbare Zellen seitlich an die Halle angebaut. An den Eckpunkten des Quadratmoduls stehen Bündelstützen aus 4 Rundstahlrohren, die durch verschweißte Stahlplatten miteinander verbunden sind. Die Hauptträger, eine Stahlrohr-Gitterkonstruktion, liegen diagonal in den Deckenfeldern. Über diesen Hauptträgern verlaufen shedförmige Oberlichter; über ihrem Kreuzungspunkt ist ein Belüftungsschacht plaziert. Da der Bau in kürzester Zeit errichtet werden mußte, wurden alle Konstruktions- und Füllteile vorfabriziert.

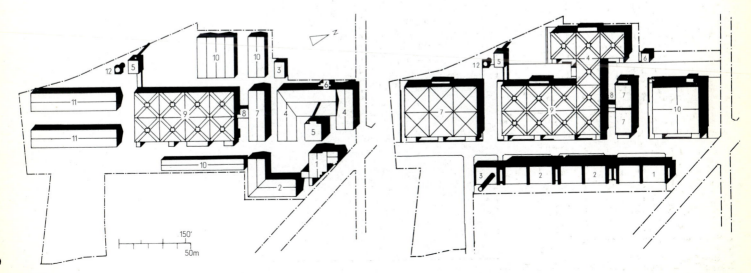

3. The service areas of the factory are placed in removable boxes attached to the perimeter on the outside. The window ribbons consist of opaque corrugated plastics.

4. Plan of factory hall. Key: 1 entrance, 2 washroom, 3 toilets, 4 tank, 5 syrup stores.

5. Interior of the hall. Daylight enters through the diagonally arranged skylights above the main girders. Above their intersections are ventilation shaft turrets.

6. The columns are already fitted with all the parts required for future extensions. This design, though governed by structural requirements, also has an aesthetic impact.

3. Die Nebenräume der Produktionshalle sind in niedrigen, austauschbaren Baueinheiten untergebracht, die als demontable Zellen vor die Fassaden gesetzt werden. Die Fensterbänder bestehen aus undurchsichtigem, gewelltem Kunststoff.

4. Grundriß der Fabrikationshalle. Legende: 1 Eingang, 2 Waschraum, 3 Toiletten, 4 Tank, 5 Siruplager.

5. Blick in die Halle, die durch diagonale Sheds über den Haupt-Gitterträgern belichtet wird. Über den Knotenpunkten die aufgesetzten Entlüftungsschächte.

6. An den Stützen sind schon alle Teile für die Erweiterung vorgesehen. Identität von konstruktiver Notwendigkeit und formaler Gestaltung.

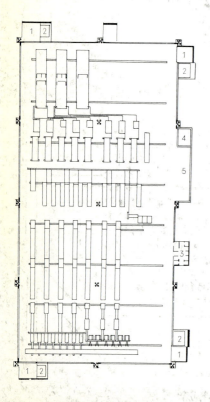

Ichiro Ebihara

Nippon Bailine Textile Factory at Moriyama near Kyoto, 1966-67

The first part oft the factory, designed by Ebihara in the early 1960's, was extended, five years later, by a second group of buildings. The extension comprises a new factory hall covering an area of 175,000 sq. ft., a social centre, as well as extensions to warehouses, laboratories and power station. All the buildings are placed on either side of a traffic artery which divides the factory grounds in the longitudinal direction (cf. Fig. 9). Whilst the older factory hall, toeing the same building line as the new one, makes a rather heavy and solid impression and is raised above ground on a platform of about 1 metre height, the new hall displays a greater lightness and elegance which bears witness to the advance in construction methods using prefabricated components. The floor of the new hall is at the same level as the road, which greatly simplifies the internal transport problems. The columns, cast in-situ, have a spacing of 65 ft. x 59 ft. Their brackets, projecting 9 ft. on either side, support the prestressed concrete I-beams which, in their turn, carry the transverse hexagonal lattice girders of tubular steel. Parts of the hexagonal prisms are glazed so as to provide top lighting. The roof panels between the lattice girders consist of corrugated steel sheeting; the full-height wall panels are of steel. The new social centre is placed between the two factory halls. Its canteen has a stage so that the room can also be used for shows. The roof, consisting of prestressed concrete channels, is supported by four columns only, spaced at 148 ft. $\times$ 105 ft. The door openings in the full-height glass curtain walls are emphasized by white markings.

Stoffabrik Nippon Bailine in Moriyama bei Kyoto, 1966-67

Der zu Anfang der sechziger Jahre von Ebihara geplante erste Teil der Fabrikanlage wurde fünf Jahre später in einem zweiten Bauabschnitt ausgebaut. Die Bauerweiterung umfaßt eine neue Produktionshalle mit 16 250 m², ein Sozialgebäude sowie die Vergrößerung von Lagerhallen, Labors und Kraftwerk. Alle Bauten liegen links oder rechts einer Verkehrsachse, die das Werksgelände in Längsrichtung unterteilt (siehe Abb. 9). Während die alte Fabrikationshalle, in deren Bauflucht auch die neue steht, eher schwer und massiv wirkt und auf einem Sockel etwa 1 m vom Terrain abgehoben ist, zeigt die neue Halle dank der Weiterentwicklung im Bauen mit Fertigteilen größere Leichtigkeit und Eleganz. Ihr Fußboden liegt niveaugleich mit der Werksstraße, was die internen Transportprobleme wesentlich vereinfacht. Die in Ortbeton ausgeführten Stützen stehen in Abständen von 19,80 x 18 m. Ihre nach beiden Seiten 2,70 m auskragenden Konsolen dienen als Auflager für vorgespannte, I-förmige Längsgurte aus Stahlbeton, auf denen in Querrichtung sechseckige Gitterträger aus Stahlrohr liegen. Eine Teilfläche des Sechsecks ist verglast, so daß die Halle Oberlicht bekommt. Die Dachflächen zwischen den Gitterträgern bestehen aus gewelltem Stahlblech, die geschoßhohen Fassadenelemente aus Stahl. Das neue Sozialgebäude steht zwischen den beiden Produktionshallen. Sein Speisesaal hat eine Bühne, da der Raum auch für Veranstaltungen verwendet wird. Das Dach aus U-förmigen, vorgespannten Betonfertigteilen ruht auf nur vier Stützen, die im Abstand von 48 x 32 m stehen. Die Wände sind vom Boden bis zur Decke voll verglast, wobei die Türöffnungen weiß markiert stark hervortreten.

1. South side of the new, 328 ft. long and 23 ft. high factory hall. The horizontal orientation of the building is rhythmically emphasized by the hexagonal box girders.
2. Detail of the south-west corner. At the glass-curtained corner of the facade stands one of the main columns, supporting the overhung girder which carries the longitudinal I-beam. It is only at the edges that the box-shaped form of the hexagonal roof girders is apparent. Inside the hall, they are designed as tubular lattice girders.

1. Südseite der neuen 100 m langen, 7 m hohen Produktionshalle. Die horizontale Gelagertheit des Baukörpers wird durch die sechseckigen Kastenträger rhythmisiert.
2. Detailansicht der Südwestecke. In der Fassade, an der verglasten Gebäudeecke, eine Hauptstütze; darüber der Kragträger, über den der I-förmige Längsgurt läuft. Die sechseckigen Dachträger treten nur in den Randzonen als geschlossene Kastenform in Erscheinung. Im Inneren der Halle sind sie als Gitterrohrträger ausgebildet.

3. The interior of the factory hall receives daylight through a high-level ribbon of windows which surrounds the building on all sides, and through top-light ribbons along the lattice girders. The supply mains for electricity, heating and ventilation are combined in the ceiling.
4. Isometric view of the structural system of the factory hall.

3. Den Innenraum der Produktionshalle belichten ein an den Seiten umlaufendes, hochliegendes Fensterband und Oberlichtstreifen in den Gitterträgern. Versorgungsleitungen für Strom, Heizung und Lüftung sind in der Deckenzone zusammengefaßt.
4. Isometrie des Konstruktionssystems der Produktionshalle.

5. North-west corner. The longitudinal I-beams project beyond the facade. The roof edge is formed by a hexagonal roof girder. The dark wall panels of steel have a circular opening near the bottom.

5. Nordwestecke. Die I-förmigen Längsgurte springen über die Fassade vor. Der Dachabschluß wird durch einen sechseckigen Dachträger gebildet. Die dunklen Wandelemente aus Stahl haben im unteren Teil eine runde Öffnung.

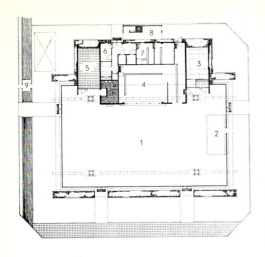

6. Plan of the social centre. Key: 1 canteen, 2 stage, 3 Tatami room, 4 kitchen, 5 dining room for guests and management, 6 office, 7 store rooms, 8 propane gas tank, 9 drainage.

7. The overhung inverted channels of the pre-stressed concrete roof units provide sun protection for the curtain walls.

8. Inside the social centre, the structural composition is clearly apparent. The photograph shows one of the four in-situ cast columns, carrying the logitudinal girder which, in its turn, supports the roof channels.

9. Site plan. Key: 1 new factory hall, 2 social centre with canteen, 3 older factory hall and stores room, 4 electric sub-station, 5 factory road, 6 laboratories, 7 administration, 8 janitor, 9 social centre, 10 hostel.

6. Grundriß des Sozialgebäudes. Legende: 1 Speisesaal, 2 Bühne, 3 Tatamiraum, 4 Küche, 5 Speiseraum für Gäste und leitende Angestellte, 6 Büro, 7 Lagerräume, 8 Propangastank, 9 Abwässer.

7. Die auskragenden U-förmigen Dachelemente aus vorgespanntem Beton geben den Ganzglaswänden Sonnenschutz.

8. Im Inneren des Sozialgebäudes ist die Konstruktion klar ablesbar. Hier eine der vier Ortbetonstützen, darüber der Längsträger, auf dem die U-Elemente aufliegen.

9. Lageplan. Legende: 1 Neue Produktionshalle, 2 Sozialgebäude mit Kantine, 3 Ältere Produktionshalle, 4 Lager, 5 Fabrikstraße, 6 Laboratorien, 7 Verwaltung, 8 Pförtnerhaus, 9 Sozialgebäude, 10 Wohnheim.

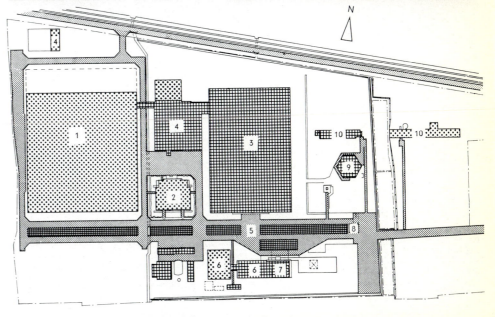

Junzo Sakakura & Associates

Shinjuku Centre, Tokyo, 1964-67

The project for a modern traffic and commercial centre on a site of about 2½ acres around Shinjuku Railway station dates back to 1957. In 1960, a beginning was made with the extension of the east wing of the station. This was followed by the construction of the south wing which spans the tracks like a bridge. Finally, between 1964 and 1967, the largest and last part of the programme, consisting of the development project for Shinjuku West Station, was realized. Today, the Shinjuku Centre is hardly less important, also in terms of traffic volume, than the near-by Tokyo Central Station which it is designed to relieve. Here, some 220,000 passengers a day use the trains of two State Railways, three private railways, and an underground railway. Some of the tracks and platforms are below ground, the different levels being accessible through passages and concourses. The most radical alterations were required on the west side of the site where a derelict backyard area with a water reservoir and old sheds has been transformed into a closely built-up precinct with offices, department stores, shops, restaurants and bars. The combination of traffic, commercial and shopping centre called for special provisions for pedestrians. This need has been met by providing an underground plaza with shopping facilities and station entrances at sub-surface level whilst the surface level of the western station forecourt is mainly reserved for vehicular traffic (including a bus station for 50 bus routes). The second basement has parking facilities for 400 cars.

Shinjuku Center in Tokio, 1964-67

Der Plan, aus dem rund einen Quadratkilometer großen Gebiet der Shinjuku Station ein modernes Verkehrs- und Geschäftszentrum zu machen, geht bis in das Jahr 1957 zurück. 1960 wurde mit dem Ausbau des östlichen Stationsgebäudes begonnen, dann folgte die Südstation, die sich wie eine Brücke über die Gleise spannt, und zwischen 1964 und 1967 wurde das größte und letzte Teilstück, das Entwicklungsprojekt für die Shinjuku West Station, verwirklicht. Heute steht das Shinjuku Center an Bedeutung und Verkehrsaufkommen kaum hinter der benachbarten Tokio Station zurück, die es als Nebenzentrum entlastet. Rund 220 000 Personen benutzen hier täglich die Züge von zwei staatlichen Eisenbahnlinien, drei privaten Bahnlinien und einer Untergrundbahn. Ein Teil der Gleise und Bahnsteige liegt unter der Erde, wobei die verschiedenen Ebenen durch Passagen und Verbindungshallen erschlossen werden. Am tiefgreifendsten waren die Veränderungen auf der Westseite des Areals, wo an Stelle eines trostlosen Bahnhof-Hintergeländes mit Wasserreservoir und alten Schuppen ein dicht bebautes Bürogebiet und eine Reihe von Kaufhäusern, Läden, Restaurants und Bars entstanden. Die Kombination von Verkehrsknotenpunkt, Büro- und Einkaufszentrum erforderte eine besondere Berücksichtigung des Fußgängerverkehrs. Ihm ist hier in der Weise Rechnung getragen, daß eine unterirdische Plaza die Einkaufsmöglichkeiten und Stationszugänge im ersten Untergeschoß erschließt, während die Oberfläche des westlichen Bahnhofsvorplatzes überwiegend dem Fahrverkehr (einschließlich einem Busbahnhof für 50 Buslinien) vorbehalten bleibt. Das zweite Untergeschoß bietet Parkgelegenheiten für 400 Autos.

1. Cross-section, east to west, through Shinjuku West Station. Key: 1 station building with sales floors of the Odakyu department stores, 2 station forecourt, 3 underground plaza, 4 deep-level garage, 5 concourse at plaza level, 6 pedestrian subway, 7 platforms of the State Railways.
2. Longitudinal section, north to south. Key: 1 longitudinal concourse at plaza level, 2 connecting passage leading to the State Railway platforms, 3 subway to underground station, 4 underground station, 5 surface platforms, 6 connecting passage to sub-surface platforms, 7 concourse for the State Railway platforms, 8 south wing of station, 9 Koshu Highway.

1. Querschnitt in Ost-West-Richtung durch die Shinjuku West Station. Legende: 1 Stationsgebäude mit Verkaufsetagen des Warenhauses Odakyu, 2 Bahnhofsvorplatz, 3 Unterirdische Platzanlage, 4 Tiefgarage, 5 Verbindungspassage auf Platzniveau, 6 Unterirdische Fußgängerpassage, 7 Bahnsteige der Staatlichen Eisenbahn.
2. Längsschnitt in Nord-Süd-Richtung. Legende: 1 Längspassage auf Platzniveau, 2 Verbindungspassage zu den Bahnsteigen der Staatlichen Eisenbahn, 3 Passage zur U-Bahnstation, 4 U-Bahnstation, 5 Oberirdische Bahnsteige, 6 Verbindungspassage zu den unterirdischen Bahnsteigen, 7 Übergang zu den Bahnsteigen der Staatlichen Eisenbahn, 8 Südliches Stationsgebäude, 9 Koshu Highway.

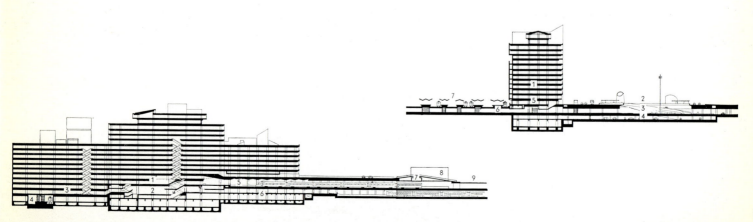

3. Aerial view of the Shinjuku Centre, from the north. In the foreground, right, surrounded by department stores and office blocks, is the western station forecourt with the bus station and the ramps leading to sub-surface plaza and deep-level garage. In the foreground, centre, the kinked building of Shinjuku West Station, followed by the Keio Department Store (dark facade). Beyond the tracks is the building of Shinjuku East Station.

3. Luftaufnahme des Shinjuku Centers von Norden. Im Vordergrund der rechten Bildhälfte, umgeben von Kaufhäusern und Bürogebäuden, der westliche Bahnhofsplatz mit dem Omnibusbahnhof und den Fahrrampen zur unterirdischen Platzfläche und zur Tiefgarage. Vorn (Mitte) das abgeknickte Bahnhofsgebäude der Shinjuku West Station, anschließend (dunkle Fassade) der Keio Department Store. Jenseits der Gleise das Stationsgebäude Shinjuku Ost.

4. Forecourt of Shinjuku West Station. In the foreground the platforms of the bus station, behind them the up and down ramps for the sub-surface plaza with the pedestrian and shopping precincts and the car parks. The skew cylinders provide air and light for the sub-surface plaza.

4. Blick über den Bahnhofsvorplatz der Shinjuku West Station. Im Vordergrund die Bahnsteige des Omnibusbahnhofs, dahinter die Ab- und Auffahrtsrampe zur unterirdischen Platzanlage mit Fußgänger- und Einkaufszone und Abstellplätzen für Autos. Die schräg abgeschnittenen Zylinder sind Ventilations- und Lichtschächte für den unterirdischen Platz.

5. At sub-surface level, a number of pedestrian subways connect with the railway and underground stations and the underground shopping parades. Here, too, are the approach roads for private cars and taxis which arrive from the station forecourt via ramps. The areas inside the ramps are decorated by fountains where the water emerges from concrete cones lined with green mosaics. The building of Shinjuku West Station also contains the sales floors of the Odakyu Department Store.

5. Auf der Ebene des 1. Untergeschosses führen verschiedene Fußgängerpassagen zu den Eisenbahn- und U-Bahnstationen und zu den unterirdischen Ladenstraßen. Ferner liegen hier die Anfahrten für Privatwagen und Taxis, die über Rampen vom Bahnhofsvorplatz herunterkommen. In den Rampenschleifen sind Bassins mit Springbrunnen angelegt, deren Wasser aus grün mosaizierten Betonkegeln hervorquillt. Das Gebäude der Shinjuku West Station enthält auch Verkaufsräume des Odakyu Department Store.

Kenzo Tange

Plan for Tokyo, 1960

The Tokyo Plan for the gradual rehabilitation of the old city and for a linear extension of the town across Tokyo Bay may here serve as an example for numerous urban renewal projects designed by Japanese architects. The traditional radial pattern of the Metropolis with its centripetal traffic system can no longer cope with the rapid increase in population (which has grown from 1.4 millions around 1900 to 9.67 millions in 1960, and is expected to grow to 15 millions by 1980). The plan produced by the research team under the guidance of Kenzo Tange is therefore designed to replace the radial system by a linear 'axis'. By concentrating the manifold functions along a single main artery, the journey time and transport requirements could be reduced to a minimum. Along the proposed axis, which is meant to be gradually extended across the Bay of Tokyo some 2 to 2.5 million people could be housed; in addition, some 5 to 6 million people would regularly commute to this axis by public transport. The existing road network would never be able to cope with such traffic demands. That is why the project envisages gyratory traffic systems with overlapping roads on three levels. All roads are one-way streets, alternately in opposite directions. The overlapping roads take the place of conventional intersections, the different levels being connected by ramps. As a first step, it is planned to build one of these gyratory traffic systems, above the present town centre. The intersections would touch ground level whilst the expressways would cross the Bay at a height of 131 ft. above sea level on suspension bridges with pylons of 1100 yards intervals. First to be erected are buildings for government offices, foreign diplomatic missions, commerce, finance and mass media. For public transport, a mono-rail system is envisaged. The residential areas are placed along spur roads of the main axis. With a total population of about 2.5 millions, each of these housing units, covering an area of about 2½ acres, would house about 100,000 people. The car parks are placed on different levels; each residential unit would have parking facilities for about 40,000 cars. The provision of an industrial estate would be vital to the new urban structure. Commercial vehicles would reach this zone on special roads below water level. Research centres would also be placed close to the industrial zone.

1. The plan envisages a connection between the present town centre of Tokyo and the Chiba District on the Bouso Peninsula across the Bay, with the building clusters concentrated on the far side. On the Tokyo side, the plan envisages the creation of an inland airport on one side and an international airport on the other side of the axis. The axis would also accommodate a new central railway station. Airports and railway station would be connected by railways below water level. The Bay would be flanked by industrial zones.

1. Eine Stadtachse verbindet das jetzige Zentrum von Tokio mit dem Bezirk Chiba auf der Halbinsel Bouso, vor deren Küste sich die Überbauung verdichtet. An der Tokioter Seite sind rechts und links der Achse ein Binnenflughafen und ein internationaler Flugplatz vorgesehen. Außerdem soll innerhalb der Achse ein neuer Zentralbahnhof für Tokio entstehen. Die Flughäfen und der Hauptbahnhof werden durch Unterwasserbahnen miteinander verbunden. Entlang der Bucht sind neue Industriegebiete geplant.

Plan für Tokio, 1960

Der Tokioplan zur stufenweisen Sanierung der bestehenden City und zur linearen Stadterweiterung quer über die Bucht soll hier als Beispiel für die zahlreichen Projekte stehen, mit denen die japanischen Architekten die Stadtstruktur verbessern wollen. Die seitherige radiale Ausdehnung von Tokio mit zentripetalem Verkehrssystem ist der rapiden Bevölkerungszunahme nicht mehr gewachsen (um 1900 1,4 Millionen Einwohner; 1960 9,67 Millionen; bis 1980 rund 15 Millionen). Der Vorschlag des Forschungsteams unter Leitung von Kenzo Tange will daher das Radialsystem durch eine lineare Stadtachse ersetzen. Durch das Verteilen der vielfältigen Funktionen in nur einer Hauptrichtung kann die Kommunikation auf ein Minimum an Zeit und Bewegung reduziert werden. An der geplanten Achse, die sich stufenweise über die Bucht von Tokio vorschieben soll, werden sich zunächst ungefähr 2 bis 2,5 Millionen Menschen ansiedeln; außerdem werden täglich etwa 5 bis 6 Millionen mit öffentlichen Massentransportmitteln ihre Arbeitsplätze in der Achse erreichen. Das heutige Straßensystem könnte einen solchen Andrang niemals bewältigen. Deshalb werden Kreisverkehrsysteme in drei Ebenen mit übereinandergreifenden Straßen vorgeschlagen. Auf jeder Straße herrscht Einbahnverkehr, aber auf zwei benachbarten Straßen jeweils entgegengesetzt. Die übereinandergreifenden Straßen dienen als Kreuzungspunkte. Rampen verbinden die einzelnen Etagen miteinander. Als erster Schritt ist der Bau einer Kreisverkehreinheit über dem heutigen Zentrum geplant. Die Kreuzungspunkte würden den Erdboden berühren, während die Schnellstraßen 40 m über der Bucht als Hängebrücken zwischen Pfeilern im Abstand von 1 km aufgehängt werden. Als erste Einrichtungen sollen Regierungsgebäude, ausländische Missionen und Bauten für Handel, Finanzwelt und Massenkommunikation erstellt werden. Für den Massentransport wird eine Einschienenbahn vorgeschlagen. Die Wohngebiete liegen an den von der Achse abzweigenden Seitenstraßen. Bei etwa 2,5 Millionen Bewohnern wird jedes Seitenglied von durchschnittlich 1 qkm Größe etwa 100 000 Menschen aufnehmen. Die Parkplätze sind auf verschiedenen Ebenen untergebracht; ein Seitenglied bietet Abstellungsmöglichkeiten für etwa 40 000 Wagen. Die Ansiedlung von Industrie ist ein lebenswichtiges Problem für die neue Stadtstruktur. Die Zulieferung für das Industriegebiet soll über Unterwasserstraßen erfolgen. Auch Forschungszentren würden in der Nähe des Industriegebietes konzentriert werden.

2. Spur roads would lead from the main axis to the residential units. Some of these units would be erected on reclaimed land, others on platforms resting on piers with foundations embedded on the sea bottom.

3. The primary feeder roads would run along either side of the main axis. Traffic would follow a one-way system where the sections of roads crossing the central ribbon would be placed on three levels. This central ribbon would serve as a general communication zone. The informally arranged, curved buildings on the right would house the city administration. On the left, office blocks forming linear framework structures. The cores of these buildings, containing lifts, stairs and lavatories, would be designed as load-bearing structures. Lifts placed in the 500 to 800 ft. high core towers would link the upper floors with the car parks in the lower floors. The vertical clearance below the building frames would be 131 ft., the span from core to core about 650 ft.

2. Von der Hauptverkehrsachse zweigen Straßen ab, die zu den Wohngebieten führen. Einige der Wohneinheiten werden auf neu gewonnenem Land stehen, andere auf Plattformen, deren Pfeilerfundamente in den Meeresboden eingelassen sind.

3. Die Hauptzubringerstraßen verlaufen auf beiden Seiten der städtischen Achse. Der Verkehr wird nach dem Einbahnsystem geregelt, wobei die Straßen im Bereich des Mittelstreifens dreistöckig übereinanderliegen. Der Mittelstreifen soll als allgemeine Kommunikationszone ausgebaut werden. Rechts in geschwungenen, freien Formen die städtische Verwaltung. Links Bürogebäude, die zu einer linearen Skelettstruktur zusammengefügt sind. Die Gebäudekerne, die Vertikalverbindungen und Sanitärräume enthalten, sind als tragende Konstruktionsglieder ausgebildet. Aufzüge in den 150–250 m hohen Kernen verbinden die Obergeschosse mit den Autoeinstellplätzen in den Untergeschossen. Die Höhe des Freigeschosses unter den Bauten wird 40 m betragen, die Spannweite von Kern zu Kern etwa 200 m.

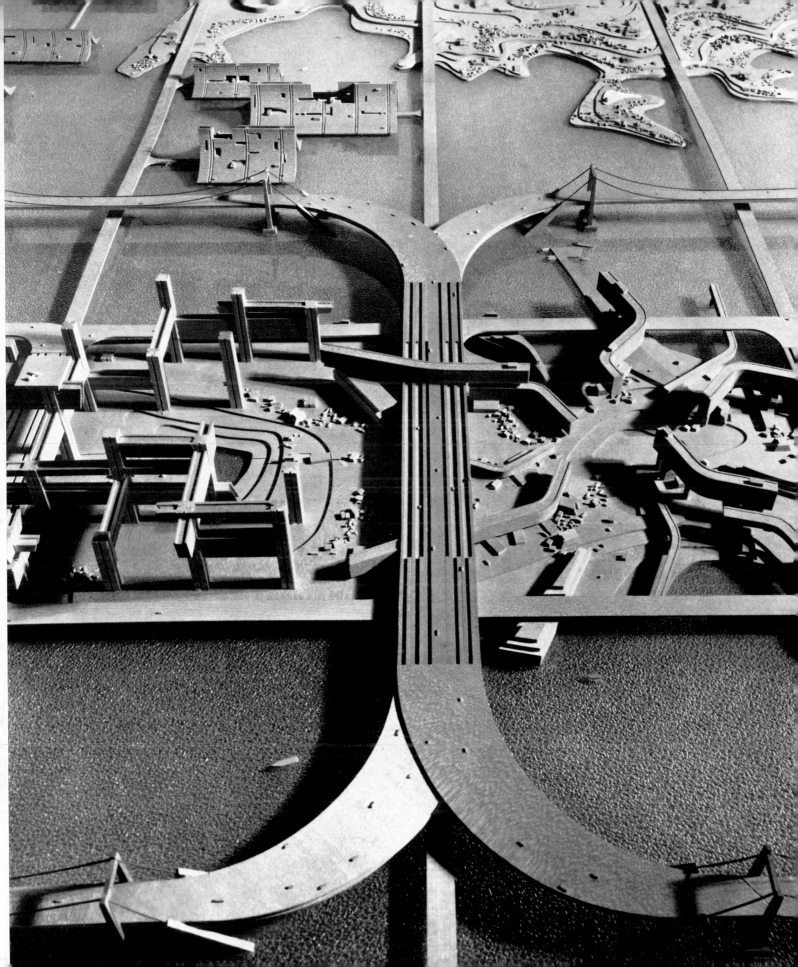